The 50+ Dog Owner:
Complete Dog Parenting for Baby Boomers and Beyond

Mary Jane Checchi

The 50+ Dog Owner
Project Team
Editor: Heather Russell-Revesz
Copy Editor: Stephanie Fornino
Indexer: Lucie Haskins
Designer: Angela Stanford

T.F.H. Publications
President/CEO: Glen S. Axelrod
Executive Vice President: Mark E. Johnson
Publisher: Christopher T. Reggio
Production Manager: Kathy Bontz

T.F.H. Publications, Inc.
One TFH Plaza
Third and Union Avenues
Neptune City, NJ 07753

Printed and bound in China

10 11 12 13 14 15 1 3 5 7 9 8 6 4 2

Library of Congress Cataloging-in-Publication Data
Checchi, Mary Jane.
  The 50+ dog owner : complete dog parenting for baby boomers and beyond / Mary Jane Checchi.
     p. cm.
  Includes index.
  ISBN 978-0-7938-0643-0 (alk. paper)
  1. Dogs. 2. Dog breeds. 3. Dogs--Selection. 4. Baby boom generation. 5. Middle-aged persons. I. Title. II. Title: Fifty plus dog owner.
  SF427.C43 2010
  636.7--dc22
                    2009052789

This book has been published with the intent to provide accurate and authoritative information in regard to the subject matter within. While every precaution has been taken in preparation of this book, the author and publisher expressly disclaim responsibility for any errors, omissions, or adverse effects arising from the use or application of the information contained herein. The techniques and suggestions are used at the reader's discretion and are not to be considered a substitute for veterinary care. If you suspect a medical problem consult your veterinarian.

Note: In the interest of concise writing, "he" is used when referring to puppies and dogs unless the text is specifically referring to females or males. "She" is used when referring to people. However, the information contained herein is equally applicable to both sexes.

The Leader In Responsible Animal Care For Over 50 Years!™
www.tfh.com

Table of Contents

Introduction

Why a Dog?

I am 62 years old, owned heart and soul by two rough-coated, sable and white Collies. I share my home, my family, and my life with Tony and Charlotte because they make me laugh, make me smile, keep me company, cheer me up, calm me down, comfort me, help me relax, and keep me moving because I have to go outside three times a day (in good weather and bad) to walk them. Although my dogs are not security dogs by nature or training, they make me feel safe at night if I am alone in the house. And they are directly responsible for introducing me to a few cherished friends and a larger number of acquaintances; I met them while walking my dogs.

Other dog owners express sentiments similar to mine, which can be summarized by the following comments: "My dog makes me happy" and "I would be lonely without a dog." Among no group are these sentiments more deeply held, or expressed more often, than among those of us over 50. In fact, a survey conducted by the American Veterinary Medical Association (AVMA) reports that most dog owners over 50 think of their dog either as a family member or as a companion.

BENEFITS TO DOG OWNERSHIP

There is more to these good feelings than sentiment. Researchers have found solid evidence that for owners the human–canine bond can:

Charlotte and Tony, my rough-coated Collies.

- reduce stress
- lower blood pressure
- lower cholesterol levels
- lower heart attack rates
- decrease the number of physician visits
- combat depression and feelings of isolation
- increase the number of social interactions
- stimulate exercise and improve fitness

The research is so compelling that at least one life insurance company has included living with a companion animal as one of the attributes that older policyholders can list as part of a healthy lifestyle—and policyholders with healthy lifestyles are eligible for lower insurance rates.

Dogs Improve Our Quality of Life

For those of us over 50, these physiological, social, and emotional benefits are especially valuable. I know many people—some acquaintances from the "dog path," others close friends or relatives—whose lives illustrate what researchers have found. Eighty-two-year-old Irene walks Toast, her part-terrier-part-something-else,

in our neighborhood twice day. "Without him," she says, "I would be a couch potato. I would have no reason to go outside. He keeps me moving."

Unlike Irene, 86-year-old Magda, a widow, is not much of a walker. On days of clement weather, she spends an hour or two sitting on a bench in her shady front yard, her two Lhasa Apsos snoozing or playing on the grass. Neighbors walking or driving by stop to chat. "I wouldn't want to sit outside alone," she explains. "But the dogs give me a reason to go out, and I stay in touch with people."

A widowed gentleman whom I know chuckles at his two terriers' morning ritual: "killing" the stuffed bear that is three times as big as the two of them combined.

Dogs can improve quality of life, especially for those of us over 50.

He likes to remind me that "Laughter is the best vitamin. I take it at least once a day, thanks to my dogs." Play is good medicine too, and it's easy to forget that, especially if there are no young children around. Dogs give us an excuse to play—fetch, catch, tag, tug-of-war—not that we should need one.

A friend whose husband passed away a few years ago mentions how good it feels to scratch, pat, and stroke her affectionate Dachshund. "You never know how important it is to touch and be touched until you are alone," she says.

Our dogs are dependent on us for daily care and attention.

Another friend, also a widow, not only tolerates but actually likes her tiny Lhasa Apso's frequent yapping. "It makes the house seem less empty," she explains.

A TWO-WAY STREET

Dogs provide us with unconditional love, diversion, and affection, as well as companionship. But the human–canine bond is not a one-way street: Our dogs are dependent on us for daily care and attention. They remind us that we are needed, even if: we have retired and are no longer "gainfully employed"; the kids have grown, have gone off to start their own lives and don't "need" us any more; we can't see or move or hear quite as well as we once did. To your dog, none of this matters: You are all-important and indispensable, regardless of a few (or many) gray hairs.

The ability to care for a dog is one of the many reasons why owning a dog contributes to overall happiness and well-being. It feels good to be needed. In fact, it feels terrific.

So here's the $64,000 question: Why do you want a dog? The answer will help you determine not only if you should get a dog but also what type of dog is best for you.

Gift Dogs

It is not unusual for well-intentioned adult children to surprise a parent with a "gift dog." Whether or not you are considering a dog of your own, do everything in your power to discourage your children from doing this. A dog will live with you 24 hours a day, 7 days a week, 52 weeks a year, for quite a few years. This is a decision that must be yours to make.

Protection

If you want a dog for protection and you plan to keep an "aggressive" dog chained in the yard or locked in the basement or garage, my advice is unequivocal: Don't do it. It is a cruel way to treat a dog and it is dangerous— for you, your family, and visitors to your home. You may open yourself up to liability. If you feel vulnerable in your home, get a home security system. It is

Owning a dog is more fun, and in some ways easier, than ever before.

safer, cheaper, easier to maintain, and more effective.

Some 30 years ago, when I was single and living alone in a downtown "transitional" (translation: scary) neighborhood, I was commended by a community police officer who at the time was being adored by my Collie: "The best protection anyone here can have is a dog. You don't need a Rambo dog or a big dog or a fierce dog. You just need a dog who will make noise if a stranger comes to the door or a window. Most people trying to break in just want to avoid the noise and the possibility of getting bitten."

I have always remembered that conversation and I like to repeat it when people tell me that they want a dog for "protection." I urge them to get a dog who simply makes them happy and fits their lifestyle, not to go looking for an "aggressive" or "protective" dog. Such dogs can be found, of course. They are large and strong and require extensive training, and they can become so protective of an individual or couple that they exhibit suspicion or resentment toward visitors, including grandchildren and other family members.

Realistic Expectations

If you are looking to a dog to cure loneliness or grief—as do some people who are recently widowed or divorced, please give yourself more time to think it over. While a dog can help alleviate sadness and the pain of loss, your expectations may be unrealistic. Wait until your life situation has stabilized before deciding whether a dog is right for you. I hope that it will be and that you find a dog to keep you company and cheer you up, but give yourself six months to a year before you tackle this major decision.

If you have recently been diagnosed with a serious illness or find yourself chronically depressed, again, please wait. A dog might be a delightful and partial antidote to these problems but will not "cure" them, so be certain that your expectations and ability to care for a dog are within the realm of possibility before you acquire one.

WHY NOT A DOG

In my opinion, there are a few reasons *not* to have a dog, including:

- Dogs are prohibited where you live.
- You cannot afford to care for a dog. Sadly, 30 percent of Americans age 65 and older say they do not have enough money to meet their own basic living expenses, so they would not be able to take on pet expenses as well. You must take care of yourself first.

Never give a dog as a gift.

Consult your heart before deciding whether and which dog is right for you.

- You do not feel physically well enough to care for a dog because you cannot walk, feed, groom, or transport him.
- You do not like dogs.

Age Issues

You may want a dog but be worried that issues associated with your age are barriers to dog ownership. You may worry that you cannot exercise your dog enough, take him with you on your travels, keep him well groomed, drive him to the veterinarian—or even hook and unhook a leash. You may worry about what will happen to a beloved dog who might outlive you.

This book will help you identify and evaluate these concerns and then show you how, in most instances, you can surmount or detour around them. At the end of each chapter you will find a "Resources Made Easy" section that will guide you to additional resources. Throughout the book you will find "Money-$aving Tip" sidebars to help you keep your budget balanced. Much has changed in the human and canine world in recent decades. There are new rules and responsibilities—laws require owners to leash their pets, vaccinate them, and clean up after them. Stunning advances in veterinary medicine keep dogs healthier longer and deter parasites that used to invade our homes and make our dogs sick or just miserable. Technological innovations allow us to microchip and track lost pets. Perhaps the biggest changes of all have been commercial. Owners can now order pet food, supplies, and equipment over the telephone or Internet and have it all home delivered; veterinarians, trainers, and groomers make house calls; pet taxis transport owners and dogs; hotels, motels, and bed-and-breakfasts nationwide open their doors to traveling canines; professional pet sitters and dog walkers supplement the options offered by old-fashioned kennels and newer pet hotels. You can even hire a company to poop scoop your yard. Owning a dog is more fun—and in some ways easier—than ever before.

If you are contemplating bringing home a dog to be your pet, companion, family member, or friend, you have a wonderful adventure ahead.

Consult Your Heart and Your Head

Before you embark on that adventure, keep this in mind: A pet should be a loved family member or companion, not a burden. Consult your heart before deciding whether and which dog is right for you. The way you feel about a dog will strongly affect your willingness to care for him and whether you enjoy this relationship at all.

I hope that you find that sharing your home and life with a dog is right for you and that you enjoy every moment of that special relationship.

RESOURCES MADE EASY

Books About the Human-Canine Relationship

- Beck, Alan. *Between Pets and People: The Importance of Animal Companionship*. West Lafayette, Indiana: Purdue University Press, 1996.

- Becker, Marty and Danelle Morton. *Healing Power of Pets: The Amazing Power of Pets to Make and Keep People Happy and Healthy*. Darby, Pennsylvania: Diane Publishing Company, 2004.

- Katz, Jon. *The New Work of Dogs: Tending to Life, Love and Family*. New York: Random Trade Paperbacks, 2004.

Part I

Finding the Right Dog for You

Chapter 1

Self Audit

How I came to share my home with Charlotte and Tony, two 60-pound (27-kg) Collies, is due partly to serendipity and partly to informed decision making. This brief tale may evoke similar memories for some readers and hopefully be both instructive and cautionary.

It began nearly 80 years ago in the small town of Calais, Maine. My paternal grandmother adopted a stray Collie-like dog off the streets. Her two sons named him Bob. I have a faded sepia photograph of my father at a very young age, dressed in a sailor suit and high-top leather shoes, standing next to Bob, who, sitting down, is taller than my dad. When Bob died, my grandmother was so distressed by her sons' anguish that she decreed there would be no more pets in the Checchi household.

Fast-forward two and a half decades. My father has married, and there are two of us children. My parents have recently moved us into the second and last house they ever owned, in a suburb of Washington, D.C. The house is an aging Dutch colonial that needs some work. Its attraction lies in the 2 acres of grass and trees that surround it.

I return from school one fall day, and when I walk into the kitchen looking for my mother, I am surprised and thrilled to find her cradling a golden ball of fluff. It is Mac, a Collie pup whom she bought as a surprise for my father's birthday. I immediately appropriated Mac as my own. He would live through my college years. Mac was joined over time by a Basset Hound (Suzie), a Heinz 57 hound (Blue), and two part-Collie mixed breeds (Sam and Pete). At one point, our family shared the house with four dogs.

When I attended graduate school in Chicago, my life felt incomplete until I added a Collie pup. And so it goes to this day: I have shared my life with a line of magnificent Collies, punctuated by an equally magnificent mixed breed, a stray whom I diagnosed as part Golden Retriever, part German Shepherd. If my grandmother had rescued a Beagle or Poodle, would I live with Beagles or Poodles

If you grew up with a particular breed, like this German Shepherd Dog, you may already be hooked on it.

today? I honestly don't know.

What I do know is that Collies and I get along very well. I tolerate their barking (moderate), I enjoy their playful, mellow nature, and I appreciate that I do not worry when they are around children, adults, or other dogs. I find that it is easy and fun to walk with them because they are docile on a leash and do not tug or pull. I like to take long walks and can easily meet my dogs' exercise needs (moderate) because there is a beautiful, safe path through woods less than two blocks from my home. We have a spacious home that accommodates their large, furry bodies. I am not terribly bothered by the fur they shed (moderate to heavy) on the carpets. Only one of my dogs developed a serious (and expensive) veterinary problem. I am able, despite some arthritis in my hands, to give my dogs a once-over light brushing. I am no longer up to bathing them because of a bad back, so I outsource their semi-annual baths.

START FROM SCRATCH

Many of you reading this book are already hooked, as I was. You grew up with a Cocker Spaniel or German

Shepherd Dog, or you raised your children alongside a beloved Golden Retriever or Dachshund—and have never looked back. Or you may have lived with and loved a succession of mixed-breed dogs (whom we inelegantly used to call mongrels). If you are thinking about adding a dog to your life now, you may fall into one of several different camps:

- **Camp Number One:** "I (we) loved that dog (those dogs) and that is the only kind of dog we will ever want."
- **Camp Number Two:** "We always stuck with one breed and had terrific luck. But that was then and this is now. Maybe it's time for a change."
- **Camp Number Three:** "I've never had a dog, but I think I would like one now that we are both retired and home during the day."
- **Camp Number Four:** "I've had dogs before, but that was years ago; I would like to have one now, but I'm in my 70s and wondering whether I can afford and care for a dog."

To all of these camps (even you long-time dog owners) I offer the same advice: Begin without preconceptions about what type or breed of dog is best for you. Start from scratch and focus on you.

- **To Camp Number One:** If you feel committed—even addicted—to a particular breed, size, or type of dog, bear in mind that you are changing and that your lifestyle is changing or may change significantly in the not-too-distant future. The breed, type, or size of dog that seemed right for you 5, 10, or 20 years ago may not be right for you now.
- **To Camp Number Two:** You are on the right track. You may end up with a new version of "Old Faithful" or an entirely different canine.
- **To Camp Number Three:** Good for you! You are in for an exciting and rewarding journey as you learn about dogs. If you discover that you really like dogs—not just the idea of one—this chapter will help you decide if dog ownership is right for you.
- **To Camp Number Four:** That's an honest and practical outlook. I can show you how to evaluate your resources to determine whether dog ownership is for you and help you assess the type of dog that will match your resources.

MUCH ADO ABOUT YOU

I'd like to share with you some of the comments offered by men and women, ranging in age from 56 to 83, with whom I have recently spoken:

- "Now that we're retired, we want to travel. We both miss having a dog, but we worry that a pet would tie us down."
- "We always had a dog—until now. We've downsized from a house with a yard to a condo. How do you live

with a dog in a high-rise?"

- "When the kids were growing up, we had Miniature Schnauzers. I was the one who took care of the dog. I don't have one now because I don't like to drive. How would I get pet chores done?"

- "It might sound silly: I'm nearly 80, and although I'm in good health now, who knows about tomorrow? What if I outlive my dog? Who will care for him?"

- "For years we had a houseful of kids and at least one Golden Retriever. The kids are out on their own now. The house seems empty, but we think that a Golden is too much for us to handle."

- "I grew up with dogs and always wanted one, but my husband was allergic to them, and honestly, didn't really want one. He passed away not long ago and now I would so enjoy the company of a dog, but I'm worried about the cost."

As you can see, each individual or couple has different concerns, just as your concerns and situation will be unique to you. Finding the "right" dog for you is, above all, about you, your personality, health, lifestyle, and resources.

There are few decisions you will make that will have a greater impact on your day-to-day life than your decision to get a dog. This addition to your family will require daily care, can live for 10 to 15 years, and can cost thousands of dollars to maintain over the course of those years. The "right" dog can add much that is fulfilling to your life. The "wrong" one can bring misery and heartache. Here are some questions and issues for you to consider as you work your way toward the right dog for you.

YOUR PERSONALITY

First, take a look at some personal things, including your likes and dislikes, habits, tastes, and preferences. It may be difficult to evaluate your own personality, but personality may be the single most important—and most frequently overlooked—issue in determining human/canine compatibility. By cataloging your personal preferences, you can determine which canine traits you are likely to like or dislike and be on your way to a better human–canine match. Ask yourself the following questions:

- Are you easygoing or tightly coiled? Flexible or rigid? If you have trouble answering questions like this, ask a spouse (if you dare) or a sibling, adult child, or friend for an opinion.

- Is a quiet, peaceful, orderly home your idea of nirvana? Or are you more a turn-up-the-music, what's-happening kind of person, who thrives on activity?

- Do you take life in stride, or are you easily rattled, so that a "dog problem" can greatly upset you?

- Do you like to express affection and do you like animals and humans who express affection back? Or do you prefer people and animals to maintain a respectful distance?

YOUR HEALTH

Next up on your dog-oriented self-audit is your health, including energy; fitness; strength; health issues (arthritis, allergies, vision or hearing impairment); and mortality.

How would you assess your overall health? Excellent, good, fair, not so good? Will the care and company of a dog improve or impose upon your health? Certainly, most people over age 55 and over 65—and many into their late 70s and 80s—are healthy and fit enough to be excellent canine caretakers. Americans are living longer and staying healthy longer than ever before; doctors now consider age 55, rather than 40, as the turning point into middle age. Chronic disability for those over 65 is steadily declining.

Consider that someone will need to take the dog outdoors in good weather and bad. While walking the dog is good for you, the weather might be

The "right" dog for you will match your personality, health, lifestyle, and resources.

problematic. Will walking in rain, snow, or extreme heat cause problems for you? If so, can you consistently find and afford dog walkers to help you exercise your dog? Giving a dog access to a yard is fine—but he still needs to be walked.

Fitness and health issues can help you determine not only whether a dog is right for you but what kind of dog is right for you. As we age, our skin thins, we are more easily bruised, and our skin tears more easily. If you have made this observation in your own case, as I have in mine, keep in mind that dogs and puppies who cannot be dissuaded from jumping on or pawing people are more of a problem for us than for younger, perhaps hardier folks.

If your immune system is compromised, seek the advice of your doctor and animal experts before bringing a dog into your family. Zoonotic diseases (diseases that can be passed from animals to humans) are rarely a problem in the United States and especially rare with dogs. This is due to improved hygiene and pet waste disposal, widespread vaccination against rabies and other diseases, use of veterinary medications that minimize internal and external parasites, and the substitution of commercial food for raw meat. Owners with a weakened immune system need to be especially careful to avoid contact with dog feces (using gardening gloves when working in the garden where a dog might have defecated) and wash their hands immediately after poop scooping. They also need to take care to avoid being bitten or scratched—an issue that can be factored into the selection of a dog.

It is common for physicians to err on the side of caution and advise patients with immunity issues to give up or not acquire pets. But Dr. Frederick Angulo, a medical epidemiologist with the Centers for Disease Control and Prevention (CDC), has said that "Many (health professionals) are not well informed about how often people catch diseases from animals. They don't know enough, so they figure it won't hurt to be extra cautious."

As one writer summarized, "A cherished pet can mean everything to a person living with weakened immunity. With solid information and simple precautions, even high-risk patients can continue to live safely with their animal companions."

Energy

How would you assess your energy level? Is it high, medium, or low? I have to admit that mine is not as great as it once was. Your dog's health and good behavior relate directly to his receiving adequate exercise, attention, and stimulation—and this in turn will affect how well the two of you get along. "Adequate" exercise varies from dog to dog.

Fitness

Fitness issues can affect your ability and willingness to exercise your dog. Is balance a problem, meaning you could be easily pulled or knocked over? Are you able to walk and to walk comfortably?

My husband's knees ache, so therefore he does not enjoy walking the dogs. Only two women I know, both in their late 80s, feel unable to walk their dogs because they are unsteady on their feet. Both hire dog walkers. If you use a cane or a walker to get around, you probably must assume that you will not be able to exercise your dog. However, if you have a yard, if you can toss a ball, if you can afford dog walkers or doggy day care, you may still be able to give a dog—especially if he's low energy—the exercise he needs.

My issue is lower back pain, not an uncommon one for people my age. With stretching and careful exercise, I am able to walk my dogs and enjoy it. As the years amble by, I turn more often to professional groomers for my large dogs. I used to wash them down outdoors using a garden hose, but I can no longer bend over for long periods without paying a price in back pain. For someone with back problems worse than mine, bending over to groom a dog, scoop poop, attach a leash, or pick up and replace food and water bowls can be a challenge. Some of these challenges can be met, for a price, with products and services described in later chapters. All of them should be taken into account when choosing a dog.

Fitness issues can affect your ability to exercise your dog.

Strength

Your level of physical strength can help determine the size, personality, and strength of the dog who is right for you. Today, I can easily pick up and carry a 5-, 10-, or 15-pound (2-, 5-, or 7-kg) dog. When I was younger, I could lift a 60-pound (27-kg) Collie, but I can't do it any more. Does this matter? It can matter in an emergency, if your dog is ill or injured and needs to be lifted into a car. It can also matter if you plan to lift your dog into a sink for bathing or onto a tabletop for grooming.

My declining strength became an issue when Dandy, one of my old Collies, developed weakness in his hindquarters, as Collies are prone to do. For more than a year, he could not walk up stairs, climb into the car, or rise from a *down* position without a boost from me. I didn't mind doing this but my back did.

An owner would not normally need to be able to lift her dog. But a dog who is injured or who is resistant to or unable to climb up stairs or into a car (as sometimes happens when a dog ages) could need boosting.

A more serious problem can arise when a dog is stronger than his owner and not under the owner's control. Two acquaintances of mine, both my age and reasonably fit, were injured by their dogs. In one case, a hefty ten-month-old pup running loose slammed into her owner and broke her leg. In the other situation, a leashed puppy pulled his owner over, resulting in a broken shoulder. Neither dog is a "bad" dog, just strong, rambunctious, and not well trained.

Health Issues

Common health issues that may affect your ability to care for a dog include arthritis, asthma, allergies, and vision or hearing impairment.

Arthritis

Osteoarthritis, the most common type of arthritis, affects most people to some degree by the time they turn 70. Several friends my age and older cope with arthritis. It does not stop them from walking their dogs—indeed, they find the exercise helpful. A few of my contemporaries complain that the arthritis that afflicts their hands can flare up if they spend more than a few minutes

grooming a dog. If your hands are painful and stiff, evaluate whether you will be able to comfortably attach, detach, and hold a leash, scoop poop, feed, or otherwise handle a dog.

Asthma and Allergies

If you suffer from asthma, allergies (including skin allergies), or other breathing problems triggered by the presence of dogs (their dander and saliva), consult your doctor before you even consider bringing a dog into your home. If your doctor clears you, some dogs will be better suited to live with you than others.

Vision and Hearing

How is your hearing and sight? Impaired hearing would not normally be an issue for dog ownership (unless you need or would benefit from a hearing-assistance dog), although problems could arise if your dog barks excessively. (Expect irate neighbors to let you know.) Inability to hear bikers or others who approach from behind when you are outside with your dog could present some danger.

Impaired vision does not have to be an impediment to caring for a dog. Owners I know who are unable to read or drive because they suffer from macular degeneration are still able to walk their dogs. However, blurred vision or lack of peripheral vision, especially if coupled with some unsteadiness, can lead to tripping or falling over a small dog underfoot.

Owners who no longer drive or own cars have other options for obtaining supplies and services. Groomers, trainers, and some veterinarians now make house calls, and food and supplies for home delivery can be ordered online or over the phone.

Mortality

More than one contemporary has told me, "Much as I would like to have a dog, I'm afraid he would outlive me." It is easier today than just a few years ago to arrange for the care of surviving pets. But more importantly, your age or health alone need not rule out a canine companion. One win-win solution is to consider adopting an older dog. Most of these pooches are homeless through no fault of their own, and many are mature, calm, mellow, and extremely lovable. They are well past the high-maintenance puppy years and desperately need homes because puppies and young dogs are the first to be adopted. Advances in veterinary care have radically extended the canine life span; small dogs routinely live past ages 12 and 4. Adopting a five- to eight-year-old dog can still bring years of happiness and companionship for both of you.

For others, the fear is that they will outlive their dog—the thought of losing a beloved pet to death is so painful that

If you suffer from allergies, consult your doctor before even considering bringing a dog home.

they avoid pets altogether. This tendency can deepen as we age, lose friends and relatives, and confront our own mortality. My advice is this: Don't deprive yourself of the joy and comfort of canine companionship because you fear the end of it. Much more than in the past, society now understands and accepts how profound the attachment to—and grief over the loss of—a pet can be. Resources and support are now widely available to help people deal with grief over the loss of a pet.

YOUR LIFESTYLE

The word "lifestyle" has crept into our everyday vocabulary yet has different meanings in different contexts. Lifestyle issues that can have a direct impact on dog ownership and care include living space; location; housekeeping; travel; visitors; and impending changes.

A careful inventory of your lifestyle issues will help you decide whether you can happily live with a dog, can influence the type of dog you choose, and can affect how, and how comfortably, you live with a dog.

Living Space

Are there legal restrictions on keeping a dog in your home? Will your home feel crowded with a dog in it? Do you have a fenced-in yard? These are all "space" issues to account for in your audit.

Legal Restrictions

Some condominium and cooperative apartment agreements, and many landlords, prohibit dogs or limit the size and number of dogs permitted. A 20-pound (9-kg) limit is typical, but I have also heard of 22-, 25-, and 30-pound (10-, 11-, and 14-kg) limits. Homeowners' associations, as well as condos, co-ops, and landlords, often restrict the number of dogs permitted to two or even one. Check your lease or the covenants that govern your home before you bring a dog home, and make certain that your new pet will be "legal." Do not try to sneak a dog into a home where dogs are not allowed; the stress is not worth it, nor is the heartache when you are inevitably forced to choose between your home and your pet.

Living Quarters

If your living quarters are small, this may affect the size of your chosen dog. A big dog can be a problem for you if you mind a large, hairy lump filling several cubic feet (m) of your living space 24/7. Are you considering a 60- to 100-pound (27- to 45-kg) dog? Picture that mass sprawled in the middle of your living room floor, roughly the size of a small area rug with a thick pile—he will not go unnoticed. Will it bother you to step over or around him several times a day for years to come? After launching their children into the world, many of my contemporaries downsized from single-family homes to condos or apartments. When the time came to choose a dog, several cited "smaller home" as an important factor in choosing a small or medium-sized dog. "It would feel crowded," explained one friend.

Yard

A fenced-in yard is a great convenience but not a necessity for canine family members and their humans. It is particularly appreciated by humans when used by dogs for early morning and late night bathroom breaks. For dogs, a yard is good for fresh air and a change of scenery. But a dog and a fenced-in yard do not equal exercise

Location

Where you live will help you determine where and how you will exercise your dog, and this in turn may influence the type of dog you choose. Take a quick accounting of your location from a dog owner's perspective. Are there sidewalks in your neighborhood? Are they well lighted at night? Is there a park nearby where you would enjoy walking your dog? Is there a park or field where you can toss a ball or flying disc for your dog to retrieve? If you are thinking about a dog who likes to swim, is there a clean creek, stream, or pond that you can access? Do you by any chance live near a dog park?

Some apartments and condos have legal restrictions about dog ownership.

Safety

If you will not feel safe walking in your neighborhood with a dog (because of the lack of sidewalks, the lack of lighting, or for other reasons), you may need to reconsider owning one or consider other options. Can you rely on someone else to walk your dog at night if that is your primary concern? Do you have a yard to use for canine bathroom breaks, and are you willing to chauffeur your dog to a park where he can get some exercise? This is not as extreme a solution as it may first appear. I live a block from a terrific walking path, and every morning at regular intervals cars, SUVs, and pickups arrive at the entrance to the park and disgorge owners with anywhere from one to four dogs each. Neither owners nor dogs seem to mind the drive. If you are fortunate enough to be able to walk or drive (every day) to a dog park, woods, park, or field where your (well-trained) dog can run free, you may decide that a high- or medium-energy dog is right for you because this proximity assures him the exercise he needs.

City Versus Country

Do you live in the heart of a city? A suburb? A rural area? Some dogs adjust much better to urban life than others. Some dogs need wide-open spaces. Most can live in suburban areas if given enough opportunity to exercise.

Legal Requirements

The jurisdiction in which you live will impose some conditions and responsibilities on you as a dog owner. Your local government will almost certainly require rabies vaccinations and licensing, prohibit dogs from running loose ("leash laws"), and require owners to clean up after their pets ("poop scoop laws"). In an effort to influence owners to spay or neuter their pets, a few jurisdictions require owners to obtain a special breeder's license if they plan to breed their dog. Some jurisdictions ban breeds considered dangerous, such as pit bull-type dogs. Your local animal shelter, veterinarian, or local government agency (usually through an agency designated "animal control") can advise you about the legal requirements of dog ownership in your area.

Housekeeping

Is a pristine home important to you? Will dog fur on the furniture or paw prints in

Assess if there is a safe place to walk your dog in your neighborhood.

the hall cause you to weep or gnash your teeth? Answers to these questions will help you decide whether you can happily share your home with a dog, and if the answer is yes, help you decide what type of dog.

Living with a dog means more housework—there is just no way around it. Be realistic about how much extra work and doggy dirt you (or your spouse) can tolerate. For some, the tradeoff is easy. I for one am not terribly finicky about the tufts of Collie fur nesting in the carpet or the scuffed-up wood floors.

Other owners, demanding a higher standard of cleanliness, have decided that the extra time spent vacuuming, wiping, and cleaning is a price worth paying for the pleasure of canine company. Some potential dog owners may love dogs and love the idea of living with one—but the anguish over shedding fur, paw prints, or chewed Chippendale furniture outweighs the benefits of a canine housemate.

Eau De Dog?

How important is air quality to you? Do slobber and drool offend you? How about bad breath in dogs? A dog's breath can vary with breed, age, and dental health, and some breeds and dogs simply slobber more than others. But rare or nonexistent is the odorless dog. Keep these factors in mind when deciding if will be happy sharing your living space with a dog.

Yard Etiquette

What does your yard mean to you? A precious plot for cultivating flowers, vegetables, herbs? A putting green? A play area for the grandchildren? A site for grilling steaks and entertaining friends? How you view and use your yard could be an issue if you decide to share it with your dog.

Regardless of your dog's habits and leisure activities, there is one thing that he is sure to do if left in the yard, and that is to use it as you would use your indoor bathroom. Poop scooping is an unavoidable outdoor housekeeping chore.

Travel

If you live with a dog, he will have to be factored into your travel plans. Whether you are planning a long weekend away from work or extensive post-retirement travel, you have three choices: take Rex with you; leave Rex at home in the care of others; or board Rex at a kennel or pet hotel.

It is easier than ever before to travel with or without your dog—for a price. Increasing numbers of people take dogs with them on road trips, and increasing numbers of hotels, motels, and bed-and-breakfasts allow pets—usually for an extra fee and advance reservations. The possibility of air travel with your dog varies by airline, destination, and his size.

A time-honored practice, at least for relatively short absences, is to hire the teenager next door to visit, feed, water, and exercise Rex at home while you are gone. Today, this role is increasingly filled by professional pet sitters. A variation is to place the dog in the home of a friend, relative, or neighbor. And the option of the old-fashioned boarding kennel has been greatly expanded (for a price, of course) to include pet motels and hotels, complete with air-conditioned units, lap pools, and individual TVs.

The option you choose will depend on your preferences, your wallet, and travel intentions, which in turn should be factored in as you consider the right size and type of dog for you.

Visitors

Some dogs are one-person dogs. If they become overly protective, you may face some training and socialization challenges when visitors come. Of greater concern is the presence of children—and for most of us, this means grandchildren who come to visit for short or long periods. If you expect young children as frequent visitors, this should be a factor when considering the type of dog that is right for your home.

Children

Children under the age of six need adult supervision when interacting with any dog, even the friendliest, gentlest dogs. Contrary to popular belief, small dogs are not "better" with children and indeed may be more easily frightened into biting. Toddlers and youngsters are naturally impulsive, active, quick, and often loud. They do not understand that smacking a dog with a bowl can cause pain or that screaming at a dog can produce fear. Indeed, as a veterinarian once told me, "Virtually every movement a toddler makes toward a dog can be viewed as threatening by the dog, including waving hands and arms in front of a dog's face, grabbing, pulling, flailing, whacking, poking." A dog who finally snaps back is not a "bad" dog, and a young child who provokes the dog is not a "bad" child. Each is simply acting and reacting as his nature and developmental stage dictate.

If young children regularly visit your home during the day, consider whether you can—and are willing—to supervise their interactions with your pet or keep pet and children separated in different rooms. (Do not crate your dog and leave him where young children can frighten or tease him, however unintentionally.) If children frequently stay at your home overnight, consider whether this will present problems. One option, if you can afford it, is to board your dog when children come to stay. Another is to defer getting a dog until your grandchildren are a little older. Or if you can put up with a little more work, continue to "supervise and separate" young children and pets.

Other Guests

In addition to children, take a quick inventory of other regular, frequent visitors, such as relatives, friends, or a housekeeper. If any of them are severely allergic to dog dander or have dog phobias, take some time to think through how—and if—you can deal with these issues. The type of dog you choose can partially alleviate the allergy problem.

Impending Changes

If you are planning major lifestyle changes, such as retirement, moving from a house to an apartment, or relocating to a different

If you expect young children as frequent visitors, this should be a factor when considering the type of dog that is right for your home.

geographic region, the optimal course would be to wait until after you have moved into your new home or settled into your retirement routine before bringing home a dog. Simply put, it will be hard for you to anticipate how that dog will fit into your new location or new life until you yourself have made that change.

YOUR RESOURCES

Time and money are resources you absolutely have to have if you want a dog. Be realistic about how much of each you have and how much you are willing to spend.

Time

How much time each day can you allocate to caring for a dog? You will need to spend an average of at least one to two hours per day to exercise and feed your dog, plus additional time (although not necessarily every day) for grooming, training, and veterinary visits. Depending on size, type of coat, age, and temperament, your choice of dog will increase or decrease the time needed for grooming, training, exercise, and possibly the need for veterinary care. Some dogs and breeds need more exercise and training than others. Some dogs have coats that require more attention than others. Puppies require far more time and attention than adult dogs. Most shelters, rescue groups, and responsible breeders are reluctant (or refuse) to hand over puppies if they are to be left alone all day. Many adoption supervisors are also leery about placing energetic adult dogs in homes where they will be alone most of the day.

By no means do you have to give up your job, golf, bridge game, or lunch with friends to stay at home full-time with a dog. But in looking at your daily schedule, make certain that you have ample time to be with and enjoy a canine buddy.

Finances

How much can you spend, on an annual and continuing basis, for 10 to 15 years, to care for a dog?

The cost of acquiring and caring for a dog over her lifetime can easily approach and exceed $10,000. The *continuing cost* of caring for a dog far exceeds *acquisition costs*. Estimating *annual costs* is hard to do because of the many variables involved: size of the dog, need for veterinary care, and choices you make about trainers and equipment.

At a minimum, annually caring for a small dog will cost about $500; for a medium dog, about $700; and for a large dog, closer to $1,000.

Acquisition Costs

Adoption fees at animal shelters range from a low of about $50 to a high of about $250; breed rescue leagues may charge more. Some shelters waive or reduce the adoption fee for adopters who are over 65. If you are interested in buying a dog, the sky can be the limit if for some reason you want to spend thousands of dollars for a "show-quality" dog, which is no guarantee that this will be the "quality pet" for you. Or you can spend several hundred to $1,500 dollars buying a mixed or purebred dog off the Internet or through a classified ad in the newspaper, a route that I (and virtually all animal welfare groups) urge you not to follow. A good option is to find your dog at a shelter or breed rescue and use the money you save to pay for training or a veterinary emergency fund.

Equipment Costs

A second one-time expense is basic equipment. Depending on your choices and regional prices, basic equipment that is perfectly adequate can cost $75, but some owners enjoy spending much more. If you have a yard that is not fenced in and plan to let your dog use it without your constant supervision, installation of a fence is mandatory and will cost from hundreds to thousands of dollars, depending on the size of your yard and the fencing that you choose.

Initial Care Costs

A third one-time expense (often included in adoption fees) is initial vaccinations and veterinary care. Spaying or neutering is no

Money $aving Tip

The continuing cost of caring for a dog far exceeds acquisition costs.

longer considered optional for responsible dog owners and costs from about $150 to $350. In some areas, low-cost spay and neuter services are available.

Training Costs
A final one-time expense is training. Unless you adopt a well-trained adult dog or are particularly adept and experienced at training, you will be better off with some professional guidance. The cost of six classes may vary from $100 to $200, and individual sessions cost substantially more. Increasing numbers of shelters offer free consultations or free classes.

Ongoing Expenses
Remaining expenses are ongoing. How much can you realistically afford to spend *each year* caring for your dog?

That price tag, excluding extraordinary veterinary expenses, varies tremendously from a few hundred dollars a year to several thousand per year, depending on regional price differences and the size, grooming, and veterinary needs of the dog you select. Food typically is the largest maintenance expense, and its price tag is dependent on the size of the dog. For some, additional costs to be factored in include boarding, pet sitting, grooming, or dog walking.

Alas, very few dogs go through life without an unexpected injury or illness. It is important and necessary for owners to be prepared for the unexpected expense—either by purchasing pet insurance or by setting aside a veterinary emergency insurance fund. I recommend a set-aside of $1,000.

RESOURCES MADE EASY

Books on Dog Behavior
- Coren, Stanley. *Why We Love the Dogs We Do: How to Find the Dog that Matches Your Personality*. New York: The Free Press, 1998.
- Horowitz, Alexandra. *Inside of a Dog: What Dogs See, Smell and Know*. New York: Scribner, 2009.
- Masson, Jeffrey. *Dogs Never Lie About Love: Reflections on the Emotional World of Dogs*. New York: Crown Publishers, 1997.
- McConnell, Patricia B. *For the Love of a Dog: Understanding Emotion in You and Your Best Friend*. New York: Ballantine Books, 2006.

Resources for Zoonotic Diseases
- Centers for Disease Control (CDC): www.cdc.gov/HEALTHYPETS/animals/dogs.htm

Chapter 2

Canine Audit

"A Labrador Retriever?" I repeated.

"Oh, yes," my friend Janet assured me. "When the kids were little, we always had Labs and loved them." Janet and her husband Phil, both recently retired, had picked out a playful chocolate Lab puppy. Six months later, without a touch of malice or intent, the adorable Lab dislocated Phil's shoulder. During their evening walk, the pup (now weighing in at nearly 50 pounds [23 kg] of muscle) spied a dog at the end of the block and took off like a rocket—while Phil, on the other end of the leash, hit the pavement with his shoulder.

Janet and Phil fell into a common trap, one that beckons to many of us who have lived with and enjoyed dogs before reaching our fifth (or sixth, seventh, or eighth) decade: "That breed was a good fit in the past, and I know and like it, so why even consider a change?"

The answer is simple: We change. And as many dog lovers will testify, there is more than one breed or type of dog that you can love.

DON'T LIMIT YOURSELF

Don't let your history limit your options. The noisy Beagle who was your best friend when you were a child, the protective German Shepherd Dog who helped you raise your own family, or the energetic mutt who was your jogging partner when you were a younger adult may still represent the right type of dog to share your life today, but there is a strong possibility that he does not. And if you have never before owned a dog, you are in for an adventure of discovery.

Don't let yourself be talked into a certain type of dog by a neighbor, friend, or well-meaning relatives. Don't be seduced by a "flavor-of-the-month" dog—the cute little Chihuahua from a television commercial or the canine hero in the latest dog-centric family movie.

It is not unusual to start with a gut feeling. You meet a friend walking a lively Corgi, you play with the Corgi, you begin to think "I could live with a dog like this." But you need to add information to that gut feeling.

In this chapter you will find information about important canine characteristics that will help you reconcile your issues, preferences, and concerns with the many aspects of "dogdom." This canine audit is your opportunity to calculate the plusses or minuses of a particular size, shape, hairstyle, personality, and gender, and to match the answers to your own personality, lifestyle, and resources.

But first, a word of caution—reconciling your concerns and preferences with canine characteristics is not going to yield an exact fit, as you would expect when you reconcile your checkbook. There is no "perfect" match, no "perfect" dog, and there certainly is no one-size-fits-all dog for everyone. But with some patience, you can find the *right* dog for you.

And now I am going to turn this chapter over to Charlotte, the most literate dog I know. She will lead you through this canine audit.

DOGS ACCORDING TO CHARLOTTE

Hello, people. I understand that you are interested in acquiring a canine friend.

Charlotte, adopted from a breed rescue, leads you through a canine audit.

You have many choices. Forgive me for bragging, but did you know that dogs, ranging in weight from 2 to 200 pounds (1 to 91 kg), vary in size more than any other species on earth?

We are special in many ways. What other species sports such a range of beautiful fur coats, from a Dalmatian's spots to a Boxer's brindle stripes, plus innumerable shades of chocolate, black, white, gold, yellow, brown, tan, red, sable, gray, liver, and silver—and seemingly endless combinations of all of these? Not to mention that these colors appear in coats that are curly, silky, long, short, coarse, dense, thin, thick, wiry, rough, and smooth. Our shapes range from the long legs of a Borzoi to very short Corgi legs, from long noses such as mine (remember, I'm a Collie) to flat Bulldog faces, from the upright pointy ears of a German Shepherd Dog to the long, floppy ears of an Irish Setter—and everything in between. The species *Canis familiaris* has greater diversity of appearance than any other species on earth.

Canis familiaris belongs to the family *Canidae*, which includes the wolf, fox, coyote, and jackal. The scientific consensus is that dogs are descended from wolves. Anthropologists believe that wolves were probably the first animals ever domesticated by humans. Thousands of years ago, dogs who were distinct and different from wolves evolved, our very nature defined by our ancient relationship to humans.

It is easy to be bewildered by the diversity of canine physical characteristics or to be bewitched by a single, adorable characteristic. It is my job to remind you that every dog has a unique *set* of physical characteristics,

that some will be more important to you than others, and that the canine personality is as unique and variable as the human personality. After all, we have been bred for many tasks, from hunting and pulling to rescuing, detecting, and protecting.

If this seems overwhelming, the good news is that there is a dog for everyone who wants one, and we are always in need of good human homes. If you don't like big, there is small. If you don't like energetic, there is mellow. If you don't like noisy, there is quiet. Searching for just the right dog can be fun. You have already audited your characteristics (in Chapter 1) as they are likely to impact one of us. This canine audit will help you evaluate our canine characteristics as they are likely to affect you.

A DOG'S PERSONALITY AND TEMPERAMENT

Although a dog's physical characteristics may be important to future compatibility, his temperament will probably play a bigger role in determining whether or not the two of you get along. Temperament can be measured in many ways. I have noticed that trainability and personality usually top the list for most people.

Our canine personalities, like people personalities, run the gamut: timid, quiet, noisy, outgoing, demonstrative, excitable, independent, dependent,

Choices, Choices

The species *Canis familiaris* (the dog family) has greater diversity of size and appearance than any other species on earth.

mellow, effusive, affectionate, standoffish, submissive, aggressive, stubborn. The challenge is to find the dog with a temperament that you can live with and enjoy.

Match Your Personality Type

Does a canine Dean Martin, Lucille Ball, or Bob Newhart fit your personality type? Here are some canine answers to the human audit personality questions you confronted in Chapter 1.

For the Easygoing Owner

If you are laid-back and easygoing, then a dog who is playful, mischievous, or even stubborn may be right for you.

Typical Playful Breeds

- Beagle
- Bichon Frise
- Collie
- English Springer Spaniel
- Golden Retriever
- Irish Setter
- Labrador Retriever

- Papillon
- Vizsla
- Many mixed breeds

For the Organized Owner

If you are well organized and feel most comfortable running a tight ship, you should probably avoid independent, high-strung, noisy dogs and instead look for an easy-to-train dog with an even temperament.

Typical Quiet Breeds

- Basenji
- Greyhound
- Whippet
- Tired, well-exercised dogs

Typical Noisy Breeds

- Beagle
- Dachshund
- Shetland Sheepdog (Sheltie)
- Some terriers (Cairn, Fox, Yorkshire)
- Some toy breeds (Maltese, Toy Poodle)

For the Outgoing Owner

If you are a "happening" kind of person and don't mind (or even enjoy) commotion and activity, you would probably get a kick out of a friendly, rambunctious, playful dog who remains puppy-like (goofy and silly) well into his later years.

Typical Friendly/Sociable Breeds

- Basset Hound
- Bichon Frise
- Collie
- English Cocker Spaniel
- French Bulldog
- Golden Retriever
- Irish Setter
- Norwegian Elkhound
- Norwich Terrier
- Pug
- Soft Coated Wheaten Terrier
- West Highland White Terrier
- Weimaraner
- Many mixed breeds

For the Peaceful Owner

If peace and quiet are important to you, seek out a gentle dog and steer away from dogs who might have a tendency to bark a lot (especially if they are left home alone too long and not given a lot of attention).

Typical Gentle Breeds

- Afghan Hound
- Bernese Mountain Dog
- Borzoi
- Chihuahua
- Collie
- Greyhound
- Mastiff
- Newfoundland
- Papillon
- Saint Bernard

Trainability

All dogs can learn. Some of us want to please you by learning the commands you teach (*sit*, *stay*, *come*), and we learn quickly. Some dogs focus their intelligence on discovering how to break out of the yard or into the garbage can and are not easily convinced of the error of their ways. Others resist your lesson plans because they are by nature independent or even stubborn. They are not "bad dogs" and not stupid but can be quite a challenge.

You might wonder "Who would want a dog who can't be easily trained?" One answer is provided by my friend Kelly, an Irish Terrier. Actually, she is more of a terror than a terrier. Although she is intelligent, she is *the* most stubborn and independent dog I have ever known. She resists all of her owner's efforts to train her—and intentionally flouts the rules. But Kelly's owner is Judith, a very nice and patient lady who so loves Kelly's quirky personality, playfulness, and loyalty that she overlooks behavior that *I* certainly would not put up with.

Typical Easier-to-Train Breeds

- Collie
- German Shepherd Dog
- Greater Swiss Mountain Dog
- Labrador Retriever
- Miniature Schnauzer
- Soft Coated Wheaten Terrier

- Weimaraner
- Many mixed breeds

Typical Harder-to-Train Breeds
- Akita
- Alaskan Malamute
- Beagle
- Chow Chow
- Most hounds
- Many terriers

Affectionate Versus Aloof

Now, about those affectionate versus more standoffish types: Extremely sociable dogs display affection and welcoming behavior, become strongly attached to their family, and may even shadow one of them from room to room. I have noticed that, to some people, this is entirely appealing canine behavior, and to others, it is anathema.

Speaking strictly from my own experience, I like to follow Mary Jane around the house. I am obviously too large to be a lapdog, which is a good thing because neither one of us would enjoy such an activity. On the other hand, my friend Anna, a Maltese who weighs about 5 pounds (2 kg), practically lives in her owner's lap. This is good for both of them because her owner is a widow who loves to cuddle Anna and might be lonely without her.

Some dogs are aloof, but this does not mean that they are not attached and loyal to their owners. They simply prefer not to be cuddled and do not engage in a lot of demonstrative behavior.

Typical Affectionate Breeds
- Beagle
- Bernese Mountain Dog
- Bichon Frise
- Boxer
- French Bulldog
- Golden Retriever
- Greater Swiss Mountain Dog
- Many mixed breeds
- Many toy breeds

Typical Aloof/Independent Breeds
- Afghan Hound
- Akita
- Chow Chow
- Rhodesian Ridgeback
- Saluki
- Schipperke
- Scottish Terrier

Puppy Versus Adult

If you rate yourself or your spouse high on a prone-to-stress scale, skip the puppy and adolescent stage and look for a calm, well-behaved older dog, one who is housetrained. I feel that I need to interject a reality check on behalf of my species: No dog is perfect (although a few of us may approach perfection). Any one of us is likely to have an accident or two in the house, have an upset stomach from time to time, forget our manners, or annoy a neighbor. But if you choose carefully and properly train and care for your dog, the stress of an occasional "dog problem" should be outweighed by the pleasure of canine companionship. How can it not?

Words to the Wise Owner

I think I should remind you that your interaction with your dog will affect his behavior only up to a point. If a quiet household is very important to you, choose a "quiet" dog. Yes, some veterinarians will remove a dog's vocal chords but *please* don't even think about it as this is a terribly inhumane choice. I shudder at the very idea. Don't bring home a dog who likes to bark and assume that you will change him. The struggle just might not be worth it, and why look for trouble when you can avoid it?

If an affectionate dog appeals to you but you don't want a cuddly lapdog, you might find a big, friendly oaf who likes to jump on people just because he is overjoyed to meet them. You can train him not to do that, but you probably will not be able to train a Chow Chow to engage in public displays of affection that he believes are beneath his dignity.

If you discover an adorable but hyper puppy or adolescent who you are panting to bring home, don't kid yourself that "He'll grow out of it." Yes, he will—but maybe not for another ten years.

In other words, be realistic.

Finally, something really important that Mary Jane will tell you about: Even the "best" and "easiest" dogs *need* and (trust me on this) *like* to be trained.

A DOG'S PHYSICAL NATURE

Dogs are physical beings, and it is important to reconcile canine and

Dogs who don't get enough physical exercise can develop problem behaviors.

human characteristics before you make your choice.

Health and Fitness

If your health concerns are a compromised immune system, balance, or fragile skin, so that it is important for you not to be scratched by a dog's nails or teeth, not to be jumped on, or not to be pulled, then your best bet is to adopt a mature, calm, well-behaved dog. Puppies, being puppies, will inevitably teethe, sometimes on a human arm or finger. They are likely to jump up on and paw at you, as will many adolescent dogs. Some dogs, despite training, tend to remain "jumpers" into their adult years, and some dogs nip. Like puppies, these dogs are not good choices if you might be knocked over because of unsteady balance or if your skin is easily torn or bruised.

If your immune system is weak, either temporarily or for the long term, there is a simple answer here too, and it will seem familiar: Adopt a mature, housetrained dog. Because a primary source for the transmission of zoonotic disease is dog feces, it is best to avoid housetraining a puppy.

If arthritis or a bad back present problems for you, consider a small dog. A small dog can be lifted onto a table or counter for grooming. Plus, a small "nonshedding" dog will require less grooming from you and your aching hands (but may require professional grooming). However, a small dog can present some challenges, such as the need to bend over to lift him or to attach or detach a leash.

Energy Level: Couch Potato or Triathlete?

Here is a mistake that I've noticed some humans tend to make: They think big dogs need exercise and little dogs don't. But size alone will not tip you off to a dog's energy level and the amount of exercise he will need. I have known 100-pound (45-kg) Newfoundlands who are really quite lazy and 20-pound (9-kg) Jack Russell Terriers who need to run, run, run.

Just like a human being, a dog's need to run, walk, play, or explore outdoors will vary with age, health, individual temperament, and genes—not just with size. When I was two years old, I could literally run my humans into the ground and even a one-hour walk would not tire me out. Today, seven years later, I am happy with 20-minute walks.

I have seen dogs older than me who still can run for miles (km).

If your self-audit does not include the time, inclination, and physical ability to spend one and a half to two hours a day outdoors exercising your dog, then avoid a high-energy or even an average-energy dog because he'll need a lot of daily activity. An unexercised dog is bored and unhappy and can annoy you half to death, pacing through your home or dropping a slimy tennis ball in your lap 500 times a day. Dogs who don't get enough outdoor stimulation and exercise can become obese and develop problem behaviors, including excessive barking, digging, destructive chewing, and house soiling.

Canine energy will also determine whether a dog's presence in your home feels comfortable or intrusive. A small- or medium-sized dog with a demanding personality and high energy level can "use" more space—and more of your energy—than a quiet, mellow couch potato at triple the weight.

Typical High-Energy Breeds

- Australian Shepherd
- Border Collie
- Dalmatian
- Pointers
- Setters
- Some hounds
- Some terriers
- Most retrievers
- Weimaraner

Typical Moderate-Energy Breeds

- Basenji
- Bernese Mountain Dog
- Bouvier des Flandres
- Briard
- Bulldog
- Chihuahua

- Great Dane
- Havanese
- Keeshond
- Mastiff
- Old English Sheepdog
- Papillon
- Saint Bernard
- Samoyed
- Shar-Pei

Strength: Mr. Atlas or Miss PowderPuff?

Does the possibility of being knocked or pulled over by a dog worry you? If it does, should you choose from among only small, frail dogs? Not at all. An owner's lack of physical strength can be offset by choosing a dog (of any size) with a docile temperament who is well trained and responsive to commands. Some dogs behave well on a leash once they are trained and are actually able to resist the temptations offered by squirrels and errant cats. Other dogs simply cannot restrain themselves.

Large dogs do not have a monopoly on strength; medium-sized dogs can be muscular, independent, and energetic. I recently heard about a Dachshund who pulled his on-leash owner over, and the owner suffered a broken hip. I know of Beagles and Beagle-type mixed breeds, weighing in at 20 to 35 pounds (9 to 16 kg), who drag their on-leash owners around the block.

Toy breeds that weigh 10 pounds

(5 kg) or less are not strong enough to pull or knock you over. On the other hand, because their bones are small and fragile, they can more easily be hurt than a bruiser Boxer. Injury can come from falls, from other dogs, from children who are too young to heed admonitions to be gentle—and accidentally from you, the owner. However, small dogs do offer advantages for owners who are not as strong as they once were. They are portable and can be lifted onto a table for grooming or into a car.

Allergies: Hypo-Allergenic Dogs?

People who are allergic to dogs are sensitive to a protein found in their saliva and skin. All dogs continually shed small particles of dead skin, called dander, and some of it falls out as the dog sheds; there is no such thing as a dog who has no dander, or a "hypo-allergenic" dog. (That would be a dog with no skin!) But one of the "nonshedding" (meaning very low shedding) breeds or a mix of two of them will drop less hair—and therefore less dander—in the house. It is important to be aware that many of these breeds need professional grooming, which can be expensive.

Breeds That May Be Good for Allergy Sufferers

- Bedlington Terrier
- Bichon Frise

- Cairn Terrier
- Kerry Blue Terrier
- Miniature Poodle
- Portuguese Water Dog
- Soft Coated Wheaten Terrier
- Standard Poodle
- Toy Poodle
- West Highland White Terrier
- Yorkshire Terrier

Mortality

Assuming good-quality care and the absence of genetic quirks, small- and medium-sized dogs usually live longer than large dogs, and large dogs usually live longer than giant dogs. Mixed-breed dogs generally have fewer health issues and live longer than their purebred counterparts.

DOGS AND YOUR LIFESTYLE

You've already taken a look at your lifestyle issues that will have a direct impact on whether or not you should own a dog. Take it from a Collie who knows—those same issues are going to affect what type of dog is right for you.

Living Space

Just like your home, dogs come in small, medium, and large sizes. We vary in weight from 2 to 200 pounds (1 to 91 kg). "Small dogs" are usually thought of as weighing 20 pounds (9 kg) or less, while "medium-sized" dogs weigh about

20 to 45 pounds (9 to 20 kg). Anything over that is considered "large," although some people further separate "large" and "giant" breeds. The size of your canine companion will affect you and your living space in important ways.

Obviously, a large dog takes up more space than a small one. If your home is small, does it make sense to share it with a canine who weighs more than 20 pounds (9 kg)? It usually is not a problem for the dog if— and *only* if— you give him plenty of outdoor exercise. Dogs don't get the exercise they need wandering around indoors, no matter how big your house is. A small, medium, or large dog can live happily and healthily in a small space if you give him enough outdoor exercise.

Location: The Weather Outside

Where you live and the kind of weather you experience can also affect your choice of breed. After all, weather is an outdoor exercise issue for us dogs as well as for people. Breeds that originated in cold climates wear heavy fur coats, so they do not tolerate hot weather well. Breeds with short muzzles tend to have respiratory problems and also struggle in hot weather—I can hear them wheezing. This is equally true of mixed breeds with thick coats or flat faces. With these dogs, you must take precautions against canine heatstroke, and it may be difficult to give them enough exercise outdoors in hot weather. This is not an insurmountable problem if you live in a temperate climate with a few months of hot weather. During hot summer days, you can walk your dog when it is coolest— very early in the morning and after dark. I have noticed that not every human is happy to embrace this schedule. Some of them don't seem to be early risers, some don't feel entirely safe walking in the neighborhood after dark, and some don't see well at night. If you live in a region where it is hot year-round, it will be much easier for you—and healthier for your dog—to choose a dog who tolerates heat.

Cold weather presents challenges to older dogs and dogs with extremely short coats. Chilling air is especially hard on small dogs with short coats because their bodies generate less natural heat. Ever more fashionable doggy coats and sweaters can help solve this problem. And there are many dogs who really like cold weather.

Breeds Affected by Hot Weather

- Boxer
- Bulldog
- Chow Chow
- French Bulldog
- Great Pyrenees
- Keeshond
- Newfoundland
- Norwegian Elkhound

- Pomeranian
- Pug
- Samoyed
- Saint Bernard
- Most heavy-coated dogs
- Most brachycephalic (flat-nosed) dogs

Housekeeping

Think about the housekeeping issues that are and aren't acceptable to you, including shedding, chewing on furniture, that doggy smell, and what can happen to your yard.

How Much Shedding Is too Much?

All dogs shed; even the "nonshedding" breeds lose a little hair once in a while. If a pristine home is important to you and you have no intention of vacuuming daily, you might want a dog who sheds very little.

Except for nonshedding breeds or mixes, most dogs shed seasonally once or twice a year and drop at least some fur year-round. Within a single breed and even within a single litter of mixed or purebred dogs, the thickness of the coat and the amount of shedding will vary with the individual dog. I am sorry to say that my coat isn't very long or thick like some Collies, so I don't shed nearly as much as my Collie housemate Tony, who has a glorious coat and sheds all over the place. Some dogs with short fur have thick undercoats and shed more

profusely than other dogs with long fur. One constant: the larger the dog, the more fur to shed.

Low-Shedding Breeds
- Airedale Terrier
- Basenji
- Bedlington Terrier
- Bichon Frise
- Maltese
- Poodle
- Portuguese Water Dog
- Puli

Furniture

If you particularly treasure the furniture in your home, including carpets, upholstery, and wood items (such as chair or table legs), think seriously about completely avoiding the puppy and adolescent stages and adopting a mature dog well past the teething and chewing stages.

Eau de Dog?

All dogs have at least some doggy odor, and some naturally have more than others. Your dog will emit less doggy odor if his coat is regularly groomed—and your house will not smell like a kennel (although I don't understand what's wrong with that).

Dogs bring the smells of the outside world into your home. If your dog swims (in a lake, creek, pond, or the ocean), he will bring a damp and possibly a salty, fishy, or polluted smell home with him. Dogs who run in the woods or the park will return with a multitude of interesting odors that will, over time, build up on his coat until you wash them away. And thank goodness, we even have remedies for bad breath in dogs.

Drooling is a different matter. There is not much you can do about a dog who naturally drools a lot except choose another dog, if that's a problem for you. Some dogs and breeds just drool more than others, and they will do it indoors and outdoors. When contemplating great but unreachable food, almost any dog can work up a good drool.

Typical "Droolers"
- Bulldog
- Boxer
- Great Dane
- Mastiff
- Newfoundland
- Saint Bernard

Yard Etiquette
Some dogs are natural diggers, bred to hunt small animals by digging into their burrows. Most terriers love to dig.

Many of us are chasers—we don't distinguish between flower beds and grass when on the trail of an annoying squirrel or trespassing cat. I am a "roller": In summer, I love to roll and sprawl in grass, ferns, geraniums, marigolds—anything soft and yielding.

In my opinion, you can't train a dog not to chase a cat or roll in the grass, and most dogs will do one or the other. What you can do is keep an eye on us, keep us out of the yard, or fence off flower beds.

Travel
A dog's size can affect your—or his—travel options or choices.

By Car
Traveling with large animals presents challenges but is getting easier. Tony and I (Collies weighing in at 60 pounds [27 kg] each) fit fairly comfortably into a small station wagon, leaving room for one driver, one human passenger, and very little luggage. A 10-pound (5-kg) dog can travel in a crate or with a harness and not affect the human passenger or luggage equation in a sedan or even a compact car.

By Air
The possibility of air travel for us dogs varies by airline. Most allow a "carry-on" dog in the cabin if he weighs less than 15 or 20 pounds (7 or 9 kg) and if his kennel will fit under a seat. Most accept dogs as cargo (something I really would not like), but some refuse to transport very large dogs. Many dog owners who we know of owned large

dogs while raising their children and now live with small dogs who weigh less than 20 pounds (9 kg); those in retirement mode cited frequent travel, both by plane and by car, as a reason to "trade down" to a small dog.

Hotels

Increasing numbers of hotels and motels nationwide allow pets in rooms, but some limit by weight the size of the dog. The weight limit varies widely, with no apparent rationale: 12, 15, 25, 45 and 50 pounds (5, 7, 11, 20, and 23 kg)—or no limit at all. Tony and I, a cumulative 120 pounds (54 kg), were recently welcomed into a very nice hotel in Annapolis, Maryland.

Visitors

If your frequent houseguests or visitors include your grandchildren, seek out a dog likely to be fond of and tolerant toward children.

Breeds Typically Good With Children

- Bernese Mountain Dog
- Collie
- Flat-Coated Retriever
- Golden Retriever
- Labrador Retriever
- Newfoundland
- Standard Poodle

YOUR CANINE CARE RESOURCES

Last, focus on the time and money you have—and are willing to spend—on a dog.

Time

How much time will you have for your dog?

Feeding and Exercise

We need to be exercised and fed every day. Filling the food bowl usually takes just a few minutes, but exercise will certainly take up more time. High-energy dogs need at least two hours of outdoor exercise daily. Medium-energy dogs should receive about one and a half hours of outdoor exercise. Couch potatoes can probably settle for about one hour a day. In addition to outdoor exercise, I hope you will give your dog lots of attention. We love to be patted and played with, and we even love to practice our obedience lessons.

Grooming

Weekly grooming is not merely a beauty treatment—it is a matter of our health. Dogs whose coats are neglected can develop infections, sores, rashes, and other skin problems. They don't just look awful. They will also start to emit a powerful doggy (or less savory) odor and shed all over your floors, furniture, clothes, and car.

All dog coats require care, including the nonshedding breeds whose coats usually require professional grooming, sometimes as often as every six weeks, and this can get expensive. Dogs with long, thick-layered coats need a thorough weekly brushing, which may take an hour or more. A few short-haired breeds also need weekly brushing, which can usually be accomplished in an hour or less. Other shorthairs need less frequent brushing.

How frequently you bathe one of us will depend on coat and lifestyle. A dog who tears through the woods, splashes in mud, or swims in the creek will need to be bathed more often than the dog who sedately walks the sidewalks with you. If you plan to bathe your dog yourself, his size and type of coat should be considered. A large dog takes more time to bathe and longer to dry than a small dog, and it may be difficult or impossible to lift him into a sink or onto a table. Short fur requires less time to wash, rinse, and dry than long, multilayered coats.

Breeds With High Grooming Requirements

Curly-Coated Breeds

- Bichon Frise
- Poodle
- Portuguese Water Dog
- Puli

Long-Coated Breeds

- Afghan Hound
- Cocker Spaniel
- Chow Chow
- Collie (rough)
- Keeshond
- Lhasa Apso
- Newfoundland
- Old English Sheepdog
- Samoyed
- Setters
- Shetland Sheepdog
- Shih Tzu
- Yorkshire Terrier

Wirehaired Breeds

- Affenpinscher
- Airedale Terrier
- Bouvier des Flandres
- Norwich Terrier
- Schnauzer
- Scottish Terrier
- West Highland White Terrier

Finances

The amount of money needed to acquire and care for a dog can vary tremendously, depending on many factors, especially size and lifestyle. Size, more than any other single factor, affects the ongoing cost of our care.

Food

Food is the single largest maintenance expense, and large dogs cost more to

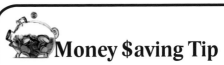
Training

Much as I hate to admit it, professional training is not optional. It is a must, even for intelligent, good dogs such as myself. Although we don't always show it, most of us enjoy being trained. The cost varies a lot, from free or low-cost classes sponsored by local governments or shelters to group classes to pricey private lessons that cost $50 an hour and more.

feed. Compare the cost of feeding a 5-pound (2-kg) Chihuahua with that of feeding a 150-pound (68-kg) Saint Bernard. The difference is astronomical! A Chihuahua might eat 1/2 cup of food a day, while a Saint can consume 10 cups or more. Large dogs cost more to groom and board, and medications based on weight and some types of veterinary care cost more for large dogs. Basic equipment can cost less than $75 or much, much more if you want to go fancy.

Veterinary Care

Another ongoing cost, basic care—an annual checkup, vaccinations, parasite prevention—is not optional. Take it from me, I don't like those trips to the vet any more than the next dog, but it keeps me free of ticks, fleas, and even worse, so it's worth it. Veterinary care for puppies and geriatric dogs typically costs more than for a healthy adult dog like me.

Some breeds do tend to present certain veterinary problems, but not every dog in that breed will suffer that problem. You should know about the likelihood ahead of time and be

Grooming

If you are able to groom your dog yourself, this expense can be as little as the price of a good brush or comb and the occasional bottle of dog shampoo. But if your dog needs—or if you choose—professional grooming, that is another matter. The type and size of dog and the frequency of grooming, as well as regional price differences, will determine how much you spend. It can range from $50 to $150 per session.

prepared for related expenses.

A word about emergencies—I've been told that some owners are shocked when they learn how much it costs to treat one of us for an illness or injury. While the cost of dog food is buried in the grocery bill each week, it's a little tough to suddenly come face-to-face with a major veterinary expenditure. Yet sadly, few of us go through life without an illness or an injury. It could be something as simple as a sore paw or infected ear or something more serious like getting hit by a car.

But—and need I say it—a good veterinarian is one of my best friends. Veterinarians are among the best-trained and (in my opinion) lowest-paid professionals in the country. Great advances have been made in animal medicine, and much more can be done for a sick or injured dog than ever before.

So please expect the best but plan a rainy-day emergency fund for your dog. Set aside, either mentally or in fact, a *veterinary emergency fund* of at least $1,000. Yes, that's right: $1,000. And hopefully you may never need to use it.

Miscellaneous Expenses

Depending on where you live and your lifestyle, you may need to factor in additional expenses, including a fence, boarding, dog sitters, dog walkers, and the many extras that we graciously accept, such as monogrammed beds, doggy doors, and car seat covers.

RESOURCES MADE EASY

Books About Dogs and Their Characteristics

- Choron, Sandra and Harry. *Planet Dog: a Doglopedia*. New York: Houghton Mifflin Company, 2005.
- De Prisco, Andrew, and James B. Johnson. *Choosing a Dog For Life*. Neptune City, New Jersey: TFH Publications, 1996.
- Morgan, Diane. *The Simple Guide to Choosing a Dog*. Neptune City, New Jersey: TFH Publications, 2003.
- Rice, Dan. *Big Dog Breeds*. Hauppauge, New York: Barron's, 2001.
- Tortora, Daniel F. *The Right Dog For You: Choosing a Breed that Matches Your Personality, Family and Lifestyle*. New York, New York: Fireside Books, 1980.
- Wood, Deborah. *Little Dogs: Training Your Pint-Sized Companion*. Neptune City, New Jersey: TFH Publications, 2004.

Chapter 3

Choosing and Finding the Right Dog

Now that you have looked over Chapter 1: Self-Audit and Chapter 2: Canine Audit, you have figured out what *type* of dog is best for you. Let's say that you've decided on a dog who weighs less than 20 pounds (9 kg), with short hair and an energy level and need for exercise that are not too high.

The next step is to look for that *individual* dog. I cannot pick out the dog for you, but in this chapter I will:

- help you evaluate whether a mixed or purebred fits the criteria you have developed
- discuss the advantages and disadvantages of adult versus puppy
- help you decide whether a male or female is best for you
- explain the pros and cons of adoption versus purchase
- detail how to find the right breeder, shelter, or rescue league
- spell out how, when you are nose to nose with a dog at the shelter, rescue, or breeder's, you can test whether this is the right dog for you
- list resources that will enable you to research breeds and locate breeders, shelters, and rescues

NARROWING THE FIELD

Mixed breed or purebred? Puppy or adult? Boy or girl? Answering the following questions will help you narrow down your search for a dog.

Mixed Breed or Purebred?

You'll need to decide if you want a purebred or if a mix is right for you.

Mixed, Shmixed

I am a huge fan of mixed-breed dogs. These pooches are often underrated and misunderstood, yet they are the most popular dogs in America.

The myth that mixed-breed dogs are unappealing mutts and mongrels is, thankfully and deservedly, on the wane. Mutts are even becoming fashionable! It's time to take stock of their wonderful qualities, including:

- the charm of being one of a kind
- the advantage of combining characteristics of two or more breeds
- hybrid vigor

For many of us, a dog like no other is the best dog. Mixed breeds come in all possible shapes, sizes, colors, and temperaments, with manifold capacities for affection, play, intelligence, obedience, loyalty, and more. A mutt can be beautiful, cute, odd, energetic, calm, stubborn, loving, and reserved. He can combine the loyalty of a German Shepherd Dog with the gregariousness of a Labrador Retriever and the short hair of a Pointer.

If information about lineage is important to you, you can pay for DNA testing for a mixed-breed dog for about $75. The results of the test can identify the breeds that contributed to a dog's genetic makeup and help you predict and understand behavioral traits and potential medical issues.

Mixes tend to be hardier than purebred dogs. They are drawn from a larger gene pool, resulting in what is sometimes called *hybrid vigor*; they are less prone to the genetic defects, both physical and temperamental, that increasingly plague purebred dogs. For the dog, this means a healthier, longer life. For the owner, this means fewer worries, less heartache, lower veterinary bills, and less short- and long-term care for ailing or disabled pets.

Purebreds

I am also a fan of purebred dogs because of their:

- predictable physical characteristics within a fairly narrow range
- somewhat predictable temperaments (likes to retrieve, swim, chase, cuddle, dig, bark, etc.)

However, these pooches are also misunderstood. I might even go so far as to call them "overrated"—not because they are bad dogs but because many people mistakenly believe that purebred

> ## Think Mix
> Mixed-breed dogs can be as intelligent, trainable, beautiful, and loving as purebred dogs—and may have fewer health problems.

Mixed breed dogs come in all possible shapes, sizes, colors, and temperaments.

and identity of registered dogs (in turn making it possible to prove ancestry). However, papers do not signify a "superior" dog. What papers promise is predictability—conformity to certain specific breed standards. Unfortunately, for many years the focus of breeding has been on perfecting physical appearance to conform with the detailed technical standards used by judges in the show ring. This focus has resulted in insufficient attention and concern to temperament and health—a trend that ethical breeders are trying to reverse.

A major concern with purebred dogs is their susceptibility to inherited physical defects, a result of being bred from a necessarily limited gene pool. Breeding within the breed multiplies the incidence of genetically transmitted defects. Every breed suffers from genetically transmitted diseases, but not every dog in a breed or given litter is afflicted.

The situation is serious: One study concluded that congenital heart disease afflicts purebreds at three times the rate as mixed breeds, and another suggested that each breed carries an average of a dozen genetic defects. The *Canine Consumer Report: A Guide to Hereditary and Congenital*

pooches come with a guarantee of good health, temperament, and brains. There is no such guarantee.

A purebred dog is one whose heritage is from two parents of the same breed, whose ancestors in turn are also purebred. Typically, they come with "papers" that document their ancestry. The papers can be filed with a recording registry—usually the American Kennel Club (AKC)—that maintains information about the lineage

Diseases in Purebred Dogs, produced by the Association of Veterinarians for Animal Rights (AVAR), is a daunting encyclopedia of genetically transmitted diseases affecting different breeds. Genetically transmitted problems include orthopedic abnormalities of the hip, knee, and elbow; blindness and deafness; allergies; extreme sensitivity to medications; ear and skin infections; and a greatly increased risk of cancer. To make matters worse, many such problems are not apparent until later in a dog's life. No matter how careful you are in evaluating a puppy's health, you cannot be certain he will be free of inherited defects.

Adult or Puppy?

I am a huge proponent of adopting adult dogs. A dog of any age can become fully attached to you and your family. It is not true, as some people believe, that only a puppy will bond with you. There are advantages and disadvantages for an owner at each stage of canine development.

Puppies: Cute but High Maintenance

There are few creatures more adorable than a puppy. They are great fun to watch, play with, and cuddle and are guaranteed to make us smile and laugh. Many people feel strongly that they want to participate in and enjoy their dog's fastest-growing first few months.

A puppy needs to spend at least the first two months of life with his mother and littermates, a crucial period of canine socialization. He also needs to be exposed to handling by humans during this period and should be adopted into a human family when he is about three months old so that he can bond with humans.

Puppies take time, money, and effort. Homes must be puppy-proofed against escapes, chewing, and soiling. Puppies need to be taken outside every few hours until they are housetrained and cannot be left alone for long periods. They can wake you up at night and need plenty of attention during the day. They require vaccinations and periodic veterinary checkups.

When you choose a puppy, a certain amount of guesswork is involved. Even with DNA tests, the adult appearance and temperament of mixed-breed pups can be hard to foresee and might surprise you in unexpected ways. There is less uncertainty with purebred puppies. Good breeding can predict within a narrow range what a puppy will grow to look like in size, shape, color, and coat type. Within that range there is some variation. For example, a Golden Retriever, very likely to be strong, muscular, and energetic, can weigh from about 55 to 75 pounds (25 to 34 kg); the coat can range from a pale blond to dark

AMERICAN KENNEL CLUB (AKC) BREED GROUPS

The AKC recognizes more than 150 breeds (with new breeds recognized from time to time). Another 300 breeds are recognized in other parts of the world.
The AKC categorizes dogs into seven groups according to the purpose for which they were originally bred. Breeds within a group share many characteristics but also display many variations. Understanding groups can help you narrow your choices. Once you decide on a specific breed that interests you, research it thoroughly.

Herding Group
- bred to herd sheep and cattle
- loyal, intelligent, sometimes intense
- 20 breeds, including Border Collies, Collies, Corgis, German Shepherd Dogs

Hound Group
- bred to hunt, not next to humans but on their own by tracking or by sight
- independent, can be stubborn and a challenge to train
- 23 breeds, including Afghan Hounds, Basset Hounds, Beagles, Bloodhounds, Greyhounds

Non-Sporting Group
- a variety of breeds, many resembling Toys, Working, or Sporting dogs
- 17 breeds, including Bulldogs, Chow Chows, Dalmatians, Schipperkes, Standard Poodles

Sporting Group
- bred to hunt alongside humans
- energetic, people oriented, friendly
- 26 breeds, including pointers, retrievers, setters, spaniels

Terrier Group
- bred to eliminate vermin from homes and farms, to hunt, to guard
- feisty, tenacious, often noisy
- 27 breeds, including Airedale Terriers, Cairn Terriers, Fox Terriers, Irish Terriers, Soft Coated Wheaten Terriers

Toy Group
- bred as companions and lapdogs
- less than 20 pounds (9 kg), affectionate, need company
- 21 breeds, including Affenpinschers, Chihuahuas, Maltese, Pugs, Shih Tzu

reddish gold; and his temperament can be mellow, submissive, hyper, stubborn, or even aggressive.

The Teenage Phase

Puppyhood ends at about 12 to 18 months. Different breeds (and even dogs within a breed) mature at different rates. For many dogs, 12 to 24 months is a period of adolescence, which typically involves chewing and teething and continued playful puppy behavior.

Adults: Grateful for a Home

By 18 months, most dogs have attained their adult size. Their energy level—low, medium, high—is usually obvious. Their personality is largely evident as well: mellow or exuberant, timid or dominant, stubborn or compliant. Choosing a dog who has reached this stage of development involves less guesswork than choosing a puppy. You have a better handle on the dog's size, strength, and temperament.

Choosing to adopt an adult dog eliminates guesswork and prediction. Whether the dog is pure or mixed, you can see with your own eyes exactly what he looks like. You can also assess his temperament. Because many genetically transmitted health problems do not become apparent until maturity, you can now evaluate an adult dog's health.

Seniors

Older dogs can make wonderful adoptees. They are mellow—they are not going to pull you around the block, knock you down, or demand endless ball throwing or heavy exercise routines. They can and will bond with new owners. Their appearance and personalities are obvious.

Some people fear that adopting an older dog will lead to high veterinary bills. This is not an inevitable scenario, although it is difficult to predict when or if this might be the case. In my experience, all but one of my adopted dogs lived into old age and passed away quickly, escaping lingering illnesses and veterinary intervention.

Some people resist adopting an older dog because of his shorter life span. But consider that a five- or six-year-old Dachshund may have nearly ten years of life remaining! An older Golden Retriever can live to be 12 or 14. If you are not comfortable making a long-term commitment to dog ownership, adopting an older dog may be right for you.

Pink or Blue Leash?

If you are choosing a purebred dog, the male will usually be larger than the female. With a litter of mixed breeds, it's hard to predict. Males are typically somewhat more assertive. Whether or not this translates into aggression depends on the breed, the individual dog, and his training and history. Both males and females should be neutered—they will be healthier, happier, and less feisty.

You'll have to decide between a puppy or an adult.

THE ADOPTION OPTION

By now you've decided on the type, size, age, and sex of dog you want. It's time to focus on whether you will adopt a dog or purchase one from a breeder. Let's look at the adoption options first.

Adoption Pros and Cons

When you adopt a dog, you are literally saving his life. Sadly, millions of dogs, many of them young and healthy, are euthanized annually simply because there is no place for them to go. At the same time, you do yourself a favor. As millions of "satisfied customers" testify, you *can* find the right dog for you at a shelter or rescue.

Both purebred and mixed-breed dogs of all ages are relinquished or abandoned by their owners. The reasons often relate to the owner, not the dog. Different regions of the country and different shelters report different likely reasons for relinquishment. Among the most common:

- The owner moves and cannot take dog.
- The owner (or a new spouse) is allergic to the dog.
- The owner has too many pets or the pets don't get along.

- The owner does not have time or cannot afford to care for the dog.
- A landlord objects to the dog.

Some dogs do develop problem behaviors, often due to lack of training or exercise, that lead to their relinquishment. Other dogs have veterinary problems that owners cannot afford or are unwilling to pay for. Divorce, death, illness, and disability of the owner can all lead to relinquishment.

A Bargain

Adoption can be cost effective for you. Fees vary tremendously from city to suburb to rural area and from state to state, from a low of about $55 to a high of nearly $250 at shelters. Purebred rescue leagues may charge more for young dogs. The fees are actually modest because they do not begin to cover the actual cost of caring for the dog prior to adoption, which can run into thousands of dollars. Some shelters provide reduced rates or free adoptions to seniors.

Adoption fees cost less than purchasing a dog and include a range of services. Here is a sample of expenses typically included in the adoption fee:
- spay/neuter surgery (or a coupon to pay for it)
- health exam
- behavior/temperament evaluation
- tattoo for identification

> **Save Some Work**
>
> Bringing home an adult dog rather than a puppy can mean less work at home.

- vaccinations
- heartworm test
- treatment for heartworm, fleas, and other parasites

Additional services might include:
- microchipping
- a month or more of free pet health insurance
- personalized identification
- telephone consultations on pet parenting or problem behaviors
- free or reduced-rate training class

Shelters and rescue leagues (also known as rescues) have "matching" programs, some very extensive, to help match you up with just the right dog. Professional staff or volunteers carefully evaluate a dog's temperament and health, and whenever possible, they obtain a history on the dog from previous owners.

Where to Adopt

There are several options for you to choose from, including shelters, breed rescue leagues, and off-site adoptions.

Animal Shelters

There was a time when I could not

walk through an animal shelter without bursting into tears, and I know of people who refuse to even consider visiting a shelter. The sight and sounds of too many needy animals add up to too much distress.

The days of the depressing "dog pound" are over in many jurisdictions, replaced by organizations run by animal welfare professionals. Thanks to aggressive spay and neuter campaigns, public education, and sophisticated, professional approaches to encourage and ensure the success of animal adoptions, the proportion of animals rehomed is steadily growing. In my local county shelter, the adoption rate approaches 90 percent.

A shelter is a great place to find your perfect dog.

Shelters operated by a government agency are required to accept all relinquished and stray animals. Sadly, this usually means that, as the shelter becomes too full, some animals must be euthanized to make room for new arrivals. Many private, nonprofit, nongovernment organizations, supported by contributions from the public, do not euthanize. But this means that, once full, they cannot accept new arrivals. The mission of both types of shelters is to take in relinquished, homeless, neglected, or abused animals and find permanent homes for them. You may find the dog you are looking for in either type of shelter. Both have purebred as well as mixed-breed dogs and puppies for adoption. Some shelters report that purebreds account for 25 to 30 percent of their dog population.

Where funds are available, shelters are reinventing themselves and becoming

Shelters

Shelters are filled to overflowing with healthy dogs who will make great pets!

Rescue a Purebred

Purebred dogs can be found in animal shelters and through breed rescue leagues.

refreshingly people and animal friendly. Rows of kennels are replaced with open, light-filled spaces and noise-reducing, glass-fronted doggy "dens" and puppy "pods." Acoustical ceilings help muffle sounds. Quieter rooms are less stressful for animals and more welcoming for human visitors. Improved air circulation and purification systems reduce odors and airborne germs. Visiting rooms and playrooms make it possible for pets and people to interact and become acquainted.

Adoption rates improve at these new shelters. In the quieter, less stressful environment of up-to-date shelters, dogs can relax into their normal personalities and human visitors find these shelters user friendly.

At the Washington Animal Rescue League in Washington, D.C., the number of adoptions increased dramatically after a major renovation of the facility. The average length of time of an animal's stay prior to adoption shortened from six weeks to three, and the average length of time a visitor spends increased from 30 minutes to 2½ hours.

Off-Site Adoptions: "Pets to the People"

Some rescues and shelters are resorting to an additional strategy: "If we can't entice people to come us, we'll go to them." Using mobile adoption vans, shopping mall parking lots, or borrowed space in pet supply stores, volunteers and professionals bring adoptable dogs into suburban and urban communities for "adoptathons" or similarly named events. Passersby are able to learn about adoptions and meet dogs in need of permanent homes. These off-site events are particularly appealing to people who find visits to shelters overwhelming. The adoption process and screening at these sites are the same that the sponsoring organization employs on a regular basis. To find off-site adoptions, check websites for local shelters and rescues and the announcements section of your newspaper.

Purebred Rescue

Many purebred adoptions take place through breed rescue organizations, although increasingly, purebred dogs can be found in animal shelters. Breed rescues are run by volunteers and are dedicated to saving and rehoming dogs of a specific breed—Akita, Chihuahua, Old English Sheepdog, and so on. The dogs whom they help come from owners who contact them and from breeders looking for a good home for a dog whose show or breeding days are over. Almost all of the volunteers are or have been breed owners themselves, and many have adopted one or more of their dogs from a rescue.

Not every geographic area has a rescue organization for every breed. The more popular a breed in a given region, the more likely that a rescue group will operate there. Some rescue groups are run by one or two volunteers, and others rely on a network of dozens of people.

A few groups provide referrals only. Members maintain a list of potential adopters—interested people who have contacted them—and refer them to local shelters when a dog of that breed becomes available, or they match them with an owner or breeder about to give up a dog. Either the shelter or the rescue screens the prospective adopters.

Many groups, either in addition to or instead of referrals, provide foster homes for dogs until a permanent placement is made, and a few provide temporary boarding in a kennel.

Foster volunteers evaluate the dog's temperament and health and may take on the tasks of training, socializing, or rehabilitating a sick or injured dog. A dog's stay in foster care may last days or months.

One of the great strengths of breed rescues lies in their thorough knowledge of a breed and their ability to match the right dog with the right family or individual. Another advantage is that adoptable dogs living in foster homes are less traumatized, more socialized, and more at ease than dogs who have been housed in shelters.

The popularity, number, and professionalism of rescues have grown quickly, thanks in part to use of the Internet. It is no surprise that the number of new AKC registrations has dropped by 18 percent from 2000 to 2004 and is expected to continue to drop as more people choose to rescue and adopt, rather than buy, purebred dogs.

At the Shelter

When you go to visit the shelter, take a "cheat sheet" with you. Jot down the most important characteristics of the dog whom you are looking for, and don't give in to "cute." Also jot down the questions that you need to have answered, such as:

- Does the shelter have a history on the dog?

- How old is he?
- Why was he relinquished?
- How long has he been in the shelter?
- Has his temperament been evaluated? What were the results?
- Is it known how well he gets along with children, cats, and other dogs?
- Does he have any health problems?
- Has he received any training at the shelter? Is he housetrained? Leash trained?
- Based on their observations, how do shelter personnel rate his energy level and temperament?

If you have your heart set on a certain breed, consider adopting from a breed rescue.

Most shelters screen dogs for health and problem behaviors before putting them up for adoption. But you should also examine the dog or puppy you are interested in:

- Are his eyes bright and clear, with no discharge?
- Is the coat shiny?
- Do the inside of the ears look and smell clean?
- Do the teeth look clean and white?

You do not need to rule out every dog with a health problem. Just like us humans, most dogs—even those who are strong and basically healthy—develop a few aches, pains, and issues over the years. A dog with a dull-looking coat may simply need better nutrition or a good bath; an older dog may need his teeth cleaned.

If you find one or more adult dogs at a shelter who seem right for you, spend time—as much time as you can—interacting with them. Most shelters have a play area for this. As you pet and play with the dogs, you will probably get a pretty strong sense of whether your personalities will click.

At the Breed Rescue

If you have found a rescue league with

a dog or puppy ready for adoption, ask the volunteer or foster caregiver the same questions you would ask at a shelter about history, temperament, and health, and also ask specific questions about the breed. The volunteer will know a lot about the breed but may not be able to answer all of your questions about an individual dog. Spend plenty of time interacting with the dog before you make up your mind. Ask yourself if the chemistry seems right before you make a decision.

The Interview

Before sending a dog home with you, shelter staff or rescue volunteers will ask you to fill out an application and/ or questionnaire and will probably interview you. A shelter or rescue may:

- insist on meeting all family members
- ask for references, probably including a veterinarian if you have had dogs before
- visit your home
- require a waiting period of 48 hours or more
- refuse to give you a dog intended as a gift or surprise for someone else
- require a letter from your landlord acknowledging that dogs are permitted in your building

Adoption counselors will try their best to help you find the right dog and a permanent, loving home for the dog. To avoid returns, even those with limited staff and funds try to socialize and train as many dogs as possible before putting them up for adoption. Despite their best efforts, not all adoptions work out perfectly, but neither does purchasing from a breeder. Most shelters and rescues will ask you to sign a contract promising to return the pet if you decide that you have made the wrong choice.

BREEDERS: A COMMERCIAL INVESTMENT

Perhaps adoption is not for you and you have decided that you want to purchase a dog or puppy.

Purchasing Pros and Cons

Purchasing a purebred puppy can be a rewarding experience for both you and the pup if you find your way to a responsible, caring, experienced breeder. Purchasing a purebred puppy from an amateur breeder or over the Internet (probably from a puppy mill) will help promote irresponsible and often cruel and inhumane breeding practices— which is bad news for you and the puppy.

Money $aving Tip

Adoption can be a bargain because fees typically include a range of services already performed, such as spay/neuter surgery, deworming, a health exam, and vaccinations.

Cost of a Purebred Dog

It is virtually impossible to predict the cost of a purebred dog from a good breeder when there are more than 150 breeds to choose from and thousands of ethical breeders. The popularity of a breed at a given time, which differs from one region of the country to another, and the number and practices of breeders in different areas will all affect the asking price. Roughly speaking— *very* roughly speaking—you can expect to pay an ethical breeder at least $1,000 (give or take a few hundred dollars on each side of that figure) for a healthy, socialized, pet-quality (rather than show-quality) puppy.

Please don't be tempted if lower prices are offered for your desired breed by a pet shop, commercial breeder, or backyard breeder. You are simply helping to support breeding that is not good for dogs, and you are likely to end up with a puppy who has health or temperament problems.

Where to Purchase

Here are three simple rules I hope you will follow. I did not dream them up myself—virtually every animal welfare group in the country, large and small, north, south, east, and west, national, state and local, agree that you should:

1. Buy only from a responsible, ethical breeder.
2. Never buy a dog from a pet store.
3. Never buy a dog over the Internet, from a large commercial breeder (a puppy mill), or from a backyard breeder.

Ethical Breeders: Two Thumbs Up

Fortunately for those of you looking for a particular breed, there are ethical, responsible breeders who know their breed and care deeply about their dogs. Good breeders:

- belong to a national or local breed club
- breed just a few litters a year (only one per year per female dog)
- own one or both parents (and will introduce you)
- have dogs who are healthy, happy, and not afraid of strangers
- are knowledgeable about the breed *and* this particular line of dogs
- will socialize the puppies
- will not let you have a puppy who is younger than eight weeks old
- will show you around the premises, which will be clean and well maintained

- will be able and happy to answer questions about the breed, about a particular litter, and about training and care for this type of dog
- will study genetics and health problems and will answer questions about hereditary issues involving the breed
- will screen for genetic defects common to the breed and be willing to provide written proof of the parents' screening
- will provide a written health guarantee
- will interview you to be certain that you understand and can handle the demands of caring for this breed of dog
- care what happens to the puppies they breed and will look for a good match by asking questions similar to those that you have already covered in your self-audit (see Chapter 1)
- will provide you with references and a written contract

Finding an ethical breeder is essential for a healthy purebred dog.

To find an ethical breeder, referrals can come from a veterinarian, groomer, trainer, or a neighborhood dog owner. One of the best sources is rescue organizations for that breed. These volunteers are likely to know the source of dogs who have been well bred and well placed—and those who are not.

Many breeders (including some good and not-so-good ones) belong to regional or national breed clubs, which can be tracked down through the AKC or on the Internet. Just plug in a breed, as in "Basset Hound Club of America."

Visiting dog shows is a good way to research and meet reputable breeders and it's fun, but the dogs you see at shows will not be for sale as pets. Some breeders place ads in newspapers and magazines, but an attractive or expensive ad doesn't ensure quality puppies.

Pet Stores: Nay to that Doggy in the Window

How difficult it is to walk by a pet shop and ignore the pleading eyes of an adorable Dachshund, Labrador Retriever, Poodle, or mixed-breed puppy! But please walk on by. The price you pay may well be higher, sometimes significantly higher, than what you would pay a reputable breeder.

All too often pet shops sell puppies who are ill, poorly socialized, poorly bred, and poorly cared for, susceptible to multiple inherited defects. Despite state pet "lemon laws" that seek to hold sellers accountable for selling sick or defective pets, there is no guarantee that the puppy in the window won't sicken and even die soon after you bring him home. Recovering your purchase price is hardly sufficient recompense. And despite federal legislation intended to protect young animals that are flown or trucked from breeders to pet shops, animals still suffer and even die en route from exposure to extreme temperatures, inadequate food and water, and long trips. To make matters worse, the pet shop supply of puppies usually comes from irresponsible sources: puppy mills and commercial breeders.

Puppy Mills and Commercial Breeders: Just Say No

Commercial breeders breed one or more purebreds or so-called "designer dogs" that mix two breeds (Pug + Beagle = Puggle) on a large scale, sometimes more than 1,000 dogs at a time, housed in cages. Puppies produced commercially are born into stressful environments, receive little individual attention, and are not well socialized, cared for, or stimulated.

Puppy mills take large-scale breeding to its worst possible extension: holding female dogs in unsanitary and often filthy conditions, breeding them over and over from a too-young age to a too-old age (even when they are sick or injured), removing their pups too early, and destroying or abandoning dogs when they are too old or sickly to continue breeding. Many of these puppies are of poor quality and doomed to behavioral or physical problems. The conditions in which their parents are kept are unhealthy and inhumane.

Large-scale breeders sell their dogs to individuals over the Internet, through newspaper ads, and through pet stores. Internet sellers offer to ship puppies almost anywhere in the country, sight unseen. Not only have you not seen and chosen the puppy, but the breeder has no idea (and doesn't care) whether this type of dog is a good choice for you.

Good Breeders

Good breeders breed for quality, not quantity. You may have to wait in line for the pup you want.

Backyard Breeders: Another Thumbs Down

Backyard breeders, who typically advertise puppies for sale in the newspaper, are either misguided amateurs or nonprofessionals hoping to make easy money. Amateurs want their own "special dog" to procreate and breed him or her just to keep a puppy for themselves while selling the rest of the litter. Others hope or plan to make money from breeding—again and again—their own dog or dogs. There are several things wrong with both plans:

A good breeder socializes her puppies.

- Overpopulation: Overpopulation is the number-one canine problem in America. Dogs who are spayed and neutered don't breed, are easier to train, have fewer health problems, and are less likely to wander, fight, or bite. "Just one litter" is not a good enough reason to breed a dog, and there is no guarantee that a parent's "special personality" will be passed on.
- Lack of Expertise: Breeding dogs demands expertise, attention, money, and hard work. It is messy and can be threatening to a dog's health. It is unhealthy and inhumane for a female dog to be bred over and over, regardless of her age.
- Quality: Many "backyard puppies," especially those intended to be money-makers, are of substandard quality. Owners don't know how or don't bother to check and control for genetic defects and provide proper nutrition, veterinary care, and socialization.

Backyard breeders, puppy mills, and large-scale commercial breeders don't like to identify themselves as such. Many prefer to sell over the Internet so that you cannot see where or how their dogs are born and raised. Avoid these sellers at all costs. You will be amply rewarded for the time that you invest in researching a breed and finding a good breeder.

At the Breeder

Before you visit the breeder, research your chosen breed ahead of time. Bring a "cheat sheet" with you that includes questions about the specific breed and especially about its genetic health problems. Good examples of the types of questions you should be prepared to ask about your chosen breed can be found in *Dog Fancy* magazine's "Ask the Breeder" sections, including:

- Do you test for the breed's specific genetic diseases (glaucoma or deafness, for example)? Can I see the results?
- Have you had trouble with any problems related to the size or structure of the breed (bloat or hip dysplasia, for example)? Can you tell me what to look for and what to do if these occur?
- Do you breed primarily for the show ring or field work?
- Can you show me how to wash the breed's ears, clip nails, groom, or perform other tasks that may be unique to the breed?

You should also ask the breeder

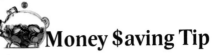

Money $aving Tip

Acquiring a puppy from a pet shop or over the Internet is a bad bargain. You will overpay for a puppy likely to have physical and behavioral problems.

general questions, including:

- Why did you choose this male and this female to create this litter?
- How long have you been working with this breed?
- How do you tell the show-quality dogs (which the breeder will usually want to keep and show) from the pets?
- How many litters do your dogs have each year?
- Is there a history of health problems with the parents or grandparents?
- How do you guarantee a puppy's health?
- How do you socialize the puppies?
- Will you be available to give me guidance as I raise a puppy?

When the litter arrives and you go to visit, spend lots of time observing and interacting with the pups who are going to be sold. It's a little hard to predict at this stage what their adult personalities will be like (the sleeping puppy may just be worn out from playing and not necessarily the mellow fellow you are looking for), but there will be some clues. The inquisitive, active, friendly pup will probably be much the same when he grows up, and the somewhat shy pup will likely be a retiring adult.

Unless your heart and your observations point you clearly toward an individual pup, a safe choice is usually the "middle-of-the-road" puppy: neither the most active nor the shyest one in the litter.

Because you are working with an ethical breeder who will give you a health guarantee, you should be able to assume that all of the puppies are healthy. This will allow you to focus on their temperament and behavior. But if you notice what you think is a health issue—such as discharge from the eyes or nose—be certain to ask the breeder about it.

Consider It Flattery

More than one would-be purchaser has been turned off by the questions a breeder asks. Consider it flattery, not an insult or invasion of privacy. These dedicated dog people have your interests at heart, as well as the dog's interests. They want to make sure that you are happy with your choice because if you are not, the dog is probably not going to stay with you. Seen in this light, it makes sense for you to:

- be asked to sign a contract agreeing to return the dog should you decide not to keep him
- be asked to provide proof that your landlord allows dogs of this size
- be asked to sign a contract agreeing to spay or neuter your pet
- answer questions about care arrangements at home and when you travel

BE PATIENT, THIS COULD TAKE A WHILE

Perhaps you have discovered that the excellent breeder you've found has no pups at the moment. (Remember, good breeders breed for quality, not quantity) Or you've checked the Internet, made a few calls, and even paid a visit to a local shelter or rescue—and found no dogs fitting the description of what you are looking for or that there are two or three applications ahead of yours for the dog you hope to adopt.

This is par for the course. You can get in line (with a deposit) to choose a puppy from the breeder's next litter. The rescue group will almost always take your application and let you know when a dog becomes available who will be a good match for you. The

Bring a list of questions to ask the breeder.

shelter will probably be receiving new animals every few days, so keep visiting so that your next application will be one of the first.

The relationship that you are about to launch with your new dog or puppy will last for years and affect you every day. Hang in there until you find the right dog.

Picky, Picky, and Picky

You may be surprised by the number of people who go looking for a small, two- to three-year-old short-haired dog but give in to impulse and the gorgeous, adorable, irresistible brown eyes of a 200-pound (91-kg), heavily shedding, drooling Newfoundland. Remember that you are bringing home an entire package. Don't choose a dog on looks alone, and don't settle on a dog because of a single characteristic, such as size or coat type.

RESOURCES MADE EASY

Books About Adoption

- Gagne, Tammy. *The Happy Adopted Dog*. Neptune City, NJ: TFH Publications, 2003.
- O'Neil, Jacqueline. *Second Start: Creative Rehoming for Dogs*. New York: Howell Book House, 1997.
- Ross, John, and Barbara McKinney. *Adopting a Dog: The Indispensable Guide for Your Newest Family Member*. New York: W.W. Norton, 2005.
- Rubenstein, Eliza, and Shari Kalina. *The Adoption Option: Choosing and Raising the Shelter Dog for You*. New York: Howell Book House, 1996.

Books About Mixed-Breed Dogs

- Bonham, Margaret H. *The Complete Guide to Mutts: Selection, Care and Celebration from Puppyhood to Senior*. New York: Howell Book House, 2004.
- DeGioia, Phyllis. *The Mixed-Breed Dog*. Neptune City, NJ: TFH Publications, 2007.
- Szabo, Julia. *The Underdog: A Celebration of Mutts*. New York: Workman Publishing, 2005.

Books About Purebreds

- Coile, D. Caroline. *The Dog Breed Bible: Descriptions and Photos of Every Breed Recognized by the AKC*. Hauppauge, NY: Barron's, 2007.
- De Vito, Dominique. *The World Atlas of Dog Breeds*, 6th Edition. Neptune City, NJ: TFH Publications, 2009.
- Van der Leyen, Katherina. *Illustrated Guide to 140 Dog Breeds*. Hauppauge, NY: Barron's, 2000.

Adoption

- American Society for the Prevention of Cruelty to Animals (ASPCA): www.aspca.org
- Humane Society of the United States (HSUS): www.hsus.org

Breed Rescues or Shelters

- Adopt a Pet: www.adoptapet.com
- American Kennel Club (AKC): www.akc.org
- Petfinder: www.petfinder.com
- Pets911: www.Pets911.com
- Look in the Yellow Pages of your phone book under "animal shelters" or "animal rescue."
- Look in your "local government" section on the Internet under "animal control" or "animal shelter."
- Use an Internet search engine and type in your state, county, or city, breed, and rescue, as in "Maryland Collie rescue."

Purebred Dogs

- American Kennel Club (AKC): www.akc.org; 212-696-8200

DNA Test for a Mixed-Breed Dog

- Canine Heritage: www.canineheritage.com; 800-362-3644
- What's My Dog?: www.whatsmydog.com
- Search the Internet for "DNA dog test."

Part II
In the Beginning

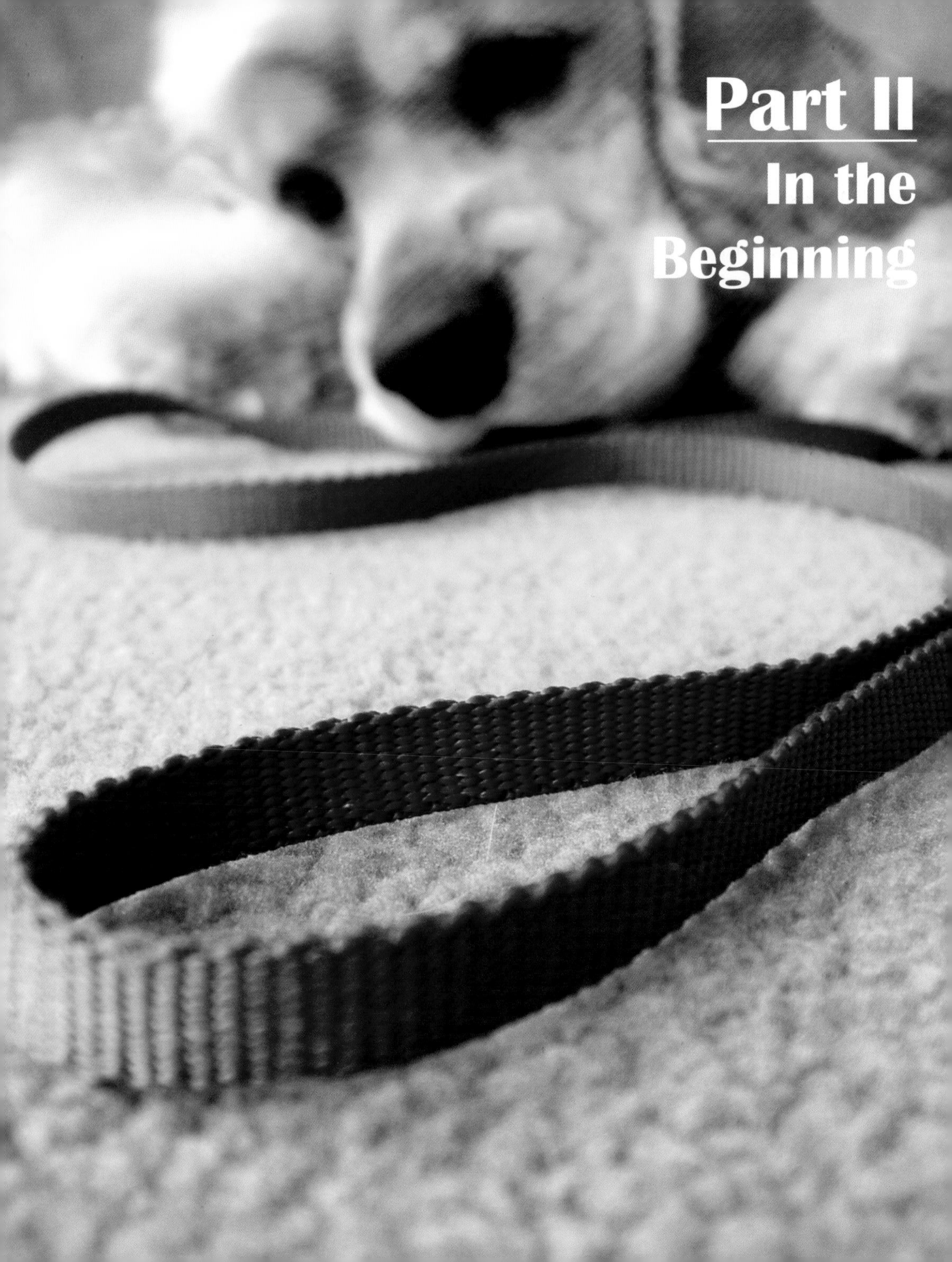

Chapter 4

Mobilizing Your Assets

To get off to a good start with your new puppy or dog, there are a few things you need to do *before* you bring him home:

1. Decide on the timing of when to bring him home.
2. Make a care plan.
3. Choose a veterinarian.
4. Buy equipment and food.
5. Puppy-proof your house if your canine is less than 12 months old.

TIMING

There are good, bad, and very bad times to bring a new dog into your home. A new home is stressful for any dog or puppy, and a new pet is stressful for any family. There are new and different chores and routines and a new animal underfoot. Both people and dogs need time to adjust.

A Good Time

To ease the adjustment, bring your new dog home at a quiet time in your household. If you are retired, this can be any time that you are not planning to travel or have houseguests. If you are working, the beginning of a long weekend or an at-home vacation is ideal.

A Bad Time

Try not to bring a new pet home during times of change, such as before, during, or after a move, during illness, or just after a major change in your household, such as marriage, death, or divorce. Your life will already be stressful enough.

A Very Bad Time

It may be obvious, but I will state it anyway: A very bad time for a new pet is the beginning of a vacation, when you will have to board your dog somewhere, leave him in someone else's care, or take him with you.

Although it sounds like fun, holidays are one of the worst times to introduce a dog into your home. Your household will be anything but calm, and holiday decorations such as tinsel, holly berries, poinsettias, and mistletoe present real danger to canines if ingested. Already nervous in a new environment, dogs and puppies can become even more anxious and unsettled during holiday bustle. Nor is this an easy time for humans, busier than usual, to establish and maintain a consistent pet care routine.

You may not even have the option of a Christmas or Hanukkah dog: Many breeders, shelters, and rescue leagues place a moratorium on pre-holiday adoptions and sales, in part to frustrate the misguided concept of giving pets as gifts.

CANINE CARE PLAN

I am a great believer in the written word. I need to write things down to keep myself organized, so I begin every day with a to-do list that I post on the refrigerator door.

Although you may not be as forgetful as I am and may not need daily reminders, I recommend that you begin canine care with a written plan that you put together ahead of time. In addition to making some basic decisions—where will the dog sleep, will he be allowed on furniture—plan a daily and weekly schedule, noting the tasks that need to be accomplished in the first few weeks and months.

Beginning Tasks

These include:

- initial veterinary visit
- any follow-up vet visits (as necessary)

Find a veterinarian with whom you feel comfortable.

Make a Plan

Every dog and every family needs a schedule of daily tasks. To help you plan yours, see Chapter 7: Everyday Care and Feeding.

Daily Tasks

Take a moment to write down a daily schedule, noting:

- timing of morning, evening, and daily walks (number of walks depends on age—puppy or dog— and energy level)
- who in the household will take charge of each walk
- feeding schedule and who will be in charge

Weekly Tasks

These will vary with your dog's needs but are likely to include:

- grooming
- training class or session (for the first few weeks or months)

CHOOSE A VETERINARIAN

Choose a veterinarian before you need one, before you bring your pooch home for the first time. You can begin your search by asking for recommendations from neighborhood dog owners, animal shelter and rescue personnel, trainers, and breeders, and check with the American Animal Hospital Association

(AAHA), which accredits 3,000 clinics nationwide (15 percent of all veterinary clinics). When you find a veterinary hospital or two that look promising, call and ask for a tour. Look for:

- clean and sanitary premises
- up-to-date equipment (ask questions, even if you're not sure what you are looking at)
- dog and cat cages in separate areas
- calm, well-organized, friendly, and courteous staff

Arrange to meet at least one of the veterinarians, and chat with some of the employees. Decide whether you feel comfortable talking with them and whether they communicate well with you. Find out about weekend and office hours. Thankfully, veterinary clinics increasingly offer extended evening and weekend hours.

Ask about prices that the clinic charges, especially for checkups and preventive care. Some facilities offer discounts to seniors or to households with multiple pets. Ask whether the clinic provides additional, nonveterinary services, such as boarding, grooming, or pet transportation, which might make it more attractive if these are services you plan to use.

Convenience Counts

A long drive or a frustrating hunt for a parking space is no fun when you have a sick or injured dog with you in the car (or even if you don't). Some clinics now offer transportation for clients and their pets, usually for an extra fee. This can be an extremely helpful service, especially if you do not drive or have trouble loading your dog into the car.

Another option, not available to everyone, is to find a veterinarian whom you like within walking distance. I lived in a city for years and enjoyed the luxury of walking my dogs to and from their animal hospital for routine checkups, but this option does not always work because of bad weather, emergencies, or when a dog is sick or injured.

Home veterinary services are becoming more popular.

Mobile Veterinary Care

Some veterinarians actually make house calls. Compared to conventional clinics, home veterinary services are few and far between but are growing in size and number, especially in urban areas. You call to make an appointment and the veterinarian arrives at your home in a specially equipped van. Most mobile veterinarians do not provide the full range of services that a clinic can offer but generally perform routine checkups and vaccinations and some diagnostic services. A few do have fully equipped mobile vans with X-ray and EKG machines, laboratory facilities, and even a surgical suite for performing minor surgery.

Vans that provide limited services will transport pets back and forth to a clinic if necessary for further in-house care. If a mobile service is offered as an adjunct to an animal hospital, the van will transport to that hospital. Mobiles that are "stand-alone" services, not working out of a particular veterinary clinic, will refer to other facilities for follow-up care.

Veterinarians and clients praise more than the convenience of mobile services.

They point out that some dogs are difficult to load into a car or become stressed and fearful in a car or a clinic. Owners, too, find it easier and far less stressful to wait for the doorbell to ring than to load a dog into a car and drive to the clinic—especially if the dog is unwell or very old.

If you plan to use home veterinary care, visit and interview the providers, just as you would a regular clinic. Also ask about fees, as mobile vets tend to be more expensive.

Emergency Care

Ask the veterinarians who run a general (or mobile) practice about emergency care arrangements during the hours that the clinic is closed. A small number of animal hospitals operate around the clock, providing general care during office hours and emergency care during off-hours. Most hospitals refer clients to another clinic during off-hours. If you choose the latter route (the most common arrangement), you can follow your clinic's advice or find your own emergency care location. In either event, check around ahead of time and find an emergency clinic with which you are comfortable. Make some calls or visit to ask questions; choose a clinic that will have at least one veterinarian, as well as support staff, present all night. Be certain that you know how to get there.

Canine Taxi Service

Urban areas increasingly are being served by "pet taxis" and "canine cabs"—commercial taxicab companies that transport pets and their owners. Usually using vans for transport, they operate like ordinary on-call cab companies: You call in advance to arrange for a pickup at your home or the animal hospital. For an extra charge, the taxi will wait for you at the veterinary clinic, and of course you will be charged for the ride to and from the clinic. Pet taxis can be pricey, so before you decide that you will rely on one, locate one or two in your area and investigate the fees. To locate a pet taxi service, begin by asking your veterinarian, who may know of one. Some of these services advertise by leaving brochures or business cards in animal clinic waiting rooms and pet shops.

BASIC EQUIPMENT

Plan to have basic equipment on hand before that big day when you bring your new dog home. You can purchase some items before you even choose your dog or puppy. The selection of other items—such as a collar that needs to

be sized to fit your pet—may have to wait until you actually know which dog will be yours. Because most breeders, shelters, and rescues do not hand over a dog on your first visit, you will probably have a waiting period between the time you choose a dog and the day you bring him home; this is the time to buy items that need to be sized.

Essential equipment need not be fancy or expensive to keep your dog happy, safe, and healthy. It is difficult to estimate the total cost of dog care items because of the variables involved (such as the size and age of your pet), but you can buy the basics for well under $75. Some equipment will cost more depending on size, and puppy equipment must be replaced to accommodate growth. Prices vary from geographic region to region, store to store, and among stores, paper, and online catalogs. A major variable is simply stylistic because you can choose between basic versions and decorative, luxury versions for most items. Basic equipment should include:

- collar
- food and water bowls
- grooming brush or comb
- identification tag
- leash
- nail clippers
- poop scoop or supply of small plastic bags
- toothbrush and toothpaste

Collar

I recommend a flat nylon or cotton web buckle collar, sized to fit your dog's neck. It should measure about 1 to 2 inches (2.5 to 5 cm) more than your dog's neck size but not be so large that it will slip easily over his head. With a growing puppy and even with adults, check the size from time to time—you should be able to easily slip three fingers of one hand between the collar and your dog's neck. As to width, small dogs can usually do with about 1/2 inch (1 cm); larger dogs can wear from 3/4 inch to 1 inch (2 to 2.5 cm). Cloth collars, depending on size and style, cost from $5 to $20.

Flat and rounded buckle collars are also available in leather, but I prefer the cloth collars because they are washable and lightweight. No matter how large or strong your dog, avoid chain, prong, or choke collars; these inflict pain and can even cause damage. Rewards and positive reinforcements are more humane and more effective. A better choice is a head collar, or for some dogs, a harness.

Money $aving Tip

You can sign up online to receive newsletters from pet supply outfits that will alert you to special sales.

A head collar is humane and helps you control a rambunctious dog.

Head Collar

A head collar is a collar made out of web cotton or nylon that rides high on the dog's neck and attaches to a strap that loops over his snout. The theory behind the head collar, which has been endorsed by training professionals and by animal welfare organizations, is that the pressure on the bridge of the snout (similar to what a mother dog might exert on a puppy) stops pulling, lunging, and jumping and prevents the choking caused by a taut collar and choke collars. Do not use a head collar without first receiving proper instruction. Depending on size and style, these collars cost from $15 to $25.

Harness

When walking a leashed dog, a harness may be preferable to a collar for toy breeds because they are predisposed to a collapsing trachea. Use of a collar and leash puts pressure on the trachea and can trigger an episode of gagging or even help to bring on the condition itself. Use of a harness, which applies pressure across the chest and shoulders rather than the neck, avoids this problem. A harness can also be used to prevent big, strong dogs from pulling you and choking themselves. A harness is also recommended by veterinary ophthalmologists for dogs with certain eye problems, such as glaucoma or weak corneas. Depending on size and style, a harness costs from $10 to $30.

If you use a harness or head collar, use it only for walking your dog with a leash attached. Do not use either as a substitute for a collar with identification tag that your dog wears at all times.

Food and Water Bowls

Get two bowls: one for water, one for food. They should be unbreakable,

Stainless steel bowls are inexpensive and dishwasher safe.

A harness may be preferable for small dogs.

are dishwasher safe, with glazes approved by the Food and Drug Administration (FDA). I recommend against using plastic bowls, which can harbor germs and be chewed.

nontoxic, and the proper size for your dog—small bowls for little dogs, large bowls for big dogs. I prefer utilitarian stainless steel bowls; they are indestructible, easy to keep clean, inexpensive, and dishwasher safe. The smallest size, 1 pint (.5 l), costs about $5.

A stainless steel bowl can be fancied up with a decorative "shell" and nonskid rubber base that helps resist tipping and slipping. A large, nonskid decorative stainless steel bowl may cost $20 to $25.

Ceramic and stoneware bowls are increasingly popular, partly because they are offered in colors and fancifully decorated or even monogrammed. If this is your preference, choose heavy bowls (less likely to slide around) that

Grooming
Brush or Comb

The type of brush or comb that you use will depend on your dog's coat. Luckily, neither costs more than $10.

Identification Tag

An ID tag is an absolute must for your dog. They come in many shapes, sizes, colors, and materials—from gold plate to neon plastic. Many pet shops will engrave one for you on the spot, or you can order one through a print or online catalog. ID tags cost $5 or less. The most important information you should include on the tag is your dog's name and your phone number. Including your address is an option that some people prefer to skip. Collars and leashes can also be ordered with your name and phone number; I prefer not to do this as it advertises this information a little too indiscriminately.

Leash

I recommend a flat (rather than rounded) 6-foot (2-m) cotton or nylon web leash (color of your choice). I prefer a 1/2-inch (1-cm) width; in any event, width should be no more than 5/8 inch (1.5 cm). These leashes are sturdy. A big dog does not necessarily require a wider or thicker leash.

I also recommend a swivel bolt clip (you'll know what I mean when you see it) for attaching the leash to the collar. It's easier to hook and unhook (even with arthritic fingers) and prevents the leash from twisting. A leather leash can burn your hands, and a chain leash can tear them up. A serviceable cloth leash will cost about $10, but you can spend more for a leather leash.

Nail Clipper

Clipping your dog's nails requires a careful hand and good equipment, which may cost about $20. Clippers can be purchased in a regular size that

Money $aving Tip

Simple stainless steel bowls—one for water and one for food—are inexpensive and indestructible.

is appropriate for most dogs and a large size for big dogs.

Poop Scoop

Cleaning up after your dog is good manners, and in most jurisdictions it is the law. In my neck of the woods, most of us use the plastic bags in which the morning paper is delivered.

There are several commercial products as well. Plastic bags for scooping are sold packaged in a small dispenser that can be attached to a leash or belt. These are quite inexpensive—$5 to $10—for a dispenser with 30 waste bags, and it costs about $10 for 90 refills. Other products include small pans, shovels, spades, and "grabbers," or scoopers equipped with long handles so that you do not need to bend over. These are useful for cleaning your yard but not convenient for carrying on a walk. They cost from $20 to $30.

Toothbrush and Toothpaste

A toothbrush for dogs is usually sold with a starter supply of doggy toothpaste for $10 or less.

An ID tag attached to your dog's collar is a neccessity.

FOOD

One of your most important jobs is to provide your puppy or dog with a healthy diet. Begin with a small supply of the same food that your pet is used to consuming. Before bringing him home, ask the breeder, employees at the shelter, or the rescue volunteers to tell you about his daily diet. You need to know what kind of food, how much, and how often he has been fed. Most of these care providers will give you a small supply of the food to take home. If they do not, either ask them for some or buy some.

When you take your puppy or dog for his first veterinary checkup within the first few days of bringing him home, ask your veterinarian to recommend a type and quantity of food and a feeding schedule. If this recommendation differs from what you already have, transition your dog or pup gradually from one food to the next. Begin by substituting a few nuggets of the new chow for the current dry food, and slowly, over a period of weeks, increase the substitution until the transition is complete.

OPTIONS, OPTIONS, MORE OPTIONS—AND CANINE LUXURY

Many of us have lots of fun buying extra equipment and gifts for our pets. There is no harm in that as long as you have the basics and as long as what you buy is safe for you and your pet. In some cases, such as the use of a harness for a

A leash with a swivel bolt clip is easier to manipulate.

small dog, the option is desirable and recommended in addition to—but not as a replacement for—the basic collar.

Automatic Feeders

These gizmos provide a constant supply of food, or in an electronic version, dispense programmed amounts of food at selected times. I cannot think of a good reason for you to purchase an automatic feeder. Dogs should not be left alone for an entire day, thus requiring automatic feeding, or have constant access to food. If unique circumstances (a health issue that requires your dog to frequently eat small amounts) lead you to consider one of these feeders, discuss the matter with your veterinarian before you purchase one. Small feeders cost $10 to $15, while large electronic dispensers cost about $75.

Bed

More money can be spent on a dog bed than any other indoor item. Does every dog need a dog bed? No, not all—some dogs prefer the floor. Years ago, one of my Collies insisted on sleeping on the stone floor of our front hall, which struck me as terribly hard and uncomfortable but which appealed to him. A favored spot on one of your home's carpets or rugs may be your dog's chosen place of rest. For others, an old blanket, towel, or

Money $aving Tip

You do not need to buy a commercial pooper scooper if you have plenty of plastic bags.

small throw rug makes perfect bedding. Or you can spend anywhere from $40 to $200 for a dog bed (or more than $300 for a therapeutic bed). If you do buy a bed, I recommend one with a removable, washable cover. Choose one that is large enough for your dog to stretch out on if he chooses.

Car Seat Covers

Seat covers to protect car bucket and backseats from doggy-delivered mud, dirt, and fur are available in different materials, from soft plush to suede, heavy canvas, and even leather. With a similar purpose in mind, dog owners can purchase large pads or pet cargo liners that fit into the back of SUVs, minivans, and station wagons. If you feel that you need such items, choose a fabric that is washable and not too slippery for your dog to stand on.

Backseat covers and large cargo liners can cost $100 to $200. A single bucket seat cover can cost $35 to $75. You can even order either a custom-fitted backseat cover or a leather backseat cover for $500. Car seat covers

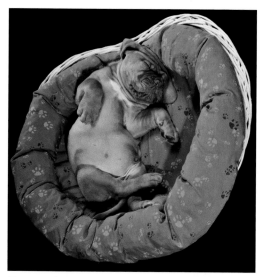

Some dogs appreciate the comfort of a dog bed.

sometimes disappoint because they refuse to stay in place.

Bear in mind that seat covers protect your car from dirt but do not protect your dog from injury should your car be in an accident, or protect him from falling if your car comes to a sudden stop. To provide the necessary protection, put your dog in a crate or carrier while traveling with him or use a doggy seat belt.

Carrier

Owners of small dogs find a carrier handy, and using one is mandatory when your small dog travels with you in

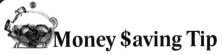

Money $aving Tip

A commercially sold dog bed is a luxury, not a necessity. An old blanket, a scrap of carpet, or a pillowcase stuffed with clean rags makes a perfectly good dog bed—and some dogs prefer to sleep on a cool floor.

the cabin of a plane. There are quite a few styles, sized by weight, for dogs up to 10, 16, 20, or 22 pounds (4.5, 7, 9, or 10 kg). Check for adequate ventilation, sturdiness, and ease of carrying. A desirable feature is a removable, washable floor pad. Prices range from $40 to $75.

Clothing

If you are into fashion, you may be tempted to share some of your style with your dog. However, I recommend that you resort to buying doggy clothing only when it's needed—as it sometimes is in the case of small, older, or short-haired dogs in cold or wet weather. Canine raincoats, sweaters, and coats cost from $15 to $50, depending on size, material, and style.

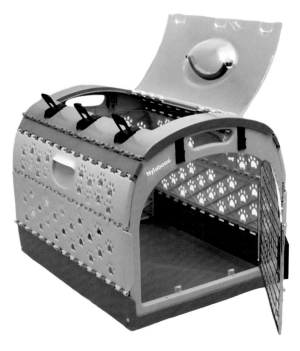

Owners of small dogs will find a carrier handy.

Crate

A dog crate is essentially a dog cage. A crate can be used as an aide in—but not as a substitute for—training. The basic model is made of wire on all sides, top and bottom, usually with a pad on the floor for comfort. Some are collapsible to make them easier to transport. A few are made of wicker or rattan for decorative effect. Crates come in many sizes, from small to extra large. If you purchase one, be sure that it is roomy enough for your dog to stand up, turn around, and lie down inside. Price can range from $75 to $200.

Dog Door

Pet doors, which allow a dog to come and go at will from your home to a fenced-in yard, involve numerous issues that any potential purchaser should research and resolve. Installation and location are threshold issues, followed closely by safety. Questions to ask include: Is your dog so large that a door big enough to accommodate him will also accommodate a human intruder? Can the door be sealed to protect your house from the cold, rain, snow, insects, and visits from unwelcome animals? Will your dog use it?

For a price, it appears that you can resolve safety issues (the door remains locked but your dog's programmed infrared collar key unlocks it) and weather issues (overlapping vinyl flaps). Depending on size and the number of features, these doors can cost from $40 to $250 plus the cost of installation.

Feeding Station

Bowls can be purchased as part of a feeding stand or station that raises the bowls off the floor; the bowl(s) and stand together are called a "feeder." Stands can be made of wood, wrought iron, plastic, or stainless steel and can be single or double, simple or decorative. Obviously, stands must be sized for the dog; a small stand is about 5 inches (13 cm) high, while a tall stand (convenient for large dogs) can be as high as 18 inches (46 cm).

A crate can be used as an aide, but not as a substitute, for training your dog.

I use a low stainless steel rack (it holds the bowls just 1 or 2 inches (2.5 or 5 cm) off the floor) with two stainless steel bowls; it costs about $15. Large, decorated wooden stands can cost $75 and up.

Stands, stations, or feeders are usually a matter of convenience, not necessity. However, if you have trouble bending over to lift and place bowls on the floor, this convenience may be important to you. It can also be helpful to a dog with joint or back problems. But you must choose a feeder with a height compatible to your dog's height. A tall feeder may be helpful to you, but a toy dog won't be able to reach it.

Fence

If you have a yard and plan to let your dog use it without benefit of your company, and especially if you plan to let your dog use a pet door, then you must fence in your yard. Choose a fence that appeals to you and will contain your dog. A low fence may not do so if he is a jumper. Small dogs can escape from many wrought iron or aluminum fences because of the spacing between the pickets. And alas, some dogs cannot restrain themselves from digging under fences.

I am not a fan of electric fences, despite their growing popularity. These systems involve underground wires (the electric fence or invisible

Use of a dog door requires a fenced-in yard.

fence) and a dog collar that transmits a shock to the dog if he approaches too close to the fence. I do not believe that transmitting pain is a good way to train or control dogs. Leaving my personal objection aside, various problems can develop with these systems. Some dogs are traumatized by the shocks and become timid or fearful. Others, tempted by a cheeky squirrel, neighborhood cat, or enemy canine, simply burst through the fence despite the shock—but the same shock dissuades them from returning to the yard in a calmer frame of mind. An invisible fence does not prevent dog theft or prevent hostile dogs from entering your yard to attack your dog. One of the worst things that has been known to happen is a shorting out of a wire or collar so that a hapless dog receives continuous shocks.

Gates

Indoor gates are a convenient way to prevent your dog from entering—or leaving—certain areas of your home. If you plan to acquire a dog and confine him 24/7 to one room, such as a kitchen or basement area, please rethink your plan because this most definitely is not a good arrangement. A gate is useful if you do not want your dog in the kitchen with you when you cook, if you need to keep him out of your bedroom, or if you prefer not to include him when entertaining guests.

Gates are pressure mounted and may be made of mesh, plastic, or wood or metal pickets. "Mini" gates for small dogs are about 18 inches (46 cm) high. Extra-tall gates run about 41 inches (104 cm) high, and there are several sizes in between. Most gates fit across a doorway, but some models offer extensions to close off wider entryways and hallways. Depending very much on size and material, prices range from about $40 to $150.

Kennel

A kennel is used for transporting a dog. It may be a convenient way to carry your small dog to the veterinary clinic. If a medium or large dog is traveling by plane, a kennel is mandatory because he will be placed in the baggage compartment. This makes safety a critical issue when you purchase a kennel. It must be approved for travel on US airlines. It should be made of reinforced high-strength plastic so as to avoid breaking, splintering, or bending. The door should have a secure lock that cannot bounce, slide, or slip open. Your dog should have plenty of ventilation, a soft washable pad on the floor, and room to stand, turn around, and lie down. Most kennels can be disassembled for storage. Sizes vary greatly, from small to very large. Prices vary accordingly, from $25 to more than $125. Choose the safest, sturdiest kennel.

Pens/Ex-Pens

An "exercise pen" (or ex-pen) does not allow much exercise. It is a containment system that is roomier than a crate or

Ex-pens can be useful for containing a puppy.

cage. An outdoor pen is a chain link or wire kennel, with or without a roof or cover, placed in a yard. Some are permanently installed and others are portable. Most are four sided, but some styles also offer additional panels to create other configurations. An outdoor pen should not be your dog's bedroom and is not a substitute for exercise. The cost varies with size and material, from about $300 to $1,000. I can't come up with any good reason for this expenditure for a family pet.

However, a collapsible, folding indoor pen can be useful for containing a puppy or small dog without resorting to the crate.

An indoor gate comes in handy for keeping a room off-limits.

Place Mats

For housekeeping, you can place a small rug (the kind you buy from a hardware store for your front door) or a plastic place mat (an old one from your kitchen table) under your dog's bowls or feeder. Or you can buy decorated "dog place mats" for this purpose, in various sizes, for from $5 to $20. I recommend mats that are nonskid and that can be wiped down (a vinyl or plastic mat) or put in the washing machine.

Pooch Potty

Yes, it has finally happened: the invention of an indoor (at least semi-indoor) dog potty. No, it does not involve teaching your dog to flush. Although sometimes advertised as indoor pet potties, this product should be used indoors only as a last (and infrequent) resort. The potty typically consists of a box 6 or 7 inches (15 or 18 cm) high covered with synthetic turf that can be removed and hosed down. Solid waste is deposited on the turf. Urine drains through the turf into a removable pan. A simpler version is a shallow plastic pan covered by a grate. Solid waste remains on the grate for removal and liquid waste drains onto newspapers or pads placed in the bottom of the pan. Sizes vary, from about 2 to 3 feet (.5 to 1 cm) square.

Except in limited circumstances, these potties are not a good idea. Let's be honest. Your house will smell. Sanitary issues will arise. You still must clean up after your pet. He still must be walked and exercised outdoors. So why bother? A potty of this type could make sense if you have a large balcony or terrace and send your dog to the potty when the weather is terribly bad or if you are ill. But at prices ranging from $200 on up (plus $50 for replacement sod) for the turf versions, it hardly seems worth it.

Retractable Leash

In recent years "retractable," "flex," or "extenda" leashes have become popular. They consist of a handle, a slender, covered reel and a simple hand control that allow you to extend, stop, lock, and retract a leash. They can be purchased with various kinds of "grips" or handles, in lengths of 10, 16, and 26 feet (3, 5, and 8 m) and in widths from 3/8 inch to 3/4 inch (1 to 2 cm), usually with a swivel bolt closure. Depending on size and style, they cost from $20 to $50. These leashes are appealing but have drawbacks.

A flex leash should not be substituted for training your dog to heel and walk by your side on a 6-foot (2-m) lead. On urban sidewalks, retractable leashes should be kept short, to no more than 6 feet (2 m), to avoid tripping pedestrians and prevent your dog from plunging into traffic—so it makes sense to just stick with the shorter leash.

Used in a park or woods, a flex leash allows your dog to roam and explore while remaining under your physical control. That control can be tested if he is ambling along on a very long lead and suddenly takes off at full speed. His lunge will immediately take up the slack in the leash, which can severely strain your arm and shoulder or pull you off your feet. A dog on a long lead can wrap himself around a tree or other objects and can trip you or others who cross his path.

Toys

Toys are good things, both indoors and out. They help keep dogs—and us—amused. Soft indoor toys are pulled, tossed, chewed, and carried about. Be certain that they are dog safe, without small parts that can easily be detached. Don't give your dog a plush toy or stuffed animal decorated with buttons and such that can be swallowed. Some small, soft dog toys, squeaky or otherwise, are available for about $5. Bigger squeaky or squawky toys (snakes, beavers, cows, pigs, monkeys) can cost quite a bit more.

Chew toys come in all sizes, shapes, and flavors, beginning

with bags of rawhide chips and graduating up to huge rawhide bones nearly 2 feet (.5 m) long—with many embellishments in between. They are available in materials other than rawhide. Nylabones, made of tough nylon, last much longer and can be nearly indestructible; some veterinarians recommend them over rawhide. Bones made of digestible cornstarch are chewed up quickly.

Retractable leashes should be kept short near busy roads.

Most dogs like to chew, and for puppies it is a must. Chewing on the appropriate material can help maintain healthy gums and teeth and preserve your furniture. Consult with your veterinarian as to what type of chew toy she recommends for your dog and how often your dog should have one. Some dogs have digestive systems that don't take well to rawhide; they can be restricted to Nylabones.

Some indoor toys can keep your dog occupied when you are not at home. Rubber hollow balls, cubes, and jugs can be stuffed with treats, challenging your dog to extract them. For dogs who like to retrieve, outdoor toys include rubber hollow chews, tennis balls, and flying discs. (Flying discs made for dogs are preferable to plastic flying discs used by people.)

Shopping for Equipment

There are many places to shop for basic equipment, including grocery stores. A wide range of equipment, both basic and optional, can be found

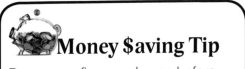

Money $aving Tip

Puppy-proofing your house before you bring your new pet home will save money on home repairs.

at big box stores, at pet supply chain stores, and at independent pet shops. The phone directory and use of a search engine on the Internet will help you locate independent pet stores and chain pet stores in your vicinity. If you prefer to shop from home, many independent pet shops, pet chain stores, big box stores, and pet supply catalog companies maintain online catalogs that allow customers to order products online or over the telephone for home delivery.

PUPPY-PROOFING YOUR HOME

To keep your puppy safe and yourself sane, survey your house and yard and take a few precautions before you bring him home. Be guided by the principal that puppies are active, curious, often explore with their mouths, will chew on just about anything, and have no concept of private property. With this principal in mind:

- Keep electrical cords out of reach.
- Don't let your unsupervised puppy hang out around wooden furniture, shoes, socks, belts, books, houseplants, cardboard boxes, or small objects (pins, nails, buttons, loose change) that can be swallowed.
- Keep medications and household, car, and garden chemicals, such as detergent, pesticides, and antifreeze, out of reach.
- Keep garbage cans and bags and other plastic bags out of reach.
- Keep human food out of reach.
- If you have a fenced-in yard, double-check to make certain that it is escape-proof and cordon off toxic plants such as rhododendrons and Japanese yews.
- Close windows or secure them with screens (especially important if you live in a multistory building).

RESOURCES MADE EASY

Finding a Veterinarian
- American Animal Hospital Association: www.healthypet.com

Pet Taxi
- Search online for "pet services" or "pet taxi." (You can also use the Yellow Pages.)

Shopping Online
- Use a search engine and type in "dog supplies."
- Go to the website of your favorite pet chain store.

Chapter 5

An Initial Investment Pays Dividends:
The First Few Hours, Days, and Weeks With Your New Dog

The big moment has arrived. You are on your way to pick up Primo, Scout, Maisy, or Tiny, your new puppy or dog. The first few hours, days, and weeks of this budding relationship are especially important because your actions during this time can help determine how easy and successful the relationship will be.

HOMECOMING
Let's take a look at what's involved in your puppy or dog's homecoming.

The Ride Home
If you are picking up a puppy, ask a friend or family member to go with you. Take a large towel or old blanket so that whoever is not driving can hold the puppy. Before you leave the breeder, shelter, or foster home, ask as many questions as you can think of about the puppy, his breed, and his care. Take notes!

If you are bringing home a dog and he is too big for you to hold, I recommend placing him in a crate. If your car cannot accommodate a crate, bring along a second person so that one of you can sit in the backseat with the dog to help him stay calm. Before you begin your drive home, extract as much care information and advice as you can from the dog's caretaker and write it down.

At Home
As soon as you arrive home, take the puppy or dog to your yard or an outdoor area, along with your plastic bag or poop scoop, to give him a chance to eliminate.

By this time, your new arrival is already wearing a collar with identification tag. If you have a fenced-in yard, stay with him and let him explore your yard. If you are walking him in a park or through the neighborhood, use your 6-foot (2-m) leash. Bring your dog inside after business has been completed outdoors. Make him feel at home! Show him where he will sleep and the location of his water bowl. Let him explore. Feed him.

Whether Tiny is a puppy or an adult, he is nervous. Your home and its surroundings are new to him. You and your family are new to him. He may be frightened by unknown sounds, smells, and sights. The familiar—his mom and siblings, a foster home, or even a shelter—are gone for good. He's thinking "Now what?" and not knowing what to expect.

This is where the information you have gleaned from his former caretaker comes into play. You should have a good idea of what Tiny's life has been like up to now. Try to maintain at least some consistency with the past, even if you plan to make changes. For the first few days, feed him the same food, at the same hours, in the same amounts. If Tiny has a "potty schedule" that has been working, try to stick to it. If you want to change it,

As soon as you arrive home with your puppy, take him out to your yard or outdoor area to eliminate.

change it gradually. If Tiny is used to a crate and likes it, by all means give him a crate.

Stay with him and keep him company, but keep the reception low key. Feel free to cuddle! Make lots of contact—scratch his ears and pat his head—and speak to him in a quiet tone of voice. Introduce family members living at home and keep visitors to a minimum. This is not a good time to invite friends and neighbors to meet the new arrival, who is trying to cope with an avalanche of new experiences. Give your furry pal a chew toy, but do not overwhelm him with a huge cache of toys. Play a little bit. If Tiny is a puppy, he will soon be ready for a nap. Even grown-up dogs usually sleep away part of the day, and the excitement of the move will tire out most adult dogs.

Nap Time

When nap time arrives, leave your dog or puppy in a limited, enclosed space—he will feel safer, and this helps prevent indoor elimination. If you choose not to use a pen or crate, leave your dog in a bathroom or kitchen with a gate across the doorway. These two rooms are practical for new pets because the floors are uncarpeted and easily cleaned. Make sure that potentially dangerous items, such as cleansers, sponges, soap, and electrical cords, are safely out of reach. Do not leave a new pet outdoors in your yard.

If Tiny will be using a crate, dog bed, or indoor pen (nice for puppies and small dogs), I recommend locating it near to, but not in the middle of, an area where you will spend a lot of time, such as a family room, kitchen, den, or living room. If you have decided that certain rooms in your house will be off-limits, have your gates in place.

Try to lure—not force—your dog or pup into what will be his "safe space." If this is a bathroom with a gate, furnish it with Tiny's bed, water bowl, and a toy. Lead him inside with a treat. If you

are using a crate or pen, try to "lead" your dog or pup inside with a treat or by gently lifting first one paw and then the other in the right direction; don't shove or force him.

THE FIRST FEW DAYS

Every dog has the same basic needs: food, water, shelter, attention, kindness, stimulation, exercise, rest, opportunities to eliminate, and a sense of security. Your dog's needs—the amount of food, exercise, rest, even what it takes to make him feel secure—will be individual to him. One 60-pound (27-kg) dog may have a high metabolism and lots of energy and will need considerably more food and exercise than the next 60-pound (27-kg) dog who has a slow metabolism and an aversion to exercise. One puppy may be full of bravado and self-confidence and ready to meet the world, while another equally endearing pup is shy and timorous and needs a lot more help to feel secure. If you have chosen a purebred puppy or know the breeds that contributed to your mixed-breed pup, you may already have a good sense of his breed-related traits and needs, such as for strenuous exercise or a propensity to dig. If you have adopted an adult, you hopefully have been able to extract a history from his caretakers.

Spend a lot of time with Tiny during his first days with you. This shouldn't be hard to do because new dogs and puppies are so much fun. As the days

Create a daily schedule that meets your dog's needs.

unfold, pay attention to your dog and try to evaluate how much exercise, food, sleep, play, and stimulation he needs. These observations will help you create a daily schedule that meets his needs. An adult dog's needs and routines will be different from those of a puppy, and a puppy's needs will change as he develops, so be ready to make adjustments in his schedule every few weeks.

When planning a daily routine, your goal is to meet your dog's needs, but you also must be realistic about what is workable for you. Some folks like to stay up late at night and walk the dog at 11:00 p.m. or midnight. This means that the

dog does not need to go out early the next morning. If you like to turn in early and your last dog walk comes at 9:30 p.m., that is okay—if you are willing to be up and out (for an adult dog) before 8:00 a.m. the next morning. A dog shouldn't be asked to "hold it" for more than ten hours. Older dogs and puppies need more frequent bathroom breaks.

Daily Routine

Establishing and following a fairly consistent daily routine (let's be realistic—you can't be perfect every day) will help your dog feel secure and prevent accidental use of the indoor bathroom (your home). A good routine will help ensure that your dog's needs for stimulation and exercise are met, making it easier to prevent problem behaviors that grow out of boredom and insecurity.

A consistent routine will help you blend dog care chores into your day and makes it easier to remember when to feed and walk your dog. I suggest that you write down your schedule and post it on the refrigerator door. If two or more people are sharing responsibility for Tiny, make note of who is responsible for which chores. Although Tiny may be delighted to receive breakfast twice— once from you and again from your spouse —there will be a price to pay if you each assume that the other has taken Tiny on his morning walk.

Maintain a consistent walking and feeding schedule *if it is working*. If there are too many indoor accidents, if your dog is gaining weight, or if he is becoming bored and destructive, *make adjustments*. You may need to feed your dog less or exercise him more, or both.

Adults

For an adult dog with "medium" exercise needs, the schedule might look like this:

8:00 a.m.	small meal
8:10 a.m.	30-minute walk
12:00 noon	15-minute walk
5:00 p.m.	30-minute walk
6:00 p.m.	main meal
10:00 p.m.	15-minute walk

Whenever your dog uses the outdoor facility, praise him. Your tone of voice will tell him you are pleased, but it also helps to use the same one or two words of praise. "Good dog!" "Good girl!" or "Good boy!" will do just fine.

Puppies

A puppy's schedule will be different because a puppy needs to eat more often and in small amounts, and he needs to pee more often—much more often. Puppies simply do not have the physical capacity to "hold it" for long, and no amount of training on your part will change that physiological fact. The good news is that a puppy's capacity to "hold it" increases with age. It is your job to teach him where to go (outdoors) and to get him there often enough.

A twelve-week-old puppy's schedule might look like this:

6:00 a.m.	10-minute outdoor walk/bathroom break (*important!*)
6:15 a.m.	small meal
6:30 a.m.	15-minute outdoor walk/bathroom break/playtime
9:00 a.m.	15-minute outdoor walk/bathroom break/playtime
12:00 noon	15-minute outdoor walk/bathroom break
12:15 p.m.	small meal
12:30 p.m.	15-minute outdoor walk/bathroom break
3:00 p.m.	15-minute outdoor walk/bathroom break/playtime

5:00 p.m.	15-minute outdoor walk/ bathroom break
5:15 p.m.	small meal
5:30 p.m.	15-minute outdoor walk/ bathroom break
8:00 p.m.	15-minute outdoor walk/ bathroom break/playtime
11:00 p.m.	15-minute outdoor walk/ bathroom break

If you are a truly hardy and committed person:

3:00 a.m.	15-minute outdoor walk/ bathroom break

Praise your puppy when he uses the outdoor bathroom. If he has an indoor accident, as is bound to happen, don't use a harsh tone of voice or punishment. Instead, reconsider your outdoor routine; you may have to add some extra walks. As your puppy grows, he will have more control over his bladder and you will be able to reduce the number of outdoor visits. In between walks and indoor play or cuddle time, give your puppy rest time in his crate, pen, or gated room.

When He's Alone

When you are away from home during these early days, leave your dog or pup in a contained indoor area, such as the crate, pen, or fenced-off kitchen or bathroom. This will help him feel secure in what is still a strange environment. Don't leave him alone in the yard, even if it is well fenced in. Don't leave him home alone all day. Someone (preferably you) needs to come for walks, company, and reassurance.

Expectations

It is not uncommon for people to have unrealistic expectations of their new pet. The expectations may spring from lack of experience, memories of a previous dog, unfamiliarity with the characteristics of this dog, or quite simply, a little too much optimism.

I've noticed that unrealistic expectations often arrive home with a new puppy and come to a head after a few of those very early morning walks or indoor accidents, usually culminating in a comment such as:

- "I didn't know (or remember) that it could be so much work!"
- "He wakes up and barks at 5:00 a.m.!"
- "He just doesn't want to be housetrained!"

These comments are conveyed in a tone containing varying degrees of exasperation, indignation, sorrow, shock, resignation—even personal outrage—as though, somehow, the puppy is defective, spiteful, or overly demanding.

TIME WELL SPENT

Puppies require a lot of time, effort, and attention and will interrupt your sleep. Investing time now will help your puppy grow into a well-behaved adult.

Alas, the human caretaker is simply too tired to think straight. Many people who choose puppies are several years removed from their last puppy experience and have been lulled into forgetfulness of puppydom by years of adult canine behavior. While you may remember taking your puppy outside in the middle of the night (10 or 15 years ago), you probably don't remember how tired you were or what it felt like in the midst of winter.

For some of my contemporaries, waking and walking with a puppy is not a problem. They regularly wake up before 5:00 a.m. and sleep only a few hours a night. Puppy routines don't seem to bother them. Others do not fare well if their sleep is interrupted or if they are awakened early in the morning. I am one of these, so you late sleepers have my sympathy.

If you are in the uncomfortable position of having a puppy, but despite the red flags of Chapters 2 and 3, you find your expectations being harshly challenged by reality—practice patience and remember that puppies grow and change quickly. Your sleep patterns *will* return to normal. Meanwhile, during the early months, your time investment will be intense but the returns will be great: a housetrained, healthy, socialized, and well-behaved dog.

At the other end of the canine age spectrum, people who adopt adult dogs sometimes expect perfect behavior

Puppies have different needs than adult dogs.

from day one. Even a dog who was housetrained while living in a foster home can (and probably will) have accidents in your home. He is new to the premises and he is nervous. Practice patience, stick to a consistent feeding and walking schedule, and try taking him on more frequent or longer walks.

THE FIRST FEW WEEKS

As you already know, owning a puppy or dog is not like owning stock. You are not a passive investor! You are an active participant in your dog's success as a healthy, happy companion. Now that both you and your dog have settled into a routine that seems to be working, it's time to think about adding critical components that will make life even better for both of you.

In the very first weeks, your immediate tasks include canine socialization, initial veterinary care, and establishing a working relationship with your new companion.

Meet 'n Greet

Politicians do it and so should your dog or puppy. He needs to meet people and other dogs, to learn to accept them and get along with them. He needs to learn to be comfortable with sidewalk traffic and automobile noise so that the two of you can walk just about anywhere. After your new pet spends a few quiet days with you and your immediate family settling into his new home, a top priority will be to socialize him.

For dogs and puppies who have already been socialized and have a friendly, outgoing temperament, this will not be much of a challenge. Dogs and puppies who are shy, timid, or fearful need to be helped and encouraged—not forced.

> ## PATIENCE
> Patience is needed as you adjust to your new dog or puppy—and as he adjusts to you.

Gradually expose Tiny to a range of people, experiences, and other dogs. The operative word is "gradually." Don't overwhelm your dog or puppy with new experiences. Some introductions will come naturally and easily as you walk your dog (who is leashed, of course) in the park or neighborhood. Allow him to approach and sniff dogs and people you know; if you don't know them, ask permission first. It's hard to believe, but not everyone likes dogs and not all dogs are friendly to their own kind. Introduce Tiny to visitors in your home, including toddlers, children, and adults. Let the "new people" in his life pat him, cuddle him, talk to him, and scratch his ears while you supervise. This will help him learn to remain calm around people both unknown and familiar and to accept handling from veterinarians, groomers, dog walkers, or house sitters.

Visiting the Dog Doctor

One of the new people Tiny must meet is his veterinarian, preferably during his first two weeks with you. Make an appointment within a day or two of bringing your pet home. Let the clinic know that this is an initial visit that should include a physical examination and routine diagnostic tests.

Take a fecal sample with you when you visit the clinic. A sample can be a small amount, carried in a plastic sandwich bag. Take a written list of questions with you and all health records and proof of

Your dog needs to meet other people and learn to accept and get along with them.

vaccinations that you receive from the breeder, shelter, or foster home. If you can, make a copy for yourself to keep at home or ask the veterinarian to make copies and return the originals to you. Keep a file at home of your dog's health records; most veterinarians will routinely provide you with an itemization of services with a bill each time you visit. Simply add them to the file.

Whether you have a new puppy or a new dog, he should receive a thorough examination. The veterinarian will listen to your pet's lungs and heart, check his abdomen and the condition of his coat and skin, manipulate his joints, and examine his teeth, gums, ears, and eyes. The veterinarian is not looking for problems—she is looking to rule them out. She wants to confirm the *absence* of a heart murmur or breathing problems; of tenderness or pain in muscles and internal organs; of infection or inflammation in the eyes or ears; of external parasites; and of bad teeth or gum disease. In addition to examining the fecal sample for internal parasites (common to puppies), the veterinarian or her technician will usually take a blood sample to rule out blood disorders.

Tell your veterinarian about any ailments you may have noticed in your pet, such as diarrhea, vomiting, or lethargy. Discuss, decide on, and make note of a schedule for return visits (especially important for puppies).

Don't be shy about asking questions. At a minimum, you should know about the following when you leave your first appointment:

- Immunizations: Up to date? Next step?
- Internal and external parasites: Is treatment needed? Preventive medications?
- Food: What type and how much? Are supplements needed?
- Spay and neuter: If your pet has not been spayed or neutered, discuss with your veterinarian the scheduling of this procedure.
- Care of teeth, ears, coat.
- Specific health or problem behaviors and suggested solutions.

Money $aving Tip

To avoid the cost of refinishing floors, repairing furniture, or cleaning rugs and carpets, do not let your newly arrived dog or puppy have the run of the house—or even a large room when you are not at home. Put him in a crate, indoor pen, or bathroom.

Mistakes, not Habits

During the first few days and weeks, it is important to establish the foundation of a canine–human working relationship. Your goal is to nip a problem behavior in the bud before it becomes a habit and more difficult to reverse.

Supervise your dog or puppy carefully when he is not in his enclosed space. Some trainers recommend the "tether" approach: keeping yourself tethered to your new pet and vice versa, even indoors, with a long leash for the first few days or even weeks. With close supervision or tethering, you will quickly learn if Tiny's housetraining is incomplete or if he is into stealing from the table or eating shoes—and you can take immediate action.

Your dog will feel more secure with clear limits on his behavior. A secure dog will find it easier to understand and conform to human rules than a dog who is insecure, nervous, and stressed.

Your new canine has no idea which behaviors are acceptable in your household and which are not. It's your job to show him what his limits will be. While households vary as to whether or not dogs are allowed on furniture, dogs and families both benefit from limits on chewing (chew toys only); barking (minimal, as in when the doorbell rings); and jumping (not on people). Stealing food, whether from garbage pails or tabletops, should be prohibited—it's plain bad manners and is dangerous to a dog's health.

Reinforcement, not Punishment

You can successfully teach your dog the rules of the house with distraction (away from negative behavior) and with positive reinforcement (toward desirable behavior).

Use positive reinforcement with your dog or puppy. Praise and reward him when he does something right, such as eliminating outside or going to his crate, pen, or bed to rest.

Don't choke, frighten, yell at, or smack your dog for breaking a rule that he doesn't even know exists. When you use force, fear, or pain to "teach" your dog, you make it difficult for him to trust you. These methods focus the dog on the fear or pain, making it less likely that he will understand or learn the message you are sending.

Be consistent, firm, and insistent (hence the need to supervise from the beginning) in correcting your dog or puppy. You are not being kind to him if

Supervise your dog carefully when he is not confined.

you do not train him. Dogs and puppies thrive with order and boundaries in their lives and an unambiguous relationship to humans. No matter how "sweet," "smart," or "good" your dog is, he will not figure out on his own how best to get along in your household. It is your responsibility to teach him.

RESOURCES MADE EASY

Books on General Care

- De Vito, Dominique. *The Well-Behaved Puppy*. Neptune City, NJ: TFH Publications, 2008.
- Morgan, Diane. *Good Dogkeeping*. Neptune City, NJ: TFH Publications, 2006.

Chapter 6

Sharing Your Home With a Dog

You are now sharing your home with a canine. Living with a dog raises issues, from muddy paw prints on the Oriental carpet to teeth marks on the Chippendale furniture to toxic plants and household products that can sicken and even kill your furry housemate. If you are or are about to be an empty nester, you may be looking forward to a more pristine environment—minus a teenager's clothes, sports equipment, and empty water bottles underfoot—and wondering how to deal with Rosie, your 90-pound (41-kg) Labrador who deposits tracks in the foyer and sheds on the furniture. Or perhaps, like many at our age and stage, you plan to downsize to an apartment or condominium, retire to warmer climes, or move to another town closer to the grandchildren. Where and how do you look for an apartment that will accommodate Rosie? And how will you and Rosie adjust to an elevator and no yard?

Whether you live in an apartment or a house with a yard, you will be confronted with similar issues of keeping Rosie safe and coexisting comfortably with a dog who tracks in dirt but doesn't know how to use a vacuum cleaner.

WHERE YOU LIVE

More than ever before, we Americans in the 50 and over crowd are relocating—from one state to another, from one community to another, to planned communities of single family homes, townhouses, high-rise condominiums, and garden apartments. More than ever before, we will find rules and regulations in place that affect us as dog owners.

Apartment Living

Some apartment building managers prohibit dogs, period. Some restrict dog-owning families to lower floors of the building. Others limit by size, prohibiting dogs over 20, 25, 30, and sometimes 50 pounds (9, 11, 14, and 23 kg). The larger the dog, the more difficult it is to find a rental unit. Some landlords prohibit certain breeds, most commonly pit-bull types, Rottweilers, and Doberman Pinschers.

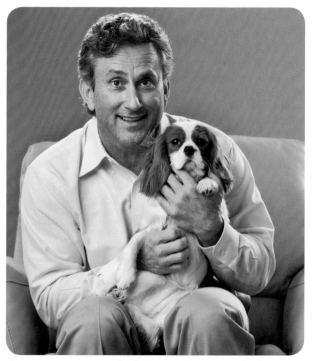

Some apartment buildings allow small dogs but may prohibit larger-sized dogs.

Luckily, some buildings welcome dogs of all sizes but may limit the number of dogs per unit. Federally assisted rental housing for seniors and the disabled are pet friendly by law, and many states allow pets in state-subsidized housing.

If you are looking for a pet-friendly apartment to rent, the search has, thankfully, become somewhat easier in recent years. In addition to checking classified ads in the local newspaper, contact the local humane society or animal shelter, which may have a list of pet-friendly apartment buildings. Some realtors specialize in helping people with pets find rentals. In my area, these realtors advertise in a free pet publication that is widely available in veterinary clinics and pet stores. Similar publications are available in other areas, and many of them include listings of pet-friendly apartments and realtors who specialize in them. Local guidebooks listing rental agents and rental units, usually found in supermarkets, often highlight pet-friendly apartments and realtors.

Why do so many landlords reject dogs, and why do some reject only larger dogs? Landlords fear destruction of property, including damage to floors; carpets, walls, or drapes being soiled, stained, and scratched; complaints from other tenants disturbed by barking or by dogs behaving badly in elevators, halls, or the lobby; and unscooped excrement in common areas around the building. As to the acceptance of smaller but not larger dogs, this is largely due to the belief held by managers that large dogs necessarily are noisier or harder to control, as well as anticipated objections from tenants.

Extras

When you do find a dog-friendly building to your liking, you may discover that renting with a pet will cost more than renting without one. Charges will vary but could include:

- extra security deposit (refundable if not used to repair damages)
- nonrefundable pet fee
- extra monthly fee (may vary with size of the dog)

Some landlords want nonmonetary assurances from prospective tenants, which may include:

- references from a veterinarian, former landlord, or trainer that verify that you are a responsible owner and your dog is well cared for
- proof of sterilization and/or vaccination

Read the Fine Print

If you are moving into an apartment or if you live in an apartment and plan to add a dog to your home, carefully read your lease and be certain that you are aware of and can live with the restrictions. Some landlords require that dogs use a front or side door instead of the front door. Others ask that dogs use only a certain elevator. Make absolutely certain that your lease allows you to have a dog and that your dog fits within the weight limit, if there is one. Do not rely on a verbal assurance that your pet is acceptable. Insist on a written, signed pet clause or pet addendum, even if your landlord does not. Do not try to "cheat" by sneaking in a prohibited pet or by claiming that your 80-pound (36-kg) German Shepherd Dog really weighs only 50 pounds (23 kg). Sidestepping the landlord's rules will lead to unpleasant results, including complaints, aggravation, threats, eviction notices, and lawsuits. All too often, a beloved but prohibited dog lands in an animal shelter. If your lease allows you to keep your dog and management changes its policy to prohibit dogs, the new policy cannot be enforced against you until after your lease has expired. In practice, dogs in this situation are almost always "grandfathered in," while new dogs are not allowed.

Condominium Living

Condominium and cooperative housing units are governed by rules and regulations embodied in covenants and bylaws that address pet ownership. As in the case of apartments, dog ownership may be entirely prohibited or limited by size, breed, or number. Sanctions for breaking the rules may include fees, fines, revocation of privileges, and litigation. If a governing board changes the pet policy to prohibit dogs, currently owned dogs are "grandfathered in" because a change in policy of this kind cannot legally be applied retroactively.

Read condominium and co-op documents carefully. They may not only regulate whether you may have a dog but prescribe canine–human behavior in the lobby, elevators, and common space. Use of a leash is usually mandatory in these areas. Some condo boards actually require that dogs be carried through the lobby!

Before getting a dog, read your lease carefully.

Planned Community Living

Owners of townhouses and single-family homes in a planned community may be governed by a homeowners' association that can adopt rules regulating pet ownership or by covenants affecting pets. These rules may limit the number of dogs per household, require fences of a certain type, require poop scooping, or prohibit dog walking in certain areas. Sanctions may include fees, fines, revocation of privileges, and litigation. Newly adopted restrictive rules affecting pets cannot be applied retroactively.

Before You Decide

A dog can live as comfortably and happily with you in an apartment as in a single-family house with a yard, with some adjustments. Before you make a move like this, consider that yard time for your dog (typically the early morning and late night bathroom break) will have to be replaced by a walk. How close is the nearest park or area where you can walk Fluffy? If Fluffy is alone during the day, is he given to barking in frustration? How can you keep him occupied? In considering issues such as these in choosing where and how to downsize, you may find yourself factoring in the cost of a pet sitter, pet walker, or doggy day care. Also consider the benefits of a balcony (safely enclosed) for a pet porta-potty, fresh air, and general entertainment for your canine.

Some pet-friendly buildings and communities are friendlier than others. If you find a building that you would like to live in, spend some time in the lobby or just outside so that you can meet and talk to tenants who are walking their dogs. Ask them about their experiences as dog-owning tenants. In some buildings, as many as one-third to one-half of the tenants have pets, so the atmosphere is generally welcoming and helpful. In other buildings, although pets are allowed, some tenants may resent the policy and complain, even about acceptable behavior, such as dogs on leashes in elevators or lobbies.

In my community of single-family homes, a small percentage of dog owners let their dogs roam, which means no poop pickup. The results are unpleasant for anyone who steps in it, and it's also unpleasant for the rules-abiding dog owners as anti-

CANINE ETIQUETTE

Lawyers who specialize in landlord–tenant, condominium, and community association law say that pet issues are contentious. People sneak dogs into buildings where they are not allowed, lie about a dog's weight, refuse to poop scoop in common areas, and allow their dogs to roam through lobbies—a litany of people behaving badly. Pet policies in condominium and apartment buildings and planned communities are not aimed at pets but at behavior by pet owners. It is an owner's job to:

- poop scoop
- keep the dog leashed and under control in the halls, lobby, and elevator
- exercise and entertain the dog (or hire dog sitters and walkers) so that he will not be left bored and barking during the day
- prevent the dog from soiling the elevator, hallway, or lobby, which may require that he be walked more often
- understand and live within the building's pet policies

dog sentiment builds in the neighborhood.

HOW YOU LIVE

Let's face it: Dogs don't care about being clean, don't care if your home is clean, don't care if you are clean…don't know from clean.

We humans take a different approach. Baths, showers, soap, shampoo, fresh sheets, polished floors, scrubbed sinks and kitchen counters, and such have a certain appeal. But each of us has a different standard of clean. I am used to mud on the floor and Collie fur on the furniture. Friends of mine who love their pets could not bear the level of dogginess present in our house. You know where you stand on this spectrum. Some of the options I offer here may appeal to you and others won't.

You can treat upholstered furniture with a protective finish to help prevent stains.

Off-Limits

Indoor pet gates, which can be found in many sizes, designs, and materials, can be used to prevent your dog from visiting rooms or areas in your home. People who have allergies and want to keep certain rooms dander-free and people who are housetraining puppies find these barriers particularly useful. Or you can set up gates simply because you want to keep some rooms in your house free of pet fur, drool, or paw prints. Gates can be purchased in various heights and widths, to be used at the bottom or top of a stairway and across doorways, rooms, or hallways.

Floors, Carpets, Rugs

This is where fur and tracked-in dirt and mud accumulate. What you do about it depends on who you are and who your dog is. Some homeowners who walk their dogs in wooded areas hose and dry their dogs' paws before letting them in the house. Swimming dogs often receive the same treatment. Other folks don't mind the prints or wait until cleaning day to remove them.

You can cut down on indoor paw prints by placing a heavy-duty doormat (available at hardware and home product stores) outside any door that your dog uses, including a dog door, and wipe your dog's paws on the mat before entering. Some stores and catalogs offer "paw mitts" and pre-dampened paw wipes that you can keep by the door. If you have a back, side, or garage door, bring your dog in that way rather than through a front foyer. Another mat inside these doors can absorb more mud and dirt. Sporting goods retailers and pet product suppliers sell mats especially for this purpose.

Carpets and rugs made from synthetic fibers withstand stains and do so better than wool and cotton, which are natural, more absorbent (of odors and stains) fibers. Commercial-grade carpets, such as those used in hotels and offices, are particularly tough and not unattractive. A protective stain repellant can be applied to new carpeting to keep moisture from soaking in. Moisture-proof padding for underneath a carpet is also available, as well as a polyethylene film backing that is laminated to the underside of a carpet to prevent moisture from soaking down into the carpet pad.

Fur, sand, and dry dirt can be swept, mopped, or vacuumed from hard floors. Slate and tile are easy to clean with a damp mop. Wood floors can be protected with a polyurethane finish, and wood laminates are an easy-to-clean option. If your dog leaves muddy paw prints, wipe the floor dry with a soft cloth or mop and wood cleaner. Keep your dog's nails trimmed to minimize scratches. More than one manufacturer now offers an electric cleaner for wood, tile, and vinyl that will both "dry" (vacuum) and "wet clean" floors. In the kitchen, place a large mat under your dog's water and food bowls to catch and absorb slobber. It can be a washable cotton rug that you throw in the washing machine every week or a plastic mat that you wipe down in the sink.

You can reduce the amount of fur your dog sheds indoors by frequently brushing him outdoors, in a basement, or on a balcony. Indoors, the tried-and-true combinations of elbow grease, mopping, and vacuuming are effective and pretty inescapable, but now, for a hefty price, there are vacuum cleaners designed specifically for pet owners. If you have a

be unavoidably delayed, leaving Fluffy no choice after being locked in the house for 12 or 14 hours. Most dogs, at some time in their lives, experience a stomach upset or urinary problem that overcomes their good manners, training, and their natural instinct and preference to use the outdoors for excretion.

An array of cleaning and odor-removal products can be found in pet shops. After blotting up any urine or feces from carpets or floors, a commercial product can be used on the spot to remove or reduce stains and eliminate odors. Some products are made specifically for wood and tile, others for carpets and fabric. Soiled areas that are not properly cleaned can invite repeat performances.

Garbage In...

When you dispose of trash or garbage in the kitchen garbage can, you want it to stay where you put it. Not all dogs agree with this proposition. Many new kitchens hide garbage pails away in a cupboard, but some dogs actually figure out how to open the cupboard door. Another solution is to buy and use a heavy metal can with a lid that opens with a foot lever. If you have a Houdini-trained dog who somehow manages to figure this one out (and some do), you can actually buy a dog-resistant trash can with a locking lid.

Money $aving Tip

Quickly clean up house soiling accidents to prevent stains that set and require professional cleaning.

Toxic Substances

For safety reasons, certain items must be kept away from your dog. To see a complete list of substances (those found outdoors as well as indoors) that are dangerous for dogs to ingest, visit a pet poison control website or toxic substance database before you have a problem, or ask your veterinarian if she can provide you with a printed list. As a safeguard, keep the phone number for the national Animal Poison Control Center handy in your phone directory, on your speed dial, or posted on the refrigerator door: (888) 426-4435.

By far the largest number of phone calls made to the Animal Poison Control hotline are for medications meant for humans that are ingested by pets, so be certain to keep your pills safely out of reach. Even if your motivation is to help your dog feel better, never give him any medication not prescribed or recommended by your veterinarian; this includes both prescription and over-the-counter drugs such as ibuprofen, cold medicines, and laxatives.

Other items toxic to dogs include:

- chocolate
- cleaning products, disinfectants, bleach
- cosmetics, hair dye
- rodent poison

During the holidays, take care to keep garlands, tinsel, mistletoe, and poinsettias away from pups and dogs. Year-round indoor plants that can be harmful if ingested include:

- amaryllis
- asparagus fern
- ficus
- ivy
- philodendron
- umbrella plant

In the garage or basement, secure products such as these from inquisitive canines:

- antifreeze
- glue
- insecticides and herbicides
- paint and paint thinner
- pool chemicals

Curly-haired breeds, like the Poodle, are practically nonshedding.

ALLERGIES

If you have reason to believe that you are allergic to dogs, consult an allergist before you bring a dog home. Be guided by her professional advice concerning your health.

People who are allergic to dogs react to a protein found in their saliva, skin, and urine. Avoiding dog drool and kisses can help minimize contact with the allergen. Dogs continually shed small particles of dead skin, called dander, containing the offending protein. Since all dogs have skin, there obviously is no such thing as a dog without dander.

Some dander falls out as a dog sheds his coat. Smaller dogs have less fur and dander to shed. So-called "hypoallergenic" breeds do not shed their coats as do most dogs, although they do lose dead hair, and while they still shed dander, there is less of it flying around in the home. To complicate matters, the chemistry of each individual dog and human varies; a person may, unpredictably, be far more allergic to one dog than another.

If you are allergic to dogs but have

determined that it is wise to share your home with one, consider adopting a small low-shedding dog. In addition, there are a number of strategies you can follow to remain comfortable:

- Keep your bedroom pet-free.
- Brush your dog frequently, outdoors.
- Bathe your dog frequently, preferably outdoors. (Even better: Have someone else bathe him.)
- Vacuum carpets often, at least weekly, and preferably with a HEPA vacuum.
- Choose low-pile carpets and have them steam cleaned two or three times a year.
- Wash throw rugs frequently in hot water.

- Sweep and wash floors often, at least weekly.
- Dust often using a damp cloth or a dust control product.
- Wash your dog's bed and blanket frequently.
- Use a HEPA air purifier (available in different sizes, depending on the size of the room) where you and your dog spend time, and change filters often.
- Wherever possible, replace carpets with hardwood floors.
- Use washable slipcovers (and wash often) or leather instead of upholstered furniture.
- Replace cloth drapes with plastic blinds or shutters.

THE YARD

Dogs and humans can, but do not always, happily share a yard. When it comes to chasing squirrels, most dogs are impervious to the beauty and fragility of flowers. Some dogs believe that gardens are meant for digging, and for all dogs, nature inevitably calls, often from your front or back lawn.

Safety

If you share your yard with a dog, the most important thing to do is install a fence that will safely contain him. If you maintain a vegetable or flower garden or flower borders, install an attractive low fence or barrier to keep your dog out.

A small, low-shedding breed could be appropriate if you have allergies.

Some vegetable gardeners build raised beds, such as a square wood frame filled with soil. Most dogs don't bother to climb into the bed.

Lawn chemicals used to kill insects, slugs, and weeds can pose a danger to your dog, especially if the liquids form puddles or if edible granules are accessible. Use products labeled "pet safe," and keep your dog out of the yard for 24 hours after you apply a chemical. Some outdoor plants can also pose problems for dogs interested in chomping on them, including:

- azalea
- narcissus
- oleander
- rhododendron
- sago Palm
- tulip

For a more extensive list of problem outdoor plants, consult a database listed at the end of this chapter.

Sanitation

The second most important task is to keep your yard clean, and this means poop scooping—no one's favorite task but an unavoidable one for reasons of both aesthetics and sanitation. (It has actually been estimated that a dog produces more than 250 pounds [113 kg] of poop per year.) You can do this with a shovel, a pet waste removal scooper, plastic bags (the kind you carry home your groceries in), or scooper

Keep your garbage can secure so that your dog won't be tempted to raid it.

bags found in pet shops and pet supply catalogs. Deposit the poop into a heavy metal garbage can that you keep in your driveway or yard, lined with a plastic bag. Follow the instructions of your local jurisdiction for disposing of this waste material. In my jurisdiction, such waste is picked up regularly every week, along with garbage and recyclables, and we are required by law to double-bag with plastic bags. Because we use small plastic bags to pick up and then toss these into a large plastic bag, we simply close up the large bag and place it and the garbage can out for regular pickups.

A fairly new development that promises to bring joy to the hearts of many dog owners is the growth of commercial poop-scooping services. There are now hundreds of these across the country. For a fee, the service providers will scoop your yard on an agreed-upon schedule, which could be weekly, biweekly, or monthly. The speedy growth of these services is proof of their early popularity with homeowners.

Another elimination problem is the creation of yellow or brown spots on grass, resulting from urine. If you see your dog urinate, hose the area down for several minutes.

Unsightly spots can be treated with special sprays. Tablets are also sold to change the chemical makeup of a dog's urine to reduce odor and staining, but these can be unhealthy for some dogs and should never be used unless recommended by a veterinarian.

Digging

Puppies and adolescent dogs love to dig. Alas, adult dogs—especially terriers—don't always grow out of this pastime. If you supervise your dog, you can issue a stern command if you see the paws and dirt start to fly. If your dog spends a lot of time in the yard alone, you have more of a challenge.

Dogs dig for fun, exercise, to bury or dig up a bone or other treasure, to create a hole large enough to lie and cool off in, and to tunnel under a fence. And they dig

Make sure that your yard is safe from toxic plants and materials before allowing your dog access.

out of boredom. One good remedy is to give your dog plenty of playtime, exercise, and outdoor toys. Another approach is compromise: "Give" your dog a digging area and make other areas off-limits. To encourage digging in one locale, bury a few toys or treats there from time to time and praise your dog for finding them.

To discourage digging:

- Fill in holes but bury a few bricks just under the surface.
- Sprinkle nontoxic but obnoxious items over and around the area: ground pepper, cotton soaked in vinegar. (Check with your veterinarian before using

commercial dog "repellants" for this purpose.)

- Watch from a distance and turn on a strategically placed sprinkler.
- Plant rosebushes, junipers, cacti, or other thorny or scratchy plants.

WANDERERS, ESCAPE ARTISTS, ADVENTURERS

What dog owner has not had at least one of these experiences (along with some serious heartburn)?

- A phone call informing you that your dog Duke is ensconced at the home of the caller (a stranger to you) miles (km) away. You thought that Duke was in the backyard, where you left him half an hour earlier.
- You were walking Duke off leash on a lovely wooded path and then spent two hours calling and searching for him because he took off running after spotting… something…moving in the underbrush.
- You go to the back door to call Duke in from the yard. No response. You have no idea how long he has been gone.

Strategies to Keep Dogs at Home

Let's face it—some dogs are born to wander. And some homebodies will suddenly shock you by disappearing when you least expect it. The best you

Money $aving Tip

The more that you exercise your dog and give him attention and stimulation, the less likely he will be destructive inside the house or the yard.

can do is to diminish the wanderer's appetite for wandering and reduce your dog's opportunities to explore the world solo.

A dog who is spayed or neutered, well exercised, stimulated with activity, treated affectionately, and trained is less likely to wander. A dog who is bored and left alone for long periods is more likely to become restless and want to escape. If your dog spends time alone in the yard:

- Provide a secure fence of the appropriate height and type.
- Make certain that there is someone at home while he is outside.
- Take a few minutes to play with him in the yard.
- Leave him with a few toys or a toy stuffed with treats.
- Walk the fence every few weeks to make sure that it is secure.
- Double-check that the gate is closed. Post a sign on it: "Please keep gate closed."

If technology appeals to you and you don't mind spending upward of $300, you can outfit your dog with a wearable GPS (global positioning system). This battery-powered device, weighing 3 to 5 ounces (85 to 141 g), attaches to the dog's collar and operates off a system of satellites. You, the owner, set an invisible boundary or safety zone; if your dog leaves the zone, an alert and his location are automatically sent to your cell phone, PDA, or computer. You'll know right away if he has left the yard and where to find him.

A secure fence is essential for keeping your dog safe.

Strategies for Finding a Lost Dog

The single most important factor in the return of a lost dog is that he is wearing a collar and identification tag. The tag must, at a minimum, have the owner's home phone number on it; adding a cell phone number is usually a good idea.

I recommend that you outfit your dog with an identifying microchip. These tiny chips, about the size of a grain of rice, are implanted under a dog's skin just above the shoulders by a veterinarian or vet technician. When the chip is scanned, the numbers and letters that it contains will identify the dog and match him with owner contact information that has been stored in a database. If your microchipped dog wanders off, is found, and is then taken to a shelter or veterinary clinic, he will almost always be scanned and you will be notified of his whereabouts. The cost varies by region and clinic, hovering at about $50. Some local humane societies offer reduced rate microchipping for as low as $15 to $25. Microchips are now routinely implanted by many animal shelters and rescue groups in dogs being adopted out. A few municipalities require owners to microchip their pets, and others may soon follow suit.

If your dog is lost:

- Grab a leash and some treats and begin walking the streets in your neighborhood, calling your pet's name. If you can, enlist friends and neighbors to help. Most lost dogs are found within 1 mile (1.5 km) of home. The sooner you start searching, the better your chances of finding your dog.

- Call your local animal control organization and animal shelters to file a report on your dog and to ask if such a dog has been reported found. Keep checking by phone, and visit shelters in person to look at the dogs.
- Make up and post flyers. Use a color photo of your dog. Add a description (weight, sex, age, special characteristics); include your phone number, and if you wish, a reward. Post as many flyers as possible within a 1- to 2-mile (1.5- to 3-km) radius; post them along main roads and on bulletin boards in as many places as possible, such as grocery stores, libraries, laundromats, veterinary clinics, and pet stores. If you do not have a computer and printer at home, take the photo to a copy and print store where your flyers can be made up.
- Post information about your lost dog and check for postings of found dogs on the internet.
- Place a classified ad in the "Lost" section of your local newspaper and check the "Found" section.
- Call local radio and television stations to ask if they would report your pet as part of a public service announcement (PSA).
- As a last resort, you can hire a "pet detective," which could cost as much as $750 per day.

Stolen Dogs

A neighbor of mine likes to leave Sammy, her Golden Retriever, outside alone in the front yard. I suggested to my neighbor that if I were in her shoes, I would be worried that Sammy would be stolen.

"No way!" she assured me. "People don't steal dogs in this neighborhood." Luckily, Sammy has not been stolen or wandered off, but my neighbor is taking a chance. Dogs do get stolen in all kinds of neighborhoods, whether they're urban, suburban, or rural—from front yards and fenced-in backyards and yards with electric fences. Dogs are stolen by people who want them for themselves (they think) or to give to a girlfriend or child. They are stolen by people who sell them to laboratories or to strangers. A few simple precautions will help protect your dog from being stolen:

- Do not tie him up anywhere—in your front yard, in front of a store or restaurant—unless you are with him.
- Do not let him roam.
- Do not leave him in your yard when you are not at home.
- Do not leave him unattended in a car.

RESOURCES MADE EASY

Books on Allergies

- Morgan, Diane. *Sneeze-Free Dog Breeds: Allergy Management and Breed Selection for the Allergic Dog Lover*. Neptune City, NJ: TFH Publications, 2006.

Books on "Clean" Coexistence

- Aslett, Don. *Pet Clean-Up Made Easy*. Avon, MA: Adams Media, 2005.
- Gagne, Tammy. *The Green Dog: The Complete Guide to Raising an Earth-Friendly Companion* (e-book) . Neptune City, NJ: TFH Publications, 2010.
- Szabo, Julia. *Animal House Style: Designing A Home To Share With Your Pets*. New York: Bulfinch Press, 2001.

Books on Sharing a Garden With Your Dog

- Smith, Cheryl S. *Dog Friendly Gardens, Garden Friendly Dogs*. Wenatchee, WA: Dogwise Publishing, 2007.

Dog Dander Reduction Products

- Miele: www.mieleusa.com; 1-800-843-7231
- National Allergy: www.nationalallergysupply.com; 1-800-522-1448
- RGF: www.rgf.com; 1-800-842-7771
- Vitaire: www.vitaire.com; 1-800-552-5533

Dog-Proof Garbage Can

- Doggy Safe: www.doggy-safe.com; 1-866-428-DOGS

GPS Dog Locator

- Global Petfinder: www.globalpetfinder.com

Hard Floor Electric Cleaners

- Bissell: www.bissell.com
- goClean: www.goCleanvacs.com; 1-888-462-5326

Indoor Pet Gates

- Check your favorite local pet retailer or pet chain (in store or online).

Indoor Pet Potties

- Always check your favorite local pet retailer or pet chain (in store or online) first.
- PetaPotty: www.PETaPOTTY.com; 1-866-PET-PAWS

Lawn Spot Eliminators

- Check your favorite local pet retailer or pet chain (in store or online).

Lost or Found Pet

- America's National Lost & Found Pet Database: www.lostfoundpets.us; 1-800-969-2241
- FidoFinder: www.fidofinder.com; 1-205-969-2241
- Petfinder: www.petfinder.com
- Pets911: www.pets911.com

Managing Allergies

- Asthma and Allergy Foundation of America (AAFA): www.aafa.org; 1-800-7-ASTHMA
- Humane Society of the United States (HSUS): www.hsus.org

Microchips

- AVID: www.avidid.com; 800-336-2843
- Home Again: www.homeagain.com
- Petlink: www.petlink.net

Pet Detectives

- Use an Internet search engine and type in "pet detective."

Pet-Friendly Rental Apartments

- Apartments.com: www.Apartments.com
- Humane Society of the United States (HSUS): www.rentwithpets.org

Pet Stain and Odor Removers

- Always check your favorite local pet retailer or pet chain (in store or online) first.
- Clean + Green: www.sea-yu.com
- Clear the Air: www.cleartheair.com; 1-800-611-1611
- Febreze: www.febreze.com
- Get Serious!: www.GETSERIOUSProducts.com; 1-844-7967
- Nature's Miracle: www.naturemakesitwork.com
- OdorZout: www.88stink.com
- OP Products: www.opproducts.com
- Oxy Clean & Protect: www.scotchgard.com
- Petastic: www.petastic.com

- Simple Solution: www.simplesolution.com; 1-800-272-6336
- Urine Gone!: www.urinegone.com; 1-800-709-0298
- Search online for the keywords "pet stain remover."

Poop-Scoop Services

- Association of Professional Animal Waste Specialists (aPAWS): www.apaws.org
- Look in the Yellow Pages or search online for "pet waste removal."

Protective Carpet/Fabric Sealant

- Crypton Super Fabric and Furniture: www.cryptonfabric.com; 1-800-crypton
- FiberSeal: www.fiberseal.com; 1-800-TUFSEAL
- Scotchgard: www.solutions.3m.com/wps/portal/3M/en_US/Scotchgard/Home/

Toxic Plant Database

- American Society for the Prevention of Cruelty to Animals (ASPCA): www.aspca.org
- Humane Society of the United States (HSUS): www.hsus.org

Vacuum Cleaners Designed for Pet Fur and Dander

- Bissell (Pet Hair Eraser and Pet Pack) : www.bissell.com; 1-800-237-7691
- Dyson (DC 17 Animal): www.dyson.com

Part III
The Middle
Years

Chapter 7

Everyday Care: Nutrition and Exercise

Compatibility, the dictionary tells us, means living together in a "harmonious, agreeable, or congenial combination." If you are unable to live "agreeably" with your dog, what should be a joy becomes an annoyance or a burden.

Most of the burden for creating harmony in this relationship depends on us, the humans, because we have the resources and the power. Ironically, because dogs cannot speak, incompatibility in a human–dog relationship is almost always blamed on the dog. But what if the dog could be heard? The other side of the ledger might sound like this:

- *"My owner visited the bathroom five or six times every 24 hours but expected me to "hold it." I tried but I couldn't. She only took me outside twice a day. I just turned a year old. Twelve hours to wait was too long for me. She dumped me here at the shelter."*

- *"My owner walks me around the block four times a day. That's enough for bathroom stuff, but I don't get any exercise at all. I'm on a short leash. And I really, really need to run. Then she gets mad at me at home because I 'pester' her."*

- *"My ears are killing me. I keep getting infections because my owner doesn't like to clean my ears like the vet told her to. The grandkids pull on my ears and nobody pays attention when I cry. One of these days I'm going to snap at someone and then it will be curtains for me."*

A dog who is ill, injured, underfed, or overfed is handicapped in his efforts to learn

Ask your veterinarian about a proper diet for your dog.

or conform to your household rules. A dog who receives insufficient exercise and stimulation is prone to engage in indoor elimination and unpleasant or destructive behavior. Instilling good canine behavior begins with an owner who provides her dog with:

- proper nutrition
- mental and physical exercise
- home health care of coat, skin, and teeth
- veterinary care, including checkups, vaccinations, and parasite control

In this chapter, we will address the first two points—nutrition and exercise.

(Chapters 8 and 9 will cover the last two points.)

NUTRITION

How does a responsible owner decide what to feed Scout, and how much to feed him? The answer to *what* is not found in advertisements for puppy and dog chow, and the answer to *how much* is not found on the packaging of the chow. Usually, too much food is recommended. Individual dogs, even those of the same breed within the same age group, have different metabolisms and varying opportunities to exercise. There is no one-size-fits-all diet that is appropriate for all dogs within a given weight or age.

If you have purchased a healthy puppy, ask the breeder for recommendations. If you have adopted a healthy adult, ask the caretaker for recommendations. Run this information past your veterinarian when you take Scout for his first checkup. If you have acquired a dog with health issues, collaborate closely with your veterinarian about proper diet. If, together with your veterinarian, you decide to change Scout's diet, do so gradually. If you are feeding a puppy, transition him gradually into adult food as he approaches 10 to 12 months of age.

Commercial Puppy and Dog Food

Nearly all of us buy commercial puppy and dog food rather than making our own. Commercial food is available in dry, semi-moist, and canned. You need not buy a fancy, high-priced "premium" brand to provide your dog with adequate nutrition. What you do need to do is meet your dog's nutritional needs, and many commercial dog foods, both regular and premium, will do that. Like human beings but in different proportions, dogs need water, protein, fat, carbohydrates, vitamins, and certain minerals for nourishment. Manufacturers are required to list on the packaging the minimum percentages of protein and fat and maximum percentages for

moisture and fiber, and they're required to list ingredients in descending order of quantity.

While dogs need more protein than humans and a higher proportion of fat, they really do not need much in the way of carbohydrates, but many commercial foods (especially kibble) contain a lot of them because they are inexpensive. Although a dog can metabolize only so much protein (about 30 percent of total calories, maximum; most "maintenance" foods contain about 20 percent), a fast-growing puppy—especially a large breed—will typically need more protein. Food for senior, sedentary dogs is generally lower in protein and fat and higher in fiber. To obtain more information and advice about a particular brand or type of food, check with your veterinarian or call the pet food manufacturer.

Kibble

Kibble is dry food that is commercially prepared. Some brands can be purchased at grocery stores, and others are available

Money $aving Tip

Dry kibble is cheaper than wet or moist food and usually recommended by veterinarians.

only in pet stores. All have a high grain content, and most are nutritionally adequate (but study the label and check with your vet).

Kibble is a good choice for most dogs and their owners. It is inexpensive and easy to store and serve. It should be stored in a cool, dry location in its original packaging or an airtight container, such as a plastic bin. It can be served dry or with a small amount of water or canned food added just before feeding. (Don't soak it in water until it becomes soggy.) I agree with the veterinarians who argue that chewing dry nuggets helps a dog maintain healthy teeth and gums, although a recent study challenges this conclusion. In any event, kibble is not a substitute for brushing your dog's teeth.

Kibble can be purchased in different-sized nuggets for small, medium, and large dogs. A single brand typically may also offer kibble formulated for puppies, adult dogs, and senior dogs. The array is bewildering: I recently counted more than 70 (yes, 70!) different kibbles for puppies alone. Some companies also formulate kibble for specific health issues, such as arthritis, weight control,

Money $aving Tip

Buy kibble in large bags—it's cheaper that way. To maintain quality, keep the kibble in the bag after opening it and place the bag in an airtight container.

sensitive skin, or stomach problems. Follow your veterinarian's advice before purchasing these products for your dog.

Canned Food

Given a choice between dry and canned food, most dogs would choose canned food. This does not mean that you, as an owner, must go along. Canned food is more meat based than kibble and contains fewer or no carbohydrates and about 75 percent water. It is more expensive than kibble. Once a can is opened, it should be refrigerated and can safely be used for another two to three days at the most.

Moist or Soft Dry Food

A third and fourth option for dogs are "moist" or "semi-moist" diets, which are sold in packets. These are more expensive than dry food, but unlike canned food, do not require refrigeration. "Soft" dry food is what it sounds like: dry, like kibble, but unlike kibble, soft rather than hard. I do not recommend moist food as a good choice for healthy meals, but one piece at a time can be used as a tiny treat.

Unsafe Snacks

Chocolate, high-fat foods, onions, garlic, grapes, and raisins are not safe snacks for dogs.

Mix It Up

My dogs thrive on a mix of kibble and canned food. Instead of water, I pour a small amount of store-bought broth (chicken or beef flavor) over the kibble just before serving and mix in a small amount of canned food for each dog.

Water

Water is as indispensable to dog survival and dog health as it is to humans. About 70 percent of a dog's lean body mass is water. Fresh, clean water should be available to puppies and dogs at all times.

Snacks

I am but one of an overwhelming number of dog owners who regularly give my dogs treats. I do it to bribe them, reward them, and just because I feel like it. I generally rely on store-bought treats because I find it helpful to read the packaging and understand just what I am giving them in terms of calories. I prefer the "hard" treats to the soft ones because I believe that they are good for their teeth, gums, and jaws.

Human food used as treats is not a bad thing in moderation. Believe it or not, many dogs like small pieces of apples, bananas, and even carrots. Don't give chocolate, fatty or greasy foods, onions, garlic, grapes, or raisins.

Snacks add calories to your dog's daily diet and can contribute to obesity. Because I give my dogs treats, I cut back proportionally on the food they receive as their main meal. If you are a snack giver, be sure to compensate by decreasing the size of your dog's regular meal or meals. A good rule of thumb is to limit snack calories to about 10 percent of your dog's daily calorie intake.

Supplements and Special Diets

A study conducted a few years ago by *Consumer Reports* found deficiencies in a few commercial and puppy and dog foods, both dry and canned. The deficiencies usually related to the proportion of minerals of potassium, magnesium, or calcium. If you have these or other concerns about food you are using, call the manufacturer or take the food manufacturer's label to your vet and ask for her assessment. Mixing two types of food—kibble and canned—can help assure a balanced diet.

Some dogs need supplements or special diets to relieve dry, itchy skin or to address a specific health problem such as allergies, arthritis, diabetes, and liver or kidney disease. Although pet product manufacturers offer supplements as well as specialized diets, consult with your veterinarian before using a supplement or special diet for your dog. If you are interested in using an "organic" or "all

Clean Tip

Wash and thoroughly rinse your dog's water and food bowls daily.

meat" or "holistic" or "vegetarian" diet for your dog, consult your veterinarian first to make certain that your dog will be receiving the proper nutrition.

Quantity

How much you feed your dog can be as important as *what* the food is. Every dog will have a different food intake requirement. Nutritionists, using a complicated formula, suggest that (roughly speaking) a healthy, neutered 10-pound (4.5-kg) dog requires about 350 calories per day; a 20-pound (9-kg) dog, 585 calories; and a 60-pound (27-kg) dog, 1,330 calories. If your dog is sedentary or extremely active, or a growing puppy, he will have a different calorie requirement.

Too Fat?

The biggest nutritional problem visited on pet dogs is not the quality but the quantity of food—about 30 to 40 percent are overweight or obese. Overweight or obese dogs are prone to serious health risks, including:

- arthritis and other orthopedic problems
- high blood pressure
- diabetes
- hypothyroidism
- respiratory difficulty

Not surprisingly, these health risks result in a shorter life span for the overweight dog and expensive veterinary care. They have a negative impact on the quality of a dog's life in many ways, from crippling arthritis to heat intolerance and breathing problems that make it sadly uncomfortable for a dog to walk, exercise, and play.

How can you tell if your dog is overweight? Some of the more obvious signs are rolls of fat around the neck and near the base of the tail and a "hanging" or bulging tummy. A dog of healthy weight will have a slight indentation at his "waist" (looking at your dog from above, this is just behind his rib cage), and his ribs will be covered by a thin, not thick, layer of fat. Just about every veterinary clinic today has a wall chart illustrating the healthy versus the overweight canine body.

The remedy for excess weight is simple: less food, more exercise. Rely on veterinary advice, common sense, and a gradual approach to both. Don't take an overweight dog for a two-hour walk for the first time in his life, and don't suddenly cut his food ration in half. Gradually decrease his food and increase his exercise, either by adding an

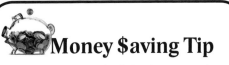

Money $aving Tip

Shop around to find the lowest price for your dog's food. Prices vary among pet shops, pet chain stores, grocery stores, and big box stores.

extra 15-minute walk each day and/or by lengthening your already scheduled walks by 5 to 10 minutes. As he begins to shed weight and feel more energetic, you can increase the number or lengths of his walks. Your goal for your dog is a gradual weight loss of 1/2 to 1 pound (.2 to .4 kg) every two weeks.

"Light, "lite," "reduced calorie," and "low calorie" canine diets are available from commercial pet food manufacturers, and others require a veterinarian's prescription. Consult with your veterinarian before substituting a "light" food for your dog's regular diet. Recently, the Food and Drug Administration (FDA) approved a prescription weight-loss medication for dogs that suppresses appetite and inhibits fat absorption. In cases of extreme obesity, particularly with life-threatening conditions, a veterinarian may suggest and prescribe such a medication.

Some puppy owners make the mistake of overfeeding, believing that puppies are meant to be roly-poly or chubby. While many (not all) puppies are indeed plump and roly-poly, a puppy who waddles instead of walking or running could be beginning life on the wrong pudgy foot. Although a puppy will not look as svelte at six months as he will at maturity, be aware that being overweight, even at a young age, is not a sign of good health. Check with your veterinarian if you

BREEDS PRONE TO OBESITY

Some breeds are more prone to obesity than others, including:
- Basset Hounds
- Cairn Terriers
- Cocker Spaniels
- Dachshunds
- Labrador Retrievers
- Pugs
- Shetland Sheepdogs

have a question about your puppy's ideal weight.

Too Thin?

Some dogs are too thin. The ribs, vertebrae, and pelvic bones on a too-thin dog are visible and easily felt. A too-thin dog might be suffering from health problems, which a veterinarian can rule in or out. These could include parasite infestation, teeth and gum problems, diabetes, kidney or heart disease, or even cancer. In a multiple-dog household, one dog may be bullied out of eating as much as he needs. Some dogs are not interested in or are too easily distracted from eating or are picky eaters. To resolve such problems:
- Take your dog for a thorough veterinary checkup and discuss his weight.
- If bullying is a problem, feed your dogs in separate rooms.

- If you have a picky dog, add chicken or beef broth to his kibble or mix in some soft food.
- If your dog is easily distracted, feed him in a quiet place, preferably a room by himself.

Some dogs are simply burning up more calories than they take in. Make certain that you are providing enough food and that it is nutritionally adequate. If your dog needs more food, increase gradually—not suddenly—the amount of food you serve until you reach the proper amount. Or you may need to change the type of food. A "senior" dog could still require an "adult maintenance" diet because he is very active. An adolescent dog who is still growing may need puppy rather than adult food.

Frequency

Experts differ in their advice about how often to feed puppies and dogs. Some puppy experts recommend feeding a puppy four times a day until he is three months old, then stepping down to three times a day for another three months, and then stepping down to twice a day. Others recommend feeding just three times a day, beginning at ten weeks, and stepping down to two at six

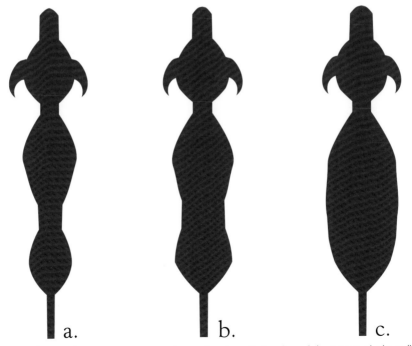

Viewed from above, here are examples of a too thin dog (a); normal dog (b); and obese dog (c).

months. I recommend following your breeder's advice and checking with your veterinarian. You will probably end up with a middle ground: feeding three times a day beginning at 3 months and then tapering down to twice a day at 10 to 12 months.

Some puppies are ready to switch from puppy food to adult dog food at about ten months of age. For others, especially large breeds that are still growing, that changeover point may not be reached until the dog is 18 months. One rule of thumb: Don't switch your puppy to adult food until he has reached about 80 percent of his expected adult body weight.

Some experts recommend feeding adult dogs twice a day, and others insist that a single feeding is better. I have reached my own compromise for my dogs: I feed a small meal in the morning and a main meal in the evening. It seems to work well.

If you have a senior dog or a dog with health problems, you may need to feed him more often, depending on your veterinarian's advice.

MENTAL EXERCISE

Simply put, "mental exercise" is a dog's "work" or some type of stimulation or activity in addition to, but no substitute for, outdoor exercise. Like humans, dogs need mental as well as physical activity.

NATURALLY THIN BREEDS

A few breeds are naturally thin, with very little fat covering their ribs, including:
- Borzoi
- Greyhounds
- Salukis
- Whippets

It has always puzzled me that some owners expect Rex to turn into a potted plant once inside the house. Rex should, apparently, shed his dogginess and patiently wait for the next meal or walk. These expectations almost always end in human disappointment and a bored, frustrated dog who may turn to incessant barking, indoor soiling, or destructive chewing. These owners miss key points of canine companionship. Our animals keep us company and pay attention to us. They are social by nature, and they need our attention in return.

Increasingly, trainers and behaviorists emphasize a dog's need for stimulation at home in addition to adequate exercise. For those tuned in to the canine–human relationship, this is a no-brainer and no effort at all. It is fun and it feels good. If you or a family member are at home most or all of the day, both you and your dog have a built-in advantage in keeping each other active.

Affection

Like humans, dogs appreciate and like physical contact and attention. Bestow affection on your dog—scratch his ears, pat his head, rub his tummy—as often as the mood strikes you. Talk baby talk, current events, or discuss movie reviews with your pet. In surveys, most owners report that they do talk to their dogs. There is no cause for concern unless your dog answers in a foreign language.

Distraction

Give your dog a chew toy now and then (not every day) or a "food puzzle"—a rubber toy filled with treats that he has to work on to get the treats. Many vets recommend Nylabones rather than rawhide. Some dogs, including my own, suffer digestive disorders if they chew and ingest a large amount of rawhide. So I indulge my dogs with Nylabones, which are available in various sizes, shapes, and flavors.

My dogs are fortunate because we have a number of French doors in our home. One or both of the dogs will plop down in front of the doors, observing the action on the street (not much, but there is the occasional squirrel or dog walker). I think of this as their television, with only one channel. My dogs do not appear to appreciate actual television shows, but in a recent survey, 36 percent of pet owners say they believe that their pets enjoy watching television and that animal-related programs such as Animal Planet are the most popular.

During mild weather, the front door of our home remains open and the dogs sit in front of the screen or storm door, which provides an equally good view. If you have a strong, impulsive dog given to running through doors, replace a screen or storm door with Plexiglas. If you have a small dog who sits on the back of a chair to look out the window, your concern, especially in a high-rise, is to guarantee that the window is escape- and crash-proof. If necessary, install bars that he cannot fall or leap through.

Games

How do you play with a dog indoors? You are never too old for hide-and-seek, take it from me. I hide, call my dogs, and they run all over the place looking for me. As I have pretty much run out of new hiding places, this game does not last long, but they do not seem to mind. They have long assumed that I'm not too bright.

I play catch with Charlotte. I show her a tennis ball, she waits expectantly

Money $aving Tip
Overfeeding your dog is a waste of money and bad for his health.

3 or 4 feet (1 m) away, I toss her the ball, and she tries (with increasing success) to catch it on the fly. I tell her to sit and try (with less success because he is less coordinated) to play the same game with Tony. If you have a little bit of indoor space, you can gently toss a soft chew toy for your pup to fetch. The object of the game is to give him something to do rather than really stretch his legs. Some dogs will search for a hidden toy or snack.

Toys

Most dogs have favorite toys that they will fetch, hunt, shake, or chew. I have a "toy box" of safe dog toys. Once or twice a day, one of my dogs will visit it, extract a toy, and begin to either chew on it or tease the other dog with it.

Dogs need affection and attention.

Stick to commercial dog toys or tennis balls. Unless you are prepared to allow your dog to chew on new slippers, shoes, or other household items, don't give him similar, old items as toys. It is not fair to expect him to make the distinction between old and new. Don't let your dog bring sticks or pine cones into the house to chew. He will make a mess and these items are not healthy to ingest.

Commercial soft toys contain batting and usually some kind of squeaker that are unsafe for your dog to ingest, although he may well try. Once he tears the toys open (as he probably will, eventually), remove the squeaker and batting yourself and throw them away. Avoid buying toys that have beads or other small objects stitched to them because they are, and probably will be, easily swallowed. Safe stuffed animals for dogs have eyes or decorations made of cloth or stitching. Among the safest toys:

- those made of cloth or tough cotton rope in small, medium, and large knots, rings, or bone shapes
- those made of nontoxic vinyl or tough rubber in small, medium, and large

cubes (you can tuck treats inside), balls, barbells, and erratic shapes

Obedience and Agility Work

One of the best indoor activities for your dog is a ten-minute practice session of *heel*, *sit*, *stay*, and *come*. This is a mental exercise for your dog. Dogs who go to classes or private training sessions almost always sleep afterward because learning and following commands are work for them. These brief sessions helpfully refresh lessons already learned.

Agility training is fun and good "work" for your dog. It need not be complicated, stressful, or competitive. You can easily create a small indoor jump in your hall or living room with a broom handle balanced on a couple of books. Commercial agility equipment, typically consisting of weave poles, jumps, ring (or "tire") jumps, and soft, collapsible tunnels can be purchased separately or as packs or play sets. The equipment is quite pricey, so if you are interested, I suggest that you start with one beginner's item before you leap in with both feet and spend a large amount of money on a complete play set. Ring

jumps and weave poles require yard space. Low jumps and some short tunnels can be used indoors. Unless you are serious about competing (in which case you should be trained by a professional), the agility challenges for your dog should be easy and fun. For safety reasons, keep jumps low!

Playmates

My two Collies hang out in the same room nearly 100 percent of the time and often play tug-of-war with their toys. I have usually had two dogs (one male, one female) at a time, and they always got along and kept each other company. There are many issues involved if you are considering two dogs instead of one:

- **costs:** twice as much for food, basic equipment, veterinary care, boarding, training, and other services such as grooming
- **space:** twice as much canine-occupied space
- **cleaning:** more fur to vacuum, more poop scooping
- **walking:** the same number of walks usually applies but with more effort

It is possible to give your dog canine companionship without acquiring another dog. Some neighbors I know arrange playdates: "Your dog can come play in my yard with my dog today, my dog will come to your house for a few hours the day after tomorrow." For compatible dogs who like to play,

> ## AGILITY
> Agility is a sport that presents dogs with an obstacle course that typically includes tunnels, A-frames, jumps, and seesaws. Dogs perform without a leash. Agility can be informal or competitive.

this is good exercise and usually exhausting. Best of all, it's a break from routine.

Doggy Day Care

This is a relatively new option, appearing and then rapidly spreading in the last ten years, largely in response to the needs of working couples who want their "latchkey dogs" to have companionship, stimulation, and attention during the workday. If you are away from home much of the day; if you are unable to exercise or interact with your dog because of illness, incapacity, or ferociously bad weather; if your home is being painted or renovated; or if you simply want to give your dog a change of pace, doggy day care may be just the thing—if you can find the right day care and if you can afford it.

Agility is a fun and exciting sport where a dog completes an obstacle course.

Doggy camp or day care comes in many forms. Quite a few facilities are adjunct to kennels, providing the option of overnight as well as day care. Some provide services on-site, such as grooming or training. Some offer indoor/outdoor play areas, while urban facilities are more likely to provide strictly indoor play space. Some indoor-only locations offer outdoor walks (sometimes for an additional charge), while others do not. Some allow dogs to play, hang out, or rest as they choose, while others require a rest period during which dogs are crated for a period, usually in the middle of the day. Some will feed dogs with food provided by owners, and some will administer medication. Some have video cams so that you can watch your dog from your home or office if you have Internet access. Some maintain vans that will pick up your dog and bring him home again. Hours vary, from 7:00 a.m. or earlier in the morning until 7:00 p.m. to 11:00 p.m. at night.

Most centers will allow dogs to visit by the hour, half day or full day. Prices vary tremendously, from $3 an hour up to $10, with discounts usually offered for purchasing "in bulk"—10, 20, 30, or a similar combination of full days in advance. This and other information will typically be available over the phone or on an Internet website.

Selecting a Day Care

It is important—indeed, mandatory—to visit a facility, or more than one, before you choose one. Observe the dogs at play, make note of what you see around you, and ask questions. A good facility will:

- require proof of current vaccinations
- require that your dog be spayed or neutered
- require that your dog receive monthly flea control medication
- screen for aggressive dogs (this typically involves temperament assessment and may include an owner's questionnaire)
- have a minimum age requirement (usually four months)
- look and smell clean, sanitary, well ventilated, and well lighted
- not be overcrowded
- have a separate area, preferably outdoors, where dogs can relieve themselves
- have a separate area for time-outs or rest periods for dogs who are older, tired, or just need to calm down
- most importantly, keep

experienced, trained staff with the dogs at all times, whether indoors or outdoors, in a ratio of 1 staff person to 10 or 12 dogs

I think that doggy day care is a swell idea for dogs who are often home alone for long periods, with two caveats:

1. A good center will be safe and fun. A strictly indoor center that is lacking in human supervision or that lets dogs eliminate in the same area where they play can be problematic. Lack of supervision can result in dogfights, bullying, and boredom. Being allowed or required to

Doggy day care is a new option for owners who can't provide care or exercise for their dogs during the day.

eliminate indoors can confuse a dog, even one who is housetrained.

2. Some dogs are very social with their own kind and love to play and be with other dogs. These dogs will like day care and benefit from it. A few dogs, by temperament or because of age, prefer to be left alone. If you do not know ahead of time, you can easily determine which category your dog falls into. Choose a good center and sign him up for a day or half day. Drop by and watch, unobserved, at some point during the day or at the end of the day. If your dog is sitting or lying in a corner, avoiding contact—this is not the place for him. If you must leave him alone during the day but want to provide exercise and stimulation, consider hiring a dog walker. *One exception to this rule*: a newly acquired dog who has not been socialized. If you have recently adopted a reclusive dog or purchased a shy puppy, give him plenty of time to get used to you and your home and to meet dogs on your neighborhood walks. If he remains extremely timid, you can take him to doggy day care for a few hours at a time. Some dogs do gradually come out of their shell over a period of months. A few will remain loners.

PHYSICAL EXERCISE

Two years ago my neighbor, a widow in her 80s, adopted a beautiful two-year-old dog from our local animal shelter. Most likely a cross between a Rhodesian Ridgeback and a chocolate Labrador Retriever, this large, muscular dog arrived housetrained, obedience trained, affectionate, and calm. I couldn't help but wonder why on earth someone would relinquish such a wonderful pet, but we will never know the answer to that question. I also regretted that her owner, Mrs. Smith, refused to even consider adopting a smaller, less energetic dog. Mrs. Smith loves and dotes on Brownie, but because of ill health, she is unable to walk her and unwilling to send her to day camp.

Brownie spends hours each day alone in a small backyard. Although still sweet tempered and affectionate, she has gradually morphed into a neighborhood nuisance, barking constantly out of loneliness and boredom. Her initially calm demeanor has been transformed into frenzied leaps when people approach her, so desperate is she for a means to expend her energy.

Brownie's story is ongoing but has taken a turn for the better. An exceptionally kind neighbor walks her every morning. This simple respite—a 30-minute walk in the park—is allowing Brownie to be a calmer, quieter dog again.

Physical exercise is indispensable to a dog's good health and good behavior. A dog who runs, plays, and walks outdoors is using and strengthening his heart, lungs, and muscles. He is engaged in his environment, exploring with his eyes, ears, and nose. A tired dog is far less likely to be an indoor or outdoor pest or to be noisy or destructive.

Walking

Dog walks are a boon to people as well as canines. As reported in getactivemagazine.com, dog owners walk an average of 300 minutes a week, compared to fewer than 170 minutes for those without pets. Another study found that older adults who own dogs engage in more physical activity and have fewer disabilities than those who do not own pets. They were likely to walk farther, walk more often, and walk faster.

Walking is by far the most popular means of exercising a dog. Most jurisdictions (and common sense) require that your dog be under your "command and control." In many areas, this explicitly requires that your dog be leashed. If not, he must be exquisitely trained to respond immediately to your call to come regardless of distractions.

As has often been said, "You should walk your dog, your dog should not walk you." This can happen with a dog who is trained to heel or walk gently on a leash without pulling or lunging. A dog who drags you along is no fun to walk and can cause you harm.

A leash is mandatory if you are walking on sidewalks, especially next to busy urban streets. Most parks also require leashes. I strongly recommend using a 6-foot (2-m) leash rather than a retractable leash.

Jogging and Biking

Many large, active dogs, such as retrievers and Dalmatians, and some smaller dogs, such as Jack Russell Terriers, love to run and make great jogging partners. If you are a jogger and want canine company on your runs, choose your path accordingly: Jogging dogs don't mix well with bikers or urban traffic. If possible, find a path where your dog can run loose as long as you are certain that he will stay near you or return to you when called. Don't let him run free unless you are certain that he will come back on command. This is not always the case, especially with dogs bred to hunt. When they catch a scent, they pretty much forget about you.

Jogging with a leashed dog is problematic at best. A jogger attached to a dog is in danger of tripping or being pulled over. A dog attached to a jogger gets his head and neck jerked upward and forward with every other step the jogger takes.

Money $aving Tip

All-day doggy day care may be too expensive, but many centers allow dogs to visit by the hour or half day. This can be a nice change for a bored dog.

Biking with a canine companion is even more problematic unless you are fortunate enough to have a safe path all to yourself. Loose dogs on biking paths are a danger to everyone, including themselves. Dogs leashed to a bike or biker are a special hazard to themselves and their owner, and most bikers travel faster than is healthy for all but the sturdiest dogs to keep up.

Fetch

Some dogs live to play fetch. I once had a Collie like this, a rare exception for the breed. Most retrievers (there are five different breeds), many spaniels, mixed breeds, hounds, and other fun-loving canines kindly allow you to stand in one place and toss a tennis ball or stick for them to chase and bring back to you. You can rest, they can run.

Of course, the basic "fetch" game has been elaborated upon. The simplest variation is the use of a tennis racket to loft the ball higher and farther. Or you can purchase a "ball launcher" or "chuckit," which allows you to throw and pick up a tennis ball without touching it, thus avoiding contact with the slobbery ball. Special dog-safe flying discs and boomerangs that won't splinter in a dog's mouth supplement the basic tennis ball or stick.

Swimming

Some dogs love to swim and some hate it. Water-retrieving breeds are usually the swimmers, and they are built for it. They have webbed feet and water-repellant coats. Other dogs, especially those with long, thick coats, should not spend much time in the water. I learned this lesson the hard way: One of my Collies loves to sit (yes, sit) neck high in our local creek. He emerges soaked through to the skin, with a soggy coat. Even though I try my best to towel him dry when we return home, his thick coat does not dry out easily or quickly. The result is severe skin irritation.

Whether your dog has access to a chlorinated pool, the ocean, or a creek, pond, or lake, here are a few tips to keep in mind:

- If your dog does not want to swim, don't force him.
- Do not let your dog swim in water that appears or smells polluted.
- Watch your dog while he is in the water.

Unless your dog is a Chesapeake Bay Retriever or similar breed with a water-resistant coat, towel him down afterward. If he has picked up salt or sand, hose him down first.

If your dog has large, floppy ears, clean them out with a canine ear-cleansing solution after he has been swimming.

Yard Work

If you have a fenced-in yard, your dog will doubtless be happy to play and run there—that is, if you are playing fetch with him or if there is another dog for him to play with. An unattended dog and a fenced-in yard do not equal exercise. Except for the sad specimen who is left alone all day, becoming so neurotic that he courses back and forth along the fence barking at every moving object (and in the process annoying all the neighbors), dogs in yards are quite sedentary. The isolated outdoor dog is missing the socialization and stimulation he needs to be a well-adjusted pet and often becomes a digger and a barker.

Yards come in handy for a late night, early morning, or emergency bathroom break for your dog. It is nice to have a yard where he can hang out from time to time during the day. I usually put my dogs in the yard for 20 to 30 minutes a few times a day, in addition to walks, mainly for a change of scenery and some fresh air.

Breeds and Exercise

- Sporting breeds need a lot of exercise. They include pointers, retrievers, and setters.
- Some breeds, including most hounds and most toys, need moderate amounts of exercise.
- Some terriers, such as the Jack Russell, Welsh, and Manchester, need a lot of exercise, while others, such as the Sealyham and Skye, usually have more moderate exercise needs.

Depending on their size, yards can provide exercise if you are willing to do your part. You can set up a small agility course consisting of a couple of jumps and a tunnel and work with your dog. Or kick a soccer ball around for Scooter to chase, throw a flying disc, or toss a tennis ball.

Dog Parks

Dog parks (parks where dogs are allowed off leash) are a great invention and I wish there were more of them. They offer the opportunity for dogs to run free and wear themselves out playing with other dogs. They offer an equally good opportunity for owners to socialize and swap dog talk.

Dog parks can be found in many metropolitan areas. If you are lucky enough to have access to one, determine whether it will offer a safe location for your dog:

- Is the fencing secure?
- Are there bags and trash receptacles available for dog waste?
- Does the area look reasonably clean and free of waste, trash, and litter?
- Are there separate sections for small and large dogs?
- Are other owners watching—and if necessary, controlling—their dogs' behavior?

Most dog parks are operated by local governments and a few are managed by volunteers. Most are free but a few are located in larger parks that charge an entry fee. These parks usually sell discounted seasonal passes. Almost all will have posted rules and regulations, although there is little on-site enforcement. Whether or not regulations are posted, it is important for dog owners to respect dog park etiquette:

- Bring plastic bags with you and always, always, clean up after your pet.
- Be certain that your dog is wearing ID tags.
- Keep an eye on your dog and call him to you for a time-out if he is being aggressive, playing too roughly, or getting overly excited.
- Do not give your dog treats while there are other dogs nearby.
- Take your dog and leave if he seems exhausted or if other dogs are misbehaving or behaving aggressively.
- Keep your dog protected against fleas, ticks, and other parasites that he may be exposed to at the park.

People who own dogs are more likely to be physically active than those who don't

Dog Walkers

In the "old days" (if they ever existed), you might pay the youngster who lives next door to walk your dog for you. Today, that youngster is probably too busy playing soccer after school to help you out, although in my neighborhood some enterprising children have established dog walking services during the summer months.

Hiring a dog walker, if you can afford it and find a good one, can be a supplement or a substitute for the exercise you provide your dog. One friend of mine relied on professional dog walkers and friends while recovering from a broken leg. My neighbor's dog Brownie would be happier and healthier if her owner hired someone to walk her midday in addition to the morning walk she receives—her only daily outing. If your dog is home alone from

9:00 a.m. to 5:00 p.m. or longer, hiring a midday dog walker is a good choice.

For most of us, dog walking help is a phone call away. My local free "pet gazette" is full of ads for dog walking services, as are the community bulletin boards at the library, grocery store, veterinary clinic, pet shop, and toy store. A membership association for pet sitters and walkers, Pet Sitters International (PSI) can provide you with a list of some (not all) of the dog walkers in your area belonging to this organization.

Most walkers charge by the half hour. Prices vary a great deal, depending on location, from $10 up to $20 for a half-hour walk.

Finding a *qualified* dog walker can be a bit more challenging than picking up the phone. Membership in PSI does not guarantee that any particular standards are being met or enforced, and most government jurisdictions do not require licenses for this type of service.

Ask for recommendations from dog walking friends, your veterinarian, or groomer. More than once I have hired veterinary technicians who work at the animal clinic who freelance on their days off. I know of more than one stay-at-home mom who walks dogs for pay during school hours. Whether or not you rely on an advertisement, a database, or word of mouth, ask for references and check them out.

Unless you know the dog walker personally, interview her before hiring. If a dog walker is not willing to come to your home and meet you and your pet

Hiring a dog walker can be a supplement for the exercise you are able to provide your dog.

before being hired, move on to another prospect. At the interview, find out:

- Is she experienced with dogs? Does she own dogs?
- Does she interact well with your dog?
- Do you like her? Do you feel comfortable with the fact that this person will have a key to your home, will be in charge of your dog, and will be in your home when you are not there?
- Does she ask questions about your dog's temperament, health, habits, training, and veterinarian?
- Will she provide references, proof of being insured and bonded, and a written contract describing fees and services?

Whether you are dealing with an individual or a service, I recommend that:

- you ask that your dog be walked at the same time every day
- you ask that the same person walk your dog each time
- your dog be walked in areas or on paths that you determine
- your dog receive individual walks rather than being walked in a pack

Weather Considerations

Extreme weather can be a threat to dogs as well as to you. Whether you leave your dog outside in a yard or are walking, jogging, or biking with him, factor in the temperature.

Too Darn Hot

Most of us have read or heard the warnings: "Never leave your dog inside a car in summer heat." If the temperature is 80°F (27°C) outside, it can rise to 120°F (49°C) in the car in less than ten minutes. A dog locked inside can die of hyperthermia (heatstroke).

Heatstroke can be a summer threat under less obviously dangerous conditions. Dogs sweat only through the pads of their feet, and they cool themselves by panting. Too much exertion in hot weather, including running, playing, and walking too far too fast, can cause heatstroke. Brachycephalic dogs (dogs with "snub," "flat," or "short" noses, such as Pugs, Boxers, and Bulldogs) are more susceptible to heatstroke. The same is true for dogs with particularly heavy coats, such as Saint Bernards, Chow Chows, and Siberian

Breeds Affected by Heat

Some breeds are at risk in hot weather, including:

- Alaskan Malamute
- Boxer
- Bulldog
- Boston Terrier
- Chow Chow
- Keeshond
- Siberian Husky
- Samoyed
- Pug
- Saint Bernard

Huskies. Also at risk are dogs who are very young, very old, or obese. Dogs with dark coats will overheat more easily than dogs with light coats.

Avoid overexertion by your dog in hot weather. Walk him in the cool of the morning and evening. Keep walks short if he is in an at-risk category. Do not leave him outside in the yard for long periods. Provide plenty of water and a cool indoor area. A heavy-coated dog can benefit from a short "haircut" during hot summer months.

Symptoms of heatstroke include heavy panting, drooling, lethargy or agitation, weakness, vomiting, diarrhea, and collapse. (Technically, hyperthermia occurs when a dog's body temperature rises from the norm of 101.5°F [39°C] to 104°F [40°C] or more.) If your dog shows signs of heatstroke, take immediate steps to cool him down. Remove him from the sun or heated area and position him near a fan or air conditioner.

Use cool water—not cold or icy water—to soak his fur. Wipe the pads of his feet with cool water. As soon as he has cooled down somewhat, take him to a veterinarian, who can administer intravenous fluids to cool him down internally.

Sunburn

A dog with light skin pigment and short hair can be sunburned if he spends too much time in strong sunlight. The obvious remedy is to keep a short-haired, light-skinned dog out of the sun. Another is to dress him in a light, white cotton T-shirt, but this will not protect the nose and ears, which burn easily. If your dog suffers a sunburn, apply towels soaked in cool water to the area and take him to a veterinarian.

The pads on the bottom of a dog's paws, tough as they are, can also be burned by asphalt or pavement that has been baking on a summer day. When temperatures are high, choose grass or dirt rather than sidewalks and streets for dog walks.

Breeds Affected by Cold

Some breeds that may have a hard time adjusting to extremely cold weather:
- Basenji
- Chihuahua
- Chinese Crested
- Dachshund (smooth coat)
- Greyhound
- Miniature Pinscher
- Pug
- Whippet

Baby, It's Cold Outside

Siberian Huskies, Chow Chows, Bernese Mountain Dogs, Saint Bernards, and similar breeds and mixed breeds with long, thick coats savor cold weather. Dogs who have very short coats, such as Whippets, Miniature Pinschers, and Greyhounds, or who are elderly, frail, or thin (especially toy dogs with these characteristics) are at risk when the temperature drops.

Any dog, including those with heavy coats, can suffer from a potentially fatal drop in body temperature known as hypothermia. Hypothermia occurs when a dog's body temperature drops too low, to 99°F (37°C) and below. Mild hypothermia, when a dog's temperature is between 97° and 99°F (36° and 37°C), will be evidenced by shivering. If body temperature falls below 97°F (36°C), the dog will lose the shivering reflex. In other words, if a dog exposed to extreme cold stops shivering, that does not mean that he is okay.

If your dog is in the shivering stage, bring him into a warm indoor area, such as near (not up against) a radiator or well-screened fire. Cover him loosely with blankets and watch him to see if, after a few minutes, he stops shivering and is able to walk around and behave normally. If he cannot stop shivering or has gone beyond the shivering stage, quickly heat some big towels in the dryer to warm them up, wrap them around your dog, and take him immediately to the veterinary clinic. Call the clinic ahead of time to let them know that you are on the way and why. The veterinarian can apply warm intravenous therapy and other techniques to warm your dog internally.

In frigid weather, you may need to shorten your walks together.

Don't let your dog get overheated in the hot weather.

To avoid exposing your pet to this danger, do not leave him outside in cold weather for long periods, and do not leave him outside all night, even if you are certain that "he loves the cold." Use your common sense or follow your veterinarian's advice in deciding how long you can safely leave your dog outside. A young, healthy Chow Chow can stay outside in winter cold much longer than an elderly Beagle! In frigid weather, you may need to shorten your dog's walks for your sake as well as for his. Again, use your common sense, taking into account your dog's age, health, size, and coat to determine how much time he can safely spend outdoors on each walk.

Some dogs need clothes in the winter. This is nothing to be embarrassed about—it is another fact of modern life. In the "old days," the dogs who survived the winters in Maine or North Dakota were hardy dogs with heavy coats, not tiny toy dogs with short hair. A cold weather outfit is simply a response to a warm weather dog living in a cold climate. There are canine coats, jackets, and sweaters in many styles, sizes, and colors from which to choose. They are usually made of wool, fleece, or nylon.

Some dogs need boots. When my Collies romp or just walk in the snow, hard

Nighttime Exercise

Walking your dog after dark can present a challenge or two. I recommend that you carry a flashlight, use a reflective leash, and that your pet wear a reflective collar or vest.

balls of ice quickly form between their toes. Every few minutes they flop down to chew the ice out. Boots protect paws from clumping ice and snow and from the salt that municipalities apply to streets and homeowners apply to sidewalks. Dog boots are sold in many sizes and styles. The human mind has worked hard to devise systems of straps, hooks, and cinches to keep them on. I must confess that, in my entire life, I have seen exactly two dogs who have consented to wear them. But it is always worth a try! As an alternative, to remove salt from your dog's paws, wipe them with a damp and then a dry towel after he comes inside on a snowy day.

RESOURCES MADE EASY

Books About Exercise and Activities

- Becker, Marty, and Robert Kushner. *Fitness Unleashed! A Dog and Owner's Guide to Losing Weight and Gaining Health Together*. New York: Three Rivers Press, 2006.
- Bonham, Margaret H. *The Simple Guide to Getting Active With Your Dog*. Neptune City, NJ: TFH Publications, 2002.
- Miller, Pat. *Play With Your Dog*. Wenatchee, WA: Dogwise Publishing, 2007.
- Morgan, Diane. *The Encyclopedia of Dog Sports and Activities*. Neptune City, NJ: TFH Publications, 2009.
- Smith, Cheryl S. *Visiting the Dog Park*. Wenatchee, WA: Dogwise Publishing, 2007.

Books About Nutrition

- Berg, John (ed). *Dog Care & Nutrition*. Medford, MA: Tufts Media Enterprises, 2004.

Doggy Day Cares

- Look in the Yellow Pages under "pets."
- Search the Internet for "dog day care" and your geographic area (town or city and state).

Dog Parks

- Look in the Yellow Pages in the "parks and recreation" section of your local government.
- Search the Internet for "parks and recreation" or "dog park" and your geographic area.

Toys

- Chain pet stores (online and in store)
- Local pet stores
- Nylabone: www.nylabone.com
- Use an Internet search engine and type in "dog toys."

Chapter 8
Good Grooming

A well-groomed dog is one whose coat, skin, eyes, ears, nails, and teeth are tended to. Grooming is essential to canine health and beauty. Regular grooming assures early detection of external parasites and of skin, eye, and ear problems. Unless your dog has a high-maintenance coat, grooming need not be onerous or time consuming. It can be broken down into the following tasks:

- brushing
- bathing
- caring for ears, eyes, and nails
- dental care

GOING PRO OR DO-IT-YOURSELF?

If you have the financial wherewithal to outsource grooming chores, you may want to consider what aspects of grooming—all, some, or none—you are going to handle yourself and which ones you are going to contract out. As you read about brushing, bathing, nail clipping, and so on, you can determine which tasks you are willing and able to do. This evaluation will vary with the dog's needs and your abilities.

If you are unsure about your eyesight or if your hands are unsteady, you should not try to clip your dog's nails, clean his ears, or use scissors or electric clippers. If you have a temperamental back, bathing a dog might not be for you. I speak from experience. Until I reached my mid-50s, I bathed my dogs in the backyard using shampoo, a bucket of warm water, and a garden hose. If I tried to do that now—bend over my dogs for many minutes at a time to shampoo and rinse—my back would ache for the rest of the day. Some friends my age who have small dogs simply lift them into a sink and bathe away. My dogs are too big for this.

I have been told that some dogs "love" being brushed or "love" being bathed. I have never personally known such a dog. When subjected to clean water from a hose or bucket as opposed to muddy creek water, my dogs react hysterically with whines and cries worthy of the hound of the Baskervilles. Any alert neighbor could have reported me to the Humane Society. Your dog's willingness to submit to various aspects of grooming rituals will determine your pleasure and pain index on this score, and this will no doubt factor into outsourcing decisions you may make. There is more than one way to approach the grooming challenge.

Decide which aspects of grooming you are able to do and which ones may need to be contracted out to a professional.

BRUSHING

Brushing is the grooming task that most of us can handle at home, and next to brushing your dog's teeth, the one that needs to be done most frequently. Regular brushing helps keep your dog's coat free of tangles and mats and keeps skin and fur healthy and clean.

How Often?

How often you brush and for how long will be determined by the two parties to the process: you and your dog.

You: How much or how little dog fur are you willing to tolerate in your home—on carpets, floors, and furniture?

Your dog: How large is he, what type of coat does he have, what is his daily "dirt level," how much does he shed?

Tolerance

I am not a fastidious housekeeper, and my family appears to have gotten used to the tufts of white and blond Collie fur floating through the house during spring and summer. On the other hand, I know families with heavily shedding dogs whose homes are pristine because the dogs are thoroughly brushed nearly every day.

Coat Type

Small dogs with short or "smooth" coats may need just a few minutes of brushing or combing every week or two, especially if their daily exercise doesn't take place around lots of dirt or mud. Dogs with long, thick, or silky coats may need daily brushing. But even within breeds, dog coats can vary. One Irish Setter may have a much longer or silkier coat than the

---

Breeds and Coat Types

Long-Coated Breeds (high-maintenance coats that require brushing more than once a week):

- Afghan Hound
- Chow Chow
- Collie (rough)
- Great Pyrenees
- Havanese
- Keeshond
- Lhasa Apso
- Malamute
- Maltese
- Old English Sheepdog
- Samoyed
- Setters
- Shih Tzu
- Yorkshire Terrier

Medium-Coated Breeds (require weekly brushing):

- Australian Shepherd
- Bernese Mountain Dog
- Border Collie
- Cavalier King Charles Spaniel
- Dachshund (long-haired)
- Golden Retriever
- Petit Basset Griffon Vendéen
- Schipperke

Short-Coated Breeds (low-maintenance coats that require weekly brushing):

- Basenji
- Basset Hound
- Boxer
- Bulldog
- Dachshund (short-haired)
- Doberman Pinscher
- French Bulldog
- Great Dane
- Greyhound
- Italian Greyhound
- Labrador Retriever
- Pug
- Rhodesian Ridgeback
- Rottweiler
- Vizsla
- Weimaraner

Wire- and Curly-Coated Breeds (best to clip or strip):

- Most terriers (and related mixes)
- Schnauzers
- Bedlington Terrier
- Bichon Frise
- Kerry Blue Terrier
- Poodle
- Portuguese Water Dog
- Soft Coated Wheaten Terrier

next and one Golden Retriever may have a much thicker coat than another. But for a rough guide to brushing:

- Long or thick coat: Brush one to three times a week and more often during shedding season.
- Medium coat: Brush weekly and more often during shedding season.
- Smooth, short coat: Brush or comb every one to two weeks and more often during shedding season.
- Curly or wirehaired coat: Clip every four to eight weeks and brush weekly.

Dirt Level

Some dogs import dirt. My big Collie Tony often returns from our walks in the woods with muddy feet and wearing a leaf and twig arrangement. The decorations are quickly combed out and I towel off the mud.

Shedding

Most dogs shed heavily once or twice a year, although some shed year-round. Your dog's genetic inheritance (whether a purebred or mixed breed) will largely determine how often and how much he sheds. The local climate, the amount of time your dog spends outdoors, and his general health and age will also have some effect on shedding.

Dare to Be Different

Some dogs and some breeds just have to be different. They don't get brushed or combed. They get stripped, plucked, or clipped. Readers who have not lived with a Schnauzer or an Airedale, Cairn, or Irish Terrier may shudder at what sounds like animal torture but is, in fact, proper grooming for some dogs.

Stripping? Plucking? What's That About?

Stripping and plucking is done by hand to remove dead hair from certain breeds (mostly terriers). It is time consuming (stripping a large dog can take hours), stressful for the dog, requires a professional groomer, is expensive—and is unnecessary unless you intend to show your dog. It is cheaper, much faster, and easier on all concerned to simply clip these dogs if and when needed.

Curls and Clips

Some dogs practically require professional grooming. Breeds and related mixes with curly hair, especially those that are "nonshedding," fall

Money $aving Tip

"Do it yourself" is the least expensive grooming option. You can prevent the need for professional grooming by brushing your dog every day and immediately removing tangles and mats.

into this category. While these dogs can be painstakingly groomed to a show standard, it makes more sense and requires fewer dollars and cents to clip them at home or have them clipped. They will look charming, feel comfortable, and stay cleaner longer.

Clipping Long Coats

Many owners of dogs with long coats, particularly smaller breeds, such as the Skye Terrier, Tibetan Terrier, and Shih Tzu, conclude that both dog and human do best when the dog has an overall short clip, sometimes called a "puppy cut." This type of cut prevents mats, tangles, excessive mud, and copious brushing or frequent trips to the groomer. A few large breeds, including the Old English Sheepdog and Polish Lowland Sheepdog, can also stand being clipped. But please do not undermine the dignity of an Afghan Hound or rough-coated Collie by clipping.

Equipment

Pet supply stores and catalogs, both online and mail order, offer quite a selection of grooming tools. Brushes and combs vary in size, shape, and material. Catalog descriptions can help narrow the choice, but I suggest that you not order from a catalog unless you have already held a similar implement and used it against your own skin. Many implements have metal teeth or "pins" that may be

as long as 1 inch (2.5 cm). After making allowances for the thickness of your dog's coat, ask yourself whether the pins or teeth could be hurtful to his skin. I also recommend that you ask someone familiar with grooming your type of dog, such as a breeder, foster or breed rescue volunteer, or professional groomer, to describe what tools she would use on a dog like yours.

One type of comb or brush does not fit all dogs, although a wire slicker works well for many dogs with medium-length coats. A soft bristle brush and possibly a comb will work just fine for a small, fragile dog, such as a smooth-coated Chihuahua. A grooming mitt or rubber curry works well on dogs with short, smooth coats, such as Doberman Pinschers and hounds. Grooming a Chow Chow, with his formidable and abundant coat, calls forth an array of heavier equipment, including a pin brush and possibly a rake.

If you have a small dog who needs copious brushing, such as a Shih Tzu or Maltese, and you are serious about grooming him yourself, you may want to invest in a folding grooming table. You can lift your dog up onto the table for grooming so that you will not have to bend over for a long period. Before you buy a table (available through catalogs), make certain that it is high enough to keep your back comfortable while you brush your dog.

How to Brush a Dog

Begin brushing your new puppy or dog within a day or two of bringing him home, for a few minutes at a time so that he can become accustomed to it. During these first few weeks, brush Sunshine daily for five or ten minutes so that he will learn that being brushed is not a fearful event. The best time to brush him is when he is tired after a long walk, run, or romp.

Grooming instruments you may need include a pin brush.

Brush or comb your dog's hair in the direction that it grows. You may need to brush small sections at a time if your dog has long fur or a thick undercoat; brush all the way down to the skin—gently. Don't stop with the back or sides: Brush or comb the front and back legs, belly, chest, ruff, and head. If your dog has long ears (like setters and spaniels), remember to (gently) brush or comb them. A few dogs, including some terriers, have long facial hair—be sure to brush that too, but always be careful to keep your brush or comb away from your dog's eyes. Follow up the session by praising him and giving him a treat.

Eventually, establish a brushing schedule that works for both of you.

BATHING

Reliable sources assure me that many dogs tolerate or even enjoy being bathed. One of my senior neighbors lives with a Portuguese Water Dog who insists on getting into the shower with him. Owners like me, who manage the dog brushing with more or less success, sometimes find that the dog bath is our Armageddon. Perfectly reasonable, gentle animals transform into squirming, wriggling beasts at the sight of the garden hose or the tub. Fortunately, many dogs do not need frequent baths if they are brushed regularly and are not prone to tramp through mud. The exceptions are allergy cases, what I call the "super mud" dogs, and dogs with high-maintenance coats whose owners prefer not to rely on the low-maintenance clip. Frequency also depends, to a large extent, on the sensitivity to doggy odor of the household's human noses and the level of doggy cleanliness that humans prefer to live with. Some people don't notice or care about doggy odor and others mind mightily. In a category by itself is the emergency bath that is triggered by the dreaded canine encounter with a skunk or the joyous roll in a foul-smelling substance.

How Often?

There is no single answer to the question, "How often should my dog have a bath?" Some dogs need to be bathed nearly every two weeks and other dogs in other households can make do with two or three baths a year. Here are factors to be considered:

- whether a super clean dog with very little canine odor is a household priority
- your dog's tendency to collect dirt and mud
- your dog's type of coat
- condition of your dog's skin
- your dog's age and health

If your nose is sensitive to doggy odors, it will probably be important to you to bathe your dog every month or even more often. A dog who runs through mud or who swims needs frequent bathing, as do dogs with very long, silky, or thick fur and unclipped dogs with high-maintenance coats, such as the Bichon Frise or Poodle. A dog with skin allergies or other skin problems may require frequent medicated baths. Older, frail dogs or dogs with health problems should be bathed no more often than a veterinarian suggests.

Some dogs may prosper with infrequent baths, including those with short, smooth coats with very little doggy odor who are naturally clean (don't jump in mud puddles) or who have coats that don't attract or hold much dirt.

Equipment

To properly bathe a dog, you will need:

- bucket (if you are bathing him outside)
- hair dryer (if necessary)
- leash or restraint harness (if necessary)
- shampoo
- conditioner (if necessary)
- towels

How to Wash a Dog

Begin by giving your dog a good walk to tire him out, then a good brushing to remove tangles, mats, and dead hair. Then gather your tools together.

Whether you choose a tub, sink, or backyard, use warm water. Bathe your dog outside only on a warm, sunny day, not in cold weather, and begin with a bucket or two of warm water from the sink. Ask your veterinarian to recommend a shampoo. Some dogs have

How often to bathe a dog depends on his coat type, age, and activity level.

dry skin and may also benefit from a conditioner.

Wet your dog down, apply a small amount of shampoo, and massage all over, including the legs and feet. Avoid the face, eyes, and inside the ears. Use no more shampoo than necessary to work up some lather, or you will be rinsing ad infinitum. Rinse with warm water if possible. If you are outside, cold water from a hose will do as long as your dog is standing in warm sunshine and is not old, frail, or ill. Keep rinsing until the water is perfectly clear and you are certain that all suds are gone.

Towel your dog down to remove as much water as possible, especially if you are indoors and your house is air conditioned. You can use a hand dryer to blow-dry the coat, but keep it turned to a low setting and do not blow it directly into your dog's face. If it is a warm day, sunshine will speed drying along—but beware! Newly washed dogs love to roll in the grass and dirt. Don't leave a wet dog outside to dry in cold weather. When your dog is dry, use a comb or brush to smooth the coat and remove any mats or tangles.

If you have a dog with a wrinkles, such as a Shar-Pei or Bulldog, be especially careful about cleaning and drying the wrinkles. It is too easy for these areas to become irritated or infected if they are damp or dirty.

DENTAL CARE: PROTECT THOSE PEARLY WHITES

A few decades ago, dental care for dogs was pretty much unheard of. I remember my entire family laughing over a television ad that promised to banish bad breath in dogs. Who cared about bad breath in dogs? That was just doggy breath, we thought.

Today, we know better. Experts say that about 75 percent of dogs over three years of age have some degree of periodontal disease (diseases of the gums and jawbone). This condition is the most common canine health problem. It can cause discomfort and pain and lead to other, far more serious health problems. Yet only a small percentage of dog owners regularly care for their dogs' oral health.

Just as in the human mouth, tiny bits of food, saliva, and bacteria combine to form plaque on the surface of a dog's teeth. Unless it is removed, the plaque eventually hardens to form tartar. The buildup of tartar can damage the teeth and gums, leading to periodontal disease.

Preventive Care

Your dog's teeth and gums need not deteriorate with age. You can help keep his teeth healthy if you:

- feed him mostly dry, crunchy food
- give him safe chews, such as Nylabones, rather than cow hooves or actual bones that can break his teeth
- give him hard, crunchy treats instead of soft treats
- do not feed him sugary or sticky treats or food
- most importantly, *brush his teeth!*

If you are at this point thinking "Are you kidding me?"—join the club. Fewer than 10 percent of dog owners say they brush their dogs' teeth daily, and nearly half of owners surveyed say they never brush their dogs' teeth. But there is a price to be paid if you are in the "Are you kidding me?" camp. Bad teeth can cause your dog to forfeit some quality

Towel dry your dog after his bath to remove excess water.

of life, and you may be paying sizeable veterinary bills for a periodontal problem that escalates. A simple cleaning can cost from $100 to $500 (because of anesthesia, blood tests, and such), and complications from neglected teeth, such as a root canal, can lead to procedures that cost thousands of dollars.

How to Brush Your Dog's Teeth

The best time to start brushing is with a new puppy, but the same technique applies for an older dog. Wrap a gauze square or corner of a washcloth around your finger, wet it with warm water, and wipe a few of your dog's teeth, especially where they meet the gums. Do this every day until he becomes accustomed to it. Every few days, wipe more teeth until you've included them all.

You now have several options. You can continue to use gauze or a washcloth or a finger toothbrush that fits on your finger, or you can switch to a dog toothbrush. You can add dog toothpaste—don't use human toothpaste, which can cause stomach irritation—on the gauze, washcloth, or toothbrush, especially if the taste is appealing to your dog.

Make brushing part of your daily routine. You might plan to do it every morning or every night after you walk with your dog. When you are finished, give him praise and a treat so that he

Brushing your dog's teeth is essential for his dental health.

will associate something good with the procedure.

In Addition to Brushing

In addition to toothpaste in filet mignon flavors designed to appeal to canine taste buds, several newer products are being advertised as promoting canine oral health and hygiene, including:

- antibacterial oral sprays
- liquids and powders to dissolve in your dog's drinking water
- specially formulated kibble
- edible dental chews to help clean teeth

Recently, the Food and Drug Administration (FDA) issued a conditional license for a vaccine said to help prevent canine periodontal disease. As always, check with your veterinarian before trying new products.

Remedial Care

Not every dog with brownish or yellowish (rather than bright white) teeth has a periodontal problem. But a brown or a yellowish brown crust of tartar near the gums is a sign of trouble. Other signs include:

- red, swollen, or bleeding gums
- difficulty eating or picking up toys
- foul breath
- unusual amount of drooling
- swelling around the mouth

If your dog exhibits any of these symptoms, take him to your veterinarian to have his teeth examined. She can advise you if a professional cleaning is needed. If it is, you will need to make a second appointment for the cleaning. Depending on your dog's age and general health, your veterinarian may take blood samples, and in some cases, chest X-rays or an echocardiogram ahead of time to evaluate whether your dog is an anesthesia risk. Dental cleanings without anesthesia pose serious risks and should be avoided.

During a dental cleaning, the veterinarian will scrape off or "scale" tartar from teeth and above the gum line; check for broken teeth and pockets of infection, bleeding gums, or unusual swelling; polish and smooth the teeth; and wash the gums with an antibacterial solution.

If a cleaning reveals serious problems, your veterinarian may take X-rays and refer you to a veterinary specialist. Just about every procedure used in human mouths—from root canals to laser surgery and implants—can be performed on your dog.

EAR CARE

Each time you brush your dog, check his ears for excess wax, unusual odor, redness, swelling, or discharge. Any of these signs could indicate an infection or the presence of ear mites and call for a visit to the veterinarian. Other symptoms include scratching and pawing of the ear, sensitivity to touch, head shaking, and loss of balance. Dogs with floppy ears, such as spaniels and some hounds, have a tendency to develop infections because their long ear flaps encourage yeast and bacteria to colonize in the ear canal.

How Often?

Each time you bathe your dog, clean his ears. Some dogs, especially those with floppy ears, need more frequent, regular ear cleaning (perhaps once a month) to prevent infections. If your dog develops infections, ask your veterinarian for advice about how often to clean his ears.

Equipment

Your equipment will be cotton balls and a veterinarian-recommended ear cleansing solution. Do not use shampoo, soap, or alcohol, which dry the skin, and do not use cotton swabs or other sharp objects.

How to Clean a Dog's Ears

Gently swab the underside of the ear flap and the ear opening with a cotton ball soaked in the solution. Squirt a small amount of solution into the ear, hold the flap or outer ear over the opening, and massage the ear to spread the solution around.

Plucking

Excess hair growing inside the ear or on the inner ear flap can trap dirt and moisture that promote infections. Some dogs, such as Poodles and Portuguese Water Dogs, are more prone to this problem than others. To prevent frequent infections in susceptible dogs, excess hair should be trimmed or plucked on a regular basis. I recommend contracting this task out to a groomer, veterinarian, or veterinary technician who is trained to use scissors or tweezers in and around a dog's ear.

EYE CARE

Check your dog's eyes each time you brush him. Use special care when using clippers, scissors, brushes, and combs near his eyes. Use a soft moist towel or moist cotton ball (no soap) to gently wipe around his eyes whenever you bathe him.

Dogs can develop a number of eye problems that require veterinary attention. Among the most common are dry eyes, excessive tearing, and cataracts. Brown tear stains, which most commonly show on dogs with white fur, can be treated cosmetically by applying a commercial product to the fur. Ask your veterinarian for recommendations about safe products, and take care that the product ends up only on fur, not in the eyes.

NAILS

Your dog's nails are too long if you can hear them clicking on the kitchen floor. Too-long nails can be uncomfortable for your dog, causing foot and gait problems.

How Often?

It is better to trim the nails regularly than to let them grow too long. How often this needs to be done varies with the dog. Nails can grow quickly or slowly, can be hard or soft, and can wear down more or less easily. Some dogs who walk or run on pavement instead of grass keep their nails worn down with exercise, compared to other dogs who receive little outdoor exercise or run only on grass.

Equipment

Doggy nail clippers or trimmers are your essential tool. Also essential: a steady hand, excellent eyesight, a calm dog, and a knowledgeable and confident human on the working side of the trimmer. Without these essentials, you can hurt your dog. Inside each nail is a vein, or "quick," that will bleed if you slip or cut the nail too short. It is all too easy to do this. I have done it and it scared me half to death because my dog yelped and the bleeding was profuse.

It is better to trim your dog's nails regularly than to let them grow too long.

Ask for Help

Experimenting and practicing on your dog, even if you are following written directions, is to be discouraged. I strongly recommend that if you are determined and able to trim your dog's nails, take lessons— as many as needed to be almost perfect—from a groomer, veterinarian, or veterinary technician. Having learned my lesson at my dog's expense, I leave nail clipping to the professionals.

Once you have mastered the art of the canine manicure (or pedicure?), take note of how quickly your dog's nails grow and plan a trimming schedule. It is best to clip off just a tiny bit of each nail with each manicure and to manicure often rather than wait until the nails grow long. Check your dog's nails each time that you brush him, and trim them frequently unless he wears them down naturally.

Check your dog for fleas and ticks after he's been outside.

EXTERNAL PARASITES

When I was growing up, the dogs who lived with us (as many as four at a time) had long, thick fur. From the time I was ten years old, my family lived in a house located on 2 acres of land, partially surrounded by woods. The dogs ran free. All summer long and into the fall they came home covered with ticks and fleas. Every few months, my mother would deliver them to the vet in the morning and pick them up at the end of the day, smelling foully chemical from a "dip" intended to stave off and kill these parasites. The odor would persist for

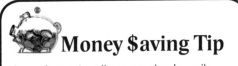

Money $aving Tip

If you learn to clip your dog's nails, the purchase of a nail clipper will quickly pay for itself.

days and was quite repugnant to humans; I remember thinking how awful it must be for canine noses. While the dogs were off being dipped, we would have to vacate the house after closing it up and scattering and detonating flea "bombs" (foggers) to kill the fleas that the dogs had generously imported into the house. It was expensive, time consuming, inconvenient, unpleasant for people and dogs alike, and not wholly effective. But it was necessary. Fleas, ticks, mosquitoes, and mites are not merely irritating; they pose real health risks to dogs, and in some cases, to humans.

Fleas

Fleas bite into the skin to obtain blood. Their saliva contains enzymes and histamine-like substances that cause itching and irritation. Some dogs and humans develop an allergic reaction to the saliva. Flea bites are a common cause of skin allergies in dogs (flea allergy dermatitis). These allergies can be chronic and are hard to control and very uncomfortable.

Ticks

Ticks also feed on blood. They attach themselves to the host with barbed mouths and secrete a glue-like substance that makes them difficult to dislodge. Neglected dogs who serve as hosts to hundreds of ticks can actually die from anemia. Ticks can transmit serious

Money $aving Tip

A dog who is walked frequently on pavement rather than soft ground is likely to wear down his nails and may not need to have them clipped.

diseases to humans and dogs, such as Lyme disease, Rocky Mountain spotted fever, Colorado tick fever, and others.

Mosquitoes

Mosquitoes are yet another bloodsucking insect. When they feed on dogs they can transmit heartworm disease, a serious and life-threatening condition that occurs when an infected mosquito deposits larvae of a parasitic worm underneath the dog's skin. When the larvae mature into worms, they migrate to and damage the heart, lungs, and nearby arteries.

Mites

Mites are too small to be visible to the naked eye but can cause a lot of damage. There are many different species of mites; three are of particular concern.

- Ear mites, which a dog can catch from contact with a cat or another dog, cause extreme irritation, can block the ear canal with excrement and wax, and invite secondary infections. Signs of ear mites are dark, dry discharge from the ear, inflammation, and itchiness.

- Sarcoptic mange mites, which live on the hair and skin, cause sarcoptic mange or scabies, a highly contagious condition that dogs catch from other dogs or from contaminated bedding and grooming tools. This condition causes intense itching and hair loss and often leads to secondary skin infections.

- Demodectic mange, caused by another species of mite, results in severe itching and irritation, hair loss, and crusty skin, usually around the head. Puppies and dogs with compromised immune systems are most susceptible.

All of these conditions should be treated by a veterinarian and can be brought under control.

You can find natural products that kill and repel fleas, ticks, and mosquitoes.

Prevention Made Easy

Times have changed for the better since the days of the infamous "dips" and "bombs," thank goodness. Instead of battling flea and tick infestations, a little effort and money invested in prevention can keep your home and your dog free of most external parasites.

Topical medications, sometimes called "spot-ons," kill and repel ticks, fleas, and mosquitoes from a dog. Some also help prevent heartworm. These liquids are usually applied monthly, in a small amount, between a dog's shoulders, a process that takes about 30 seconds. These products are said to be water resistant, but a dog who is a daily swimmer may need more frequent applications.

Oral medications, usually given in monthly doses, prevent heartworm, kill fleas, and control the flea population by preventing eggs from hatching. Available in chewable form, these medications also typically prevent roundworms, hookworms, and whipworms, which are intestinal parasites. Do not begin using heartworm preventive on your dog unless he has first been given a heartworm test by a veterinarian. If your dog has undetected heartworm disease, giving him the preventive can cause severe reactions or create diagnostic confusion.

The "old-fashioned" remedies still abound and have their use. If your home and pet are already infested with fleas or ticks, you may want to turn to foggers or bug bombs to fumigate the rooms of your home, or you can call on professionals to exterminate ticks, fleas, mosquitoes, eggs, and larvae. Over-the-counter sprays and powders can be used on carpets, rugs, and dog beds. If your dog is covered with fleas or ticks, you can use a flea-and-tick spray, powder, shampoo, or dip for a quick fix, or send your dog to a veterinarian or groomer to be treated. Treated collars that kill fleas and ticks are best used to prevent the return of these pests.

Not all over-the-counter flea and tick products are safe for all dogs. Before you choose any preventive measure, ask your veterinarian whether she recommends topical or oral medications for your dog, and ask for specific recommendations about brands. Your dog's breed, health, and age should all be considered in choosing the best preventive mode.

Dogs who are sick, elderly, pregnant, or very young should not be given these medications unless a veterinarian specifically recommends it. Do not use multiple products (shampoo, dip, oral medication) without first consulting your veterinarian.

Some people prefer to avoid using chemicals on their dog or in the home. If you are one of these, you can find natural products made from botanicals that kill and repel fleas, ticks, and mosquitoes. These include shampoos, sprays, powders, dips, collars, and topical spot-ons but not oral medications.

GOING TO THE PROS

Some people enjoy brushing and bathing their dog, and some enjoy it much less. For others, grooming chores are overly challenging, not worth the effort, or even painful. You may want to go to a pro if you:

- do not have a yard where you can wash your dog
- have a dog who is too big for your bathtub
- cannot comfortably lift your dog into a tub or sink
- want to avoid the flying, damp fur that fills your yard, kitchen, or bathroom after a dog bath
- have a dog with a high-maintenance coat, so keeping him properly groomed is very time consuming
- find that brushing or washing a dog's

coat may be difficult or unpleasant for you because it hurts your hands, arms, or back

- have an allergy that is triggered by grooming your dog

Fortunately, help is available for those of us who choose to contract out all or some grooming chores. Some smaller tasks, such as nail clipping, ear cleaning, and checking and emptying anal glands, can usually be handled by a veterinary technician at your local clinic, while professional groomers handle the full range of bathing, brushing, and clipping, as well as nail, eye, and ear care.

If your dog has a high-maintenance coat, you should consider using a professional groomer.

Finding a Groomer

Professional pet groomers, nearly unheard of a few decades ago, now number nearly 50,000. They work out of pet salons, grooming parlors, veterinary clinics, doggy day care centers, kennels, mobile vans, and pet hotels.

A good way to begin your search is by asking for recommendations from dog-owning friends or your veterinarian. Follow up by logging onto the websites of recommended groomers. I like websites that clearly state pricing and cancellation policy and provide background

information about the groomers. If you do not use a computer, or even if you do, call the groomer and ask questions about her experience, background, range of breeds, and number of dogs that she typically works on. Be prepared to ask questions specific to your dog on topics such as pricing; what accommodations, if any, are given to an older dog in brushing, bathing, and blow-drying; trimming and cleaning of problem ears; and drop-off and pick-up time. The conversation that you have with the groomer will probably leave you feeling either good or bad about handing over

Sunshine for a grooming session. My advice is to trust your instinct.

Visit the grooming facility before you make an appointment. Satisfy yourself that:

- cages are clean and large enough for comfort
- grooming area is clean (dog fur notwithstanding)
- grooming area has a doggy and shampoo odor but nothing worse
- groomers handle the dogs kindly and professionally

What Happens at the Groomer?

A professional grooming will include:

- thorough brushing to remove dead hair
- bath
- "blow out" (blow-drying)
- nail clipping
- ear cleaning
- trimming of fur around paws

Typically, a dog is dropped off at the groomer in the morning and picked up four to six hours later, although actual grooming time is much less. Some groomers work alone or with a single assistant, but in many salons and parlors they work in teams. With a team approach, the dog is rotated through several stations: one for brushing, one for bathing, another for nails and ears, etc. Using an assembly line approach, a groomer at each station performs a specific task. After being bathed, the dog is returned to a kennel or cage and a blow-dryer is directed into the cage. Actual grooming time for a dog with a coat in average condition requiring no special care ranges from one and a half to nearly three hours. Dogs with long, thick coats, dogs who are difficult to handle, and dogs with coats in poor condition may take much longer to groom.

Some dogs don't seem to mind this process, and others hate it or quake with fear.

Some owners object to the blow-drying; or to the dog being forced to stand in place on a grooming table by a "noose" that holds his head up; or to the dog being kept for several hours, waiting in the cage much of the time. I am one of these, even though I know groomers who do exceptionally good work. Like me, you may decide to choose another option for your dog. For my Collies, I have turned to a mobile grooming service. (See below.)

Pricing

Prices vary from region to region, from groomer to groomer, and from dog to dog. Condition and type of coat, breed, and size of dog all contribute to pricing. Small dogs who do not require special care cost less than large dogs. Dogs with short coats cost less than those with medium and long coats. Groomers will charge extra for procedures that take added time. Special handling for older dogs who cannot stand for long periods or dogs who are toweled dry cost more. A dog whose coat is tangled and matted will cost more. Some dogs require special medicated baths or conditioner or need special care of the ears, eyes, or nails; these services cost more, as does emptying of the anal sacs. Many groomers have a separate price schedule for clipping, trimming, special cuts, and stripping.

Grooming a small dog with an average coat may cost from $35 to $65. Grooming a larger dog or one with a long coat may cost from $85 to $120.

Different Strokes: Mobile Groomers

Pet grooming is a fast growing field, and the segment that is growing the fastest is the mobile groomer. These entrepreneurs come to your home with a van equipped with a tub and warm water for bathing, a grooming table, and all other necessary equipment. Some will need to plug into your electrical outlet, while others are completely self-contained.

Mobile groomers, provided they meet your standards of quality, offer several advantages:

- More convenient for you: No need for you to drop off and pick up your pet.
- Easier for your dog: Because the groomer is handling only one dog at a time—yours—your dog spends much less time being groomed,

typically one to two hours.
- Less stressful for your dog: He is alone in a quiet van, not confined to a cage, hearing other dogs bark. Especially if he is groomed often, he will get to know the groomer.

The disadvantage of mobile groomers is that they typically, but not always, charge somewhat more than groomers who are based in a single location. Some do not handle large dogs.

Laundromutts

An even newer innovation than grooming vans is self-serve pet washes, now numbering 2,000 to 3,000 around the country. These establishments offer a middle ground between hiring a professional groomer and washing your dog at home. They usually provide:

- raised tubs so that you can avoid bending over
- walk-up dog ramps to the tubs so that you can avoid lifting your dog
- shampoo and towels
- hair dryer

Some self-serve washes offer additional options, including brushes and combs, nail clippers, special

Money $aving Tip

If professional grooming is a must, ask about discount packages.

shampoos and conditioners, wipes for the ears and eyes, and a waterproof apron for humans. Depending on the establishment, some options may be free and some will cost extra.

Laundromutts are much less expensive than professional groomers because you do the work. Prices may vary with the dog's size and type of coat—from as little as $15 for a small dog with short hair and no extras up to $50 and more for a large dog with long hair and extras (conditioner, special shampoo). Most self-serves offer discounts for packages of 6, 10, or 12 sessions. Sometimes they are operated by grooming salons, which is a nice arrangement because you can usually pay the groomer to clip nails if you are not comfortable doing it. An advantage of laundromutts is that your dog is with you, and although he may not appreciate being bathed, he is less likely to be frightened or stressed.

RESOURCES MADE EASY

Books About Grooming

- Adamson, Eve, and Sandy Roth. *The Simple Guide to Grooming Your Dog*. Neptune City, NJ: TFH Publications, 2003.
- Young, Peter. *Groom Your Dog Like a Professional*. Neptune City, NJ: TFH Publications, 2009.

Dental Care

- Humane Society of the United States (HSUS): www.hsus.org

Finding a Groomer

- Look in the Yellow Pages under "pet grooming" or "pet services."
- Look on the Internet for "pet grooming," "mobile pet grooming," and your county and town or city and state.

Grooming and Dental Products

- Chain pet stores (online and in store)
- Local pet stores
- Search the Internet for "dog grooming products."

Pests and Skin Care

- American Animal Hospital Association (AAHA): www.healthypet.com

Self-Service Dog Wash

- Look in the Yellow Pages under "pet self-serve wash" or "pet grooming."
- Look on the Internet for "pet grooming" or "pet self-serve wash" or "dog self-serve wash" and your county and town or city and state.

Chapter 9

Canine Health and Safety

Canine health and safety begin at home. Your investment in safety and preventive care will pay huge dividends in your pet's quality of life.

YOUR VET IS YOUR PARTNER

Your partner in your dog's health care is your veterinarian. Your role in this partnership is an active one. It is up to you to give your dog preventive care, take him for regular checkups, observe and report symptoms to your veterinarian, ask questions, and take advantage of your veterinarian's training and expertise.

I have heard from veterinarians that they appreciate the concern, attention, and follow-through that we "mature" pet owners bring to caring for our pets. My favorite veterinarian, Dr. Kathleen Dougherty of Bethesda, Maryland, comments that "older people seem more attuned to the symptoms of disease in their pets."

More than a few of us have experienced or cared for people with health issues similar to those of our pets: arthritis, failing vision or hearing, a broken bone, gastrointestinal problems, cancer. I believe that these experiences give us extra empathy, patience, and understanding. Our perspective motivates us to monitor our pets and to carefully follow directions for administering medications or restricting activities for a sick or injured dog.

Canine medicine has made remarkable strides in recent decades in preventive care and in more esoteric fields. Ailing pets can receive acupuncture, physical therapy, massage, kidney transplants, and hip and shoulder replacements. Veterinary medicine has developed numerous specialties: dermatology, surgery, internal medicine, oncology; ophthalmology, radiology, neurology, orthopedics, and cardiology. A referral from your veterinarian is usually advisable before you seek out a specialist.

What Makes a Good Vet?

Good veterinarians are attuned to the needs of their human and canine clients. Good communication—a two-way street—is an essential part of your partnership. The best veterinarians are not only technically and professionally proficient. They listen, return phone calls, and establish a rapport with you and your dog. They show that they care. Some veterinarians offer helpful accommodations, including:

- providing pet medication containers that are distinctive in color (green, red, purple) so that they will not be confused with human medication containers
- providing pet med container lids that are easy to open
- cutting pills in halves or quarters when dosage calls for it (especially helpful for the tiny ones) rather than leaving this task to the human client
- delivering medications
- picking up and delivering pets
- scheduling appointments during nonrush hours or before darkness
- selling "pill pockets"—yummy dog treats with a hollow center for a pill

Information on the Web

Information about canine health abounds on the Internet and can be a useful resource but should not be a substitute for a hands-on examination and diagnosis of your dog by his own personal veterinarian. Internet sites vary in quality. Those that are reviewed by veterinarians or sponsored by veterinary schools provide the most reliable information.

Internet sites can be useful for gathering general information—for example, about vaccinations, parasite prevention, allergies, and for learning about a specific disease or problem after a veterinarian has given a diagnosis for your dog.

Annual Checkup

Every dog (every healthy dog, that is) needs, at a minimum, an annual checkup beginning at about two months of age. Puppies, older dogs, and dogs with chronic health problems should visit the veterinarian more often. Worrisome conditions or emergencies also call for a visit.

At the annual examination, the veterinarian will check Sampson's heart, lungs, abdomen, skin, eyes, ears, teeth,

Money $aving Tip

Veterinary and animal welfare associations offer free canine health information on the Internet.

Your veterinarian is your partner in your dog's health care.

and weight. She will check for external parasites and will ask you to bring a fecal sample so that she can check for the presence of intestinal parasites. The cost of a simple health exam, which varies by region and veterinary clinic, may start at about $50 but is also likely to include additional charges for vaccinations, fecal sample tests, and blood tests.

SPAYING AND NEUTERING

Because this book is written for those living with companion dogs, not the professional breeder or show dog owner, I can state that spaying or neutering is a mandatory procedure.

Sterilization improves safety, health, and longevity for both males and females. The procedure reduces roaming and aggressive behavior; prevents cancer and infections of the reproductive organs; and reduces the incidence of mammary cancer and diseases of the prostate. Spayed females are spared uncomfortable heat cycles that occur every six to nine months, and their owners are spared the messy and stressful ordeal of dealing with protective "diapers" and howling, circling male dogs. Contrary to popular myth, spaying or neutering does not cause dogs to gain weight or become lazy. Too much food and too little exercise are to blame for those particular problems.

If you are thinking about breeding your dog because you "want another one just like her," or because your friend, neighbor, or a relative "wants one like her," or because you have heard the myth that "it's healthier for a female to have one litter before being spayed," or because you think it will be fun or even profitable—please don't do it. Overpopulation is the number-one canine problem in America. Every puppy that your dog produces simply adds to the problem. Breeding is hard work, expensive, messy, and can threaten your dog's health.

Sterilization can be performed on a puppy as early as six months, as well as on healthy adult dogs. The dog is anesthetized and sometimes kept overnight at the clinic. Depending on the clinic and the region, the cost of the procedure varies tremendously. It may begin at $150 for a male and $200 for a female. A dog's age, weight, need for an overnight stay, blood tests, and other issues may increase the cost. Many local humane societies and animal welfare groups offer the procedure to the public at reduced costs.

Sterilization will improve safety, health, and longevity for both males and females.

PREVENTIVE CARE

Preventive care protects your dog from disease and parasites and allows him to live longer and healthier. Preventive care is less stressful, less time consuming, and less expensive than treating a sick dog.

Vaccinations

Puppies should be vaccinated against four viral diseases: adenovirus, distemper, parainfluenza, and parvovirus; and against rabies. In many areas, immunization against bordetella (kennel cough) is also recommended. Puppies normally receive an initial vaccination (except for rabies) at six to eight weeks and two more boosters. It is extremely important to follow your veterinarian's recommended schedule and complete all vaccinations because several of these diseases are highly contagious and often fatal.

- Adenovirus (type 1), transmitted in nasal discharge and urine, causes canine hepatitis, a disease of the liver. It is contagious and life threatening, especially for puppies and young dogs.
- Distemper is highly contagious and life threatening, causing neurological, gastrointestinal, and respiratory damage. Young puppies are highly susceptible and are at great risk if not protected through vaccination.
- Parainfluenza, contracted by contact with the nasal secretions of other dogs, causes respiratory tract infection.
- Parvovirus is an extremely contagious, dangerous, and often fatal disease transmitted by dog to dog contact, usually through fecal waste. It attacks the intestinal tract, white blood cells, and even the heart muscle.
- Rabies, a deadly virus that attacks the brain and nervous system, is usually transmitted through an animal bite. Each of the 50 states mandates rabies vaccinations for dogs, and in 2007 the Centers for Disease Control and Prevention (CDC) declared that the United States is free of the type of rabies previously found in dogs. "The elimination of canine rabies in the United States represents one of the major public health success stories in the last 50 years," said a CDC spokesman.
- Kennel cough is a highly contagious upper respiratory infection characterized by a hacking cough. It can be picked up in many places, not just kennels. In most cases, the cough will clear up in a few weeks, but in some dogs the infection can develop more serious symptoms and consequences.

Your veterinarian may recommend additional vaccinations, depending on the geographic area that you live in, including ones for Lyme disease, leptospirosis, and coronavirus.

Money $aving Tip

If asked, some veterinarians will make an effort to provide subsidized care, defer payment, or stretch out payments over a period of months.

Frequency

In the "old days," adult dogs were revaccinated annually after completing a series of puppy shots. More recently, most veterinarians have changed their recommendations for frequency of revaccinations. Some vaccines provide lifelong protection, and others need to be renewed at three-year, rather than yearly, intervals. In some cases if there is risk of contracting a disease, protection might need to be renewed more often. For example, a dog who is repeatedly kenneled or exposed to many other dogs in an indoor setting (dog shows, day care) may need to receive the bordetella (kennel cough) vaccine every six months.

Intestinal Parasites

Dogs and puppies are most commonly preyed upon by four types of worms: roundworms, tapeworms, hookworms, and whipworms. These parasites threaten canine health and in some cases can be transmitted to humans.

Prevalence and Prevention

Most dogs are infested with some type of intestinal parasite at one time or another and develop a natural immunity. Stressful events, such as pregnancy, illness, surgery, or moving to a new home can suppress the immunity and activate dormant larvae.

Additionally, dogs can easily become infested and reinfested. It is difficult to prevent them from exposure to the eggs and larvae of intestinal parasites that are excreted in feces and therefore found on grass and dirt, but there are some proactive steps that you can take:

- Remove feces from the yard.
- Do not let your dog eat feces.
- Keep your dog free of fleas and lice because they are intermediate hosts of tapeworms and roundworms.
- Wash dog bowls regularly.
- Consult with your veterinarian about choosing a monthly heartworm preventive medication that also prevents and controls roundworms, hookworms, and whipworms.
- Regularly disinfect the inside of his crate or kennel.

An adult dog should be dewormed only if a veterinarian has examined a fecal sample and determined that eggs or parasites are present. There are several types of deworming medications, each effective for one or more different parasites. No one

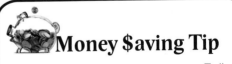

Money $aving Tip

Prevention will save you money. Follow your veterinarian's recommendations for vaccinations and for guarding against infestation by internal and external parasites.

medication is effective against all species of worms. Your veterinarian will identify the parasite affecting your dog and select the medication that is appropriate and safe.

Most puppies are infested with worms and are routinely dewormed multiple times, according to a schedule. As with adult dogs, it is advisable to rely on a veterinarian's supervision and prescription rather than on an over-the-counter medication. It is important to follow and complete the deworming schedule.

Hookworms are common in puppies.

Hookworms

These parasites are also common in puppies, transmitted in utero and through nursing. Dogs ingest them in feces, and hookworms can also enter the body by penetrating a paw pad. Hookworms feed on blood and tissue and can cause fatal blood loss in a puppy.

As with roundworms, adult dogs do not always exhibit symptoms; those who do may have diarrhea, a dull coat, weakness, weight loss, anemia, and dehydration. A veterinarian can detect the presence of hookworms by examining a fecal sample and will treat the dog with a dewormer twice over a period of one to two weeks.

Roundworms

Almost all puppies are born with roundworms, which are acquired in utero and later through nursing. Adult dogs become infested by eating feces contaminated with roundworm eggs that hatch in the intestine. Larvae pierce through the intestinal wall and enter the bloodstream, migrating throughout the body.

Puppies are treated for roundworms at 4, 6, and 8 weeks of age, and their stool is checked again at about 12 weeks to determine if more treatment is needed. Multiple treatments are necessary because they are effective only on the adult stage of the worm.

Symptoms of roundworm infestation include abdominal pain, bloated belly, dull coat, diarrhea, and respiratory problems. Adult dogs will not always show obvious symptoms of roundworms, but their overall health will suffer. Left untreated, roundworms can cause serious canine health problems, including pneumonia and obstruction of the bowel. A veterinarian can determine the presence of roundworms by examining a fecal sample. Treatment is important not only to the health of the dog but also to humans because roundworm infestations are contagious to people.

Tapeworms

A dog contracts tapeworms by eating fleas or lice infested with the eggs or by eating parts of an intermediate host, such as a rabbit or rat. Tapeworms can reach several feet (m) in length, feeding off the dog's intestine. They shed body segments, described as looking like a grain of rice, which are excreted in the dog's feces. Tapeworms are not usually a major health threat except to a dog who is ill, old, frail, or too thin. Most dogs do not have symptoms, but some will suffer from weight loss and loose stool. Controlling fleas in your dog's coat and environment is the best way to avoid these parasites.

Whipworms

Whipworm eggs remain infective for years—in your yard, the park, and along walking paths where they have been deposited in feces. A dog ingesting feces or other contaminated material swallows the eggs, which hatch in the intestines and mature into worms. The worms feed on the dog's blood and tissue fluids, causing weight loss, pain, loose or bloody stool, dehydration, and anemia. Multiple dewormings, prescribed by a veterinarian, are necessary to rid your dog of this pest.

ACCIDENTS, INJURIES, ILLNESS

Sometime during your dog's life he will almost certainly make a nonroutine trip to the animal clinic. He may have been injured or showing symptoms that depart from his normal behavior.

Worrisome Symptoms

Your dog cannot tell you when he feels sick or when or where he hurts, but his behavior can alert you that something is wrong. If your companion is a puppy or an elderly dog, be extra vigilant for unusual behavior and quickly contact your veterinarian. Puppies do not have fully developed immune systems, and elderly dogs may have compromised immune systems, and they can both become dehydrated or overcome by infection more easily. Worrisome symptoms that indicate the need for a call or visit to your veterinarian include:

- blood in the urine or feces
- diarrhea for more than a day
- excessive panting
- excessive scratching
- hair loss
- limping
- listlessness, lack of energy
- little or no urination
- loss of appetite
- lumps
- persistent coughing
- refusal to drink water or excessive drinking
- repeated vomiting
- uncharacteristic housetraining accidents (applies to dogs, not puppies)
- weight loss

Symptoms may indicate a minor, manageable problem, no problem at all—or signal trouble ahead. Only your veterinarian can make this determination. Many dogs develop noticeable lumps that are simply fatty tumors and completely benign. In fact, about one-third of all canine tumors are skin tumors, and more than three-quarters of these are benign. But a lump can also indicate a cancerous growth.

A brief bout of diarrhea or vomiting may be due to the fact that Duke found a delicious decayed animal part in the woods and consumed part of it while you were not watching. But a continuance or repetition of such symptoms could be symptomatic of a serious gastrointestinal problem.

Excessive scratching may be due to a flea invasion or to an allergy that could worsen, can lead to infections, and can make your dog miserable if left untreated. A limping dog may simply have a sore paw—or a hidden wound, broken bone, or torn ligament.

Many canine ailments are treatable, including cancer, diabetes, heart disease, kidney disease, inflammatory bowel syndrome (IBS), and ulcers. The sooner that these and less serious illnesses are detected by the veterinarian, the better and longer your pet's quality of life.

Emergency Symptoms

Some situations are so threatening to your dog's health that you should proceed immediately to the veterinarian or emergency clinic, regardless of the hour of day or night. Call ahead to tell them you are coming, and tell them why. If you are wondering whether or not you have a "true emergency" on your hands, err on the side of caution

 **Money $aving Tip**

Topical and oral parasite medications are usually less expensive when ordered from catalogs, but follow your veterinarian's advice about brands and dosage.

and take your dog to the clinic. This is no time to begin online research of your pet's symptoms! Emergency symptoms to look out for include:

- bleeding from the eyes, nose, or mouth
- bloated or tender abdomen
- choking
- collapse
- copious, violent vomiting and retching
- exposed bone or suspected fracture
- growling, snapping, or shrinking away when touched
- heavy bleeding from a wound
- hypothermia or hyperthermia
- inability to urinate or defecate
- partial or complete paralysis
- puncture wound in the abdomen, chest, or neck
- severe burn
- shaking, trembling, groaning, or whimpering
- walking stiff legged, with arched back

Common Injuries and Ailments

Despite our very best efforts, accidents happen and our pets are injured. Because you—not your veterinarian—are on

At the first sign of worrisome symptoms, contact your veterinarian.

the spot with your dog, you are his first line of defense and care. Keep calm and keep your wits about you, and you will undoubtedly be of help and comfort to your beloved pet.

Auto Accidents

More dogs die from being hit by cars than from any other kind of accident. Prevention is simple: Keep your dog leashed whenever you are walking him near traffic. If he is struck by a car, move him as little as possible. Bring your car to him rather than carrying him to your car. If he is too large for you to lift into the car, make a stretcher out of a piece of plywood or a blanket and get someone to help you lift him onto the stretcher and into the car. Transport him immediately to your veterinarian or an emergency clinic whether or not you see signs of distress or injury. Call ahead to tell them you are bringing him in and why. If he feels cold to you, cover him in something warm. If he is bleeding, press a clean, dry cloth against the wound.

Burns

Your dog can be burned by exposure to extreme heat (exhaust pipe of a car or motorcycle, outdoor grill), chemicals (acid, kerosene, gasoline), or electric shock (chewing on an electric cord). As we humans know, burns are painful, including first-degree or the "mildest" of burns, and they can easily become infected.

If your dog has come in contact with a toxic chemical, immediately flush the area with large amounts of cool water. If you detect absolutely no signs of burned skin (redness, blistering), wash the area lightly with a mild soap and rinse thoroughly. If you see signs of burned skin or if your dog has been burned in any other way, take him to a veterinarian.

Choking

A dog can die if his air supply is cut off or blocked. A dog should not be tied out on a chain, rope, or leash or left inside wearing a choke collar. Both situations present the possibility of a dog choking to death. Some dogs choke themselves by actually swallowing objects such as racquet balls, sponge balls, and small toys.

If your dog is gagging, coughing, or pawing at his muzzle and you can see an object blocking his airway, try to extract it with your fingers. If you saw your dog swallow an object and he is unable to breathe or make any sound at all:

- Put gravity to work: If your dog is small, lift him off the ground by his hind legs and hold him head down; if your dog is too large for this, lift his rear legs off the ground as high as you can.
- Apply a canine version of the Heimlich maneuver: Wrap your arms around your dog's abdomen, place one hand open over the fist of your other hand, and quickly squeeze three to five times.

Take your dog as quickly as you can to the veterinarian for emergency treatment.

Cuts and Wounds

Most dogs sooner or later end up with a cut or punctured paw, having stepped on a piece of glass or a sharp object. After all, they are not wearing shoes. Some dogs sustain wounds fighting with other dogs or with wildlife.

A puncture wound, whether from a tack or a canine tooth, may not look serious but can easily become infected and warrants a trip to the veterinarian. If your dog is bleeding profusely from a wound, apply pressure to the area with a clean cloth and head for your veterinarian or emergency clinic. If blood is spurting from the wound, head there even faster while maintaining pressure. Veterinary attention is needed for these injuries because stitches and a bandage may be called for.

Hot Spots

A hot spot is known to veterinarians as "acute moist pyoderma," "pyotraumatic dermatitis," or a similar phrase and is well known to owners of dogs of any breed, any age, in any climate. It is an inflamed, infected skin lesion, usually instigated by allergies, an insect bite (flea, tick, mite, spider), sting (bee, wasp), burrs, or an external injury such as a scrape or minor wound. The dog responds to the irritation by constant licking, chewing, or scratching at the site, and this can quickly (within a matter of hours) produce hair loss, redness, pus, and pain. Left untreated, the inflammation can spread quickly and the dog will become increasingly uncomfortable and agitated.

Your dog is depending on you, so be prepared in the event of an emergency.

Poison

If you see your dog lapping up a household cleanser or antifreeze, or come home to discover an empty 5-pound (2-kg) chocolate box, or find him consuming prescription or nonprescription medications, including the plastic bottle:

1. Collect the evidence, such as the cleanser or prescription bottle.

2. If your dog is having seizures, having trouble breathing, or is unconscious, take him immediately to your veterinarian or an emergency clinic, calling ahead first to tell them the problem and let them know that you are on your way. Take the evidence with you.

3. If your dog is not showing symptoms, call your veterinarian or call a pet poison control hotline. (See "Making it Easy.") Be prepared to describe the "evidence" and your dog by age, breed, weight, and sex.

Snake and Insect Bites

Bees, wasps, spiders, and snakes are most likely to sting or bite a dog on the face or legs. For most dogs, a single spider bite or bee or wasp sting needs not be serious. Apply a cold pack to the site and watch your dog carefully for at least an hour. If the site swells rapidly or if your dog seems agitated, pants heavily, breathes irregularly, or vomits, he may be having an allergic reaction that could send him into shock. Take him immediately to the veterinarian. If your dog is stung multiple times, take him to a veterinarian right away.

Most snakes are not poisonous, and most snake bites are not a mortal threat to your dog. But if you live or hike in areas of the country where rattlesnakes, water moccasins, cottonmouths, copperheads, or coral snakes are

Money $aving Tip

Expect and save for unexpected veterinary costs due to injury or illness.

common, learn how to identify and avoid them. They are poisonous.

A dog bitten by a poisonous snake is in danger of dying. His wound will swell, he will feel pain and weakness, and he will soon have difficulty breathing. Take him to a veterinarian as quickly as possible (and it's helpful if you can identify the snake). On the way, minimize your dog's movements. The more he moves, the more the venom circulates in his body.

Caring for a Sick or Injured Dog at Home

After your dog has been diagnosed with an illness, undergone surgery, or received stitches, a cast, or bandages, he will return home with you for follow-up care. Your veterinarian will give you instructions. I recommend that you ask for them in writing or write them down yourself. If you have trouble reading directions (including those on a pill bottle or other medication), ask your veterinarian to provide them printed in large type. Follow them carefully and completely. It helps to post them on the refrigerator door.

Elizabethan Collar

A common follow-up procedure is for your dog to wear an Elizabethan collar to prevent him from chewing on or licking or scratching at wounds and stitches. Sympathy is pretty universal when people see a dog dressed in an Elizabethan collar, and dogs don't like them. But (trust me) it is better to keep the collar on, no matter how sorry you feel for your dog, than to remove it and let him remove his stitches—this will require a new trip to the clinic, new stitches, and a prolongation of the healing process.

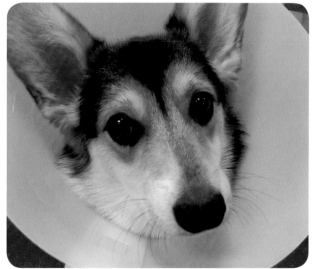

An Elizabethan collar will prevent a dog from chewing or licking wounds.

Giving Medications

A veterinarian will often prescribe a course of oral medication for your dog. If you are asked to give half a tablet at a time, check to see if you are able to cut or break the tablets before you leave the clinic; you may want to ask a veterinary technician to do this for you.

The easiest way to give a pill is to wrap it in a piece of soft cheese or hot dog. You can also purchase "pill pockets," tasty treats with a pocket where the pill is inserted. If for some reason your dog will not swallow pills, discuss options with your veterinarian. Some medications can be compounded into a tasty liquid to be mixed with food or a transdermal paste that is smeared on a hairless area, such as inside the ear, and absorbed through the skin.

You may be called upon to change bandages, cleanse a wound, or apply ointments or salves to the eyes, ears, or skin. In addition to written instructions, ask your veterinarian to demonstrate the proper technique. Do not hesitate to ask questions!

THE COST OF CARE

It is impossible to predict the cost of caring for a dog who becomes ill or injured. The cost of care varies from region to region and from clinic to clinic, and different veterinarians may suggest (and you may choose) different treatment options. Each dog responds differently to treatment, just as humans do. One study suggests that the average yearly veterinary bill for a dog is about $100—a figure that includes routine care—and this estimate is an average. You may be lucky enough to pay, in a single year, $100 or less for routine care only, but your neighbor may pay thousands of dollars for canine cancer surgery and chemotherapy. Even the cost of preventive care will vary, depending on the size and age of your dog, geographic region, and frequency of exposure to parasites. If you are confronted with a major veterinary issue and unsure about treatment choices, it is appropriate to seek a second opinion from another veterinarian or a specialist.

When it comes to pet medications, a little comparative shopping can save you money. Products for flea, tick, and heartworm prevention can usually be purchased at the animal clinic, where they tend to be expensive; at grocery and pet stores at varying prices; and through Internet and paper catalogs, where they are usually cheapest. Products for arthritis and dry skin and some medications that require a veterinarian's prescription are also available online and through catalogs. Follow your veterinarian's advice about which products to use, regardless of where you buy them. Purchasing online or from a catalog saves you a trip to the store. Some of these services deliver for free but others do not, and the delivery charge can reduce potential savings.

Taking preventive measures to ensure your dog's health and safety can help you avoid pricey veterinary bills. But accidents and illnesses do occur even with the best of care, and older dogs develop geriatric problems, which is why it is important to plan for a canine rainy day from the outset. If paying for veterinary care poses financial problems, a few clinics and shelters make reduced-cost services available. Some clinics will arrange for payment in monthly installments, and a few shelters will extend no-interest loans to cover emergency care.

PET INSURANCE: MEDICARE FOR POOCHES?

Not exactly. Only about 3 percent of dogs in America are covered by pet insurance, which was first introduced in 1983, and it is 100 percent private, having nothing to do with the government.

Pet insurance is similar to private fee-for-service health care insurance that we humans purchase. The pet owner purchases a private plan,

paying a monthly or annual premium; the plan reimburses the owner or the veterinarian a stated percentage for veterinary care given to the pet or pets covered by the policy.

A Good Idea?

Whether or not you buy insurance for your dog is a personal and financial decision. You do not need to be embarrassed because you want to insure good veterinary care for your dog!

The cost of quality pet care has been increasing rapidly and will continue to do so. Caring for a dog who has been injured or is seriously can run into thousands of dollars. If an accident occurs and your dog is covered by insurance, you will not have to worry about balancing the love of your dog against your pocketbook—an agonizing decision that people do face. With insurance, you can focus on making health care decisions for your dog.

If you are in the enviable position where money is no object when taking care of a beloved dog, insurance may hold no appeal for you. Or if you are disciplined about financial matters, make a "donation" every month to a "pooch fund," which can be a cookie jar or an interest-bearing bank account. This should be an emergency fund, while routine veterinary costs, such as vaccinations, checkups, and heartworm and flea prevention must be factored into your monthly pet budget, along with dog food.

The sobering reality is that most dogs will require emergency attention at least once. A few of my "minor" experiences, which are typical:

- Charlotte stepped on a piece of glass and required stitches for the laceration.
- Tony developed eye infections— twice.
- Dandy developed a hot spot that became infected.
- Tony received multiple bee stings on his nose, a life-threatening situation.
- Sunny chewed a prescription bottle and swallowed the contents.
- Brooks swallowed a sock.

Other dog owners have faced more serious health challenges for their dogs, including cancer treatment, joint replacement, and ongoing problems such as allergies, chronic ear infections, and diabetes.

Choosing a Plan

The most important thing to do when investigating and choosing a plan is

Money $aving Tip

Some shelters and rescue leagues can offer assistance with veterinary expenses.

Whether or not you buy insurance for your dog is a personal and financial decision.

to get all of your questions answered and read the fine print. Make certain that you are dealing with reputable companies by first determining if they are licensed to do business in the state where you live. Here is a list of important issues and questions.

Cost

Most policies call for monthly premium payments but a few are annual. Depending on the amount of coverage you buy, the premium will vary from as low as $10 a month for minimal coverage to as much as $75 per month for a "Rolls Royce" plan with extensive benefits. The average monthly cost is about $25. Some plans offer a discount for multiple pets.

Reimbursement

Most plans reimburse from 80 to 85 percent of covered procedures. One plan, which functions more like an HMO, requires owners to use "network" veterinarians who charge discounted rates and reimburses 50 percent.

Coverage

Coverage can vary greatly, depending on how much insurance you want and how much you are willing to pay. The least expensive plans cover treatment for emergency situations and accidents, including:

- if your dog is hit by a car
- if your dog steps on a nail or piece of glass
- if your dog jumps off a high deck and breaks his leg

Higher levels of coverage could include reimbursement for treatment for:

- illness, such as Lyme disease
- preventive care, such as vaccinations and checkups
- chronic and long-term conditions, such as diabetes

Exclusions

Many policies do not cover pre-existing, congenital, or hereditary conditions. It is extremely important to learn what conditions or diseases are not covered, or you may end up buying pet insurance that is of little value to you.

Limits

Most plans have a maximum benefit or limit of some kind. The limit can apply to an "incident," such as a broken bone or illness or it can cap the yearly benefit that will be paid, or both.

The limit varies with the type and cost of coverage. A "Rolls Royce" plan with extensive coverage, including for chronic conditions, could have an annual limit of $12,000 to $15,000 and an incident limit of $3,500 to $5,000. A basic plan with more modest coverage might have an annual limit of $5,000 to $8,000 and an incident limit of $1,500 to $2,500.

Deductible

Like human health insurance, most pet insurance policies have a deductible. It may be either an annual amount, typically about $100, or a "per incident" amount, typically about $50.

RESOURCES MADE EASY

Books About Canine Health and First Aid

- Arden, Darlene. *The Angell Memorial Animal Hospital Book of Wellness and Preventive Care for Dogs*. New York, NY: McGraw-Hill, 2002.

- de Laforcade, Armelle (ed). *Canine Medicine: Common Conditions, Diseases and Treatments*. Medford, MA: Tufts Media Enterprises, 2005.

- Eldredge, Debra A., DVM, Luisa D. Carlson, DVM, Delbert G. Carlson, DVM, and James M. Giffin, MD. *Dog Owner's Home Veterinary Handbook* (Fourth Edition). Hoboken, NJ: Wiley Publishing, 2007.

- Fogle, Bruce, DVM. *What's Up With My Dog? A Visual Guide to Symptoms and First Aid*. New York: Dorling Kindersley, 2002.

- Kay, Nancy, DVM. *Speaking for Spot: Be the Advocate Your Dog Needs to Live a Happy, Healthy, Longer Life.* North Pomfret, VT: Trafalgar Square, 2008.

Health

- American Animal Hospital Association (AAHA): www.healthypet.com
- American Kennel Club (AKC): www.akc.org
- American Society for the Prevention of Cruelty to Animals (ASPCA): www.aspca.org
- American Veterinary Medical Association (AVMA): www.avma.org/careforanimals/default.asp
- Cornell University College of Veterinary Medicine: www.vet.cornell.edu/library/vetaccess.htm
- Humane Society of the United States (HSUS): www.hsus.org
- Pet Place: www.petplace.com
- University of Illinois College of Veterinary Medicine: www.cvm.uiuc.edu
- Washington State University College of Veterinary Medicine: www.vetmed.wsu.edu

Medications

- 1-800PetMeds: www.1800petmeds.com; 1-800-738-6337
- PetRx: www.petrx.com; 1-800-844-1427

Pet Insurance

- American Kennel Club (AKC): www.akcphp.com
- American Society for the Prevention of Cruelty to Animals (ASPCA): www.aspcapetinsurance.co
- PetAssure: 888-789-7387
- PetCare: www.petcareinsurance.com; 866-275-738
- Petplan: www.GoPetplan.com; 866-467-3875
- PetsBest: www.PetsBest.com; 877-738-7237
- Petshealth: www.petshealthplan.com; 800-807-6724

Poison Control Hotlines

- Angell Animal Poison Control Hotline: www.mspca.org; 877-226-4355
- Animal Poison Hotline: 888-232-8870
- ASPCA Animal Poison Control: www.aspca.org/apcc; 888-426-4435 ($60 charge)

Chapter 10

Dogs Behaving Well

When I met with Lisa LaFontaine, President and Chief Executive Officer of the Washington, D.C., Humane Society, she told me about one of the most important lessons she learned running a large shelter in New England:

"We offered a puppy training course for puppies adopted from our shelter, but it was not mandatory. We began to notice that puppies who had been through the course were not being returned to the shelter. Puppies who had *not* been through the course were still being returned. So we made the class mandatory and that cut down sharply on our return rate. The lesson was clear. People were happy with puppies who were trained. They became good pets."

Lisa continued, "After the new policy was instituted, a gentleman well into his 70s adopted a puppy from us. He had adopted from the shelter before and reacted angrily when told of the mandatory classes, arguing that he had always trained his own dogs and done just fine, thank you. The shelter's adoption counselor held firm and the man, whom I'll call Mr. Jones, eventually reluctantly gave in and signed up for the puppy classes. Some weeks later, Mr. Jones stormed into the shelter, demanding to see the counselor. Nervously, she presented herself. 'I just wanted to thank you,' he amazed her by saying. 'This training you do now is much easier and more fun than the way I used to do it.'"

Perhaps you can relate to Mr. Jones. I can. My parents were two of the most softhearted animal-loving pet owners you could want to meet. Yet some 50 years ago, they did what most dog owners did: rubbed a puppy's nose in his own feces when he had an accident indoors or swatted him with a rolled-up newspaper. Maybe you can admit to doing the same thing or watching your parents do it years ago. But it's a brave new world of positive dog training, one based on research and greater understanding of canine psychology.

THE BASICS OF CANINE BEHAVIOR AND TRAINING

Lisa LaFontaine's experience at her shelter is backed up by statistics. The majority of dogs relinquished to shelters is less than one year old and are usually relinquished because of "problem behaviors," including inappropriate elimination. Too many of these relinquishing owners seem not to realize that a dog has no clue of how to fit into a human household until he is taught the rules.

I am sure that you do not want to fall into this trap. To avoid it, think of your task as "behavior modification": modifying innate canine traits so that human and dog can comfortably get along. Innate characteristics, which vary with the individual dog, are likely to include eating whatever smells appealing and is within reach, including garbage in garbage cans and food on counters and tabletops; chewing (especially for puppies) whatever is lying around, including shoes, furniture, and carpets; eliminating wherever convenient, including inside the home (especially true for puppies); jumping up on people when excited; chasing cats, children, and other small critters for the fun of it; paying no attention to your words or commands (because he has no idea you are talking to him); and wandering and roaming when the mood strikes. When your new dog or puppy exhibits these traits, he is not being "bad"—he is being a dog.

You do not need to take the dogginess out of your dog and I hope you don't want to. You do need to show him which behaviors are acceptable and which are not and make it worth his while to "do the right thing."

Building Blocks

Training your puppy or retraining an adopted dog begins with commonsense building blocks:

Positive dog training works by understanding dog behavior and psychology.

1. *Make certain that your dog is healthy and receiving the proper nutrition.* Recent research has revealed a link between certain types of doggy diets and canine aggression. A dog with a toothache or earache is not going to be able to pay attention. A dog with digestive problems or one who is overfed is not going to be able to maintain an outdoor elimination schedule.

2. *Exercise your dog.* As the saying goes, a tired dog is a good dog. A bored dog with pent-up energy is—you get the picture. This is a dog likely to dig, chew, bark incessantly, jump all over you, and have a hard time calming down.

3. *Pay attention to your dog.* Spend time with him and establish a relationship with affection, games, and fun. A dog who is isolated—banished to the yard, garage, or basement and left alone in the house 12 hours a day—can hardly be expected to calmly behave when allowed to have human company.

4. *Establish a routine for feeding and exercising your dog.* This helps with housetraining. The order and boundaries that you give your dog with routines and training will provide him with a needed sense of security.

5. *Manage potential pitfalls and canine temptations.* Put your garbage can

Money $aving Tip

Some shelters offer one or more free or reduced-rate training classes to adopters. Plus, some shelters and rescue leagues offer free "counseling" to adopters for canine problem behaviors—either in person or by telephone.

out of reach. Don't leave food on the table or countertop. Keep your shoes in the closet with the door closed. Don't give your dog or pup the run of the house unless and until he is 100 percent housetrained. Confine him to a crate or behind a gate when guests arrive.

HOUSETRAINING

Some dog training establishments offer seminars on housetraining. These may be useful, but housetraining by definition must be done at home and that means that the humans living in the house are responsible for teaching Tiny where to take care of business.

If you have adopted an adult dog described as fully housetrained, you should nevertheless supervise him for the first few days at home and be tolerant. It is not unusual for a housetrained dog to make a mistake or two when adjusting to a new home and new routine.

TRAINING "DOS" AND "DON'TS"

The way that you interact with your dog on a daily basis will help determine his behavior and can make it easier or harder for you to housetrain and obedience train him. These guidelines—the Dos and Don'ts of how you train your dog—will carry both of you through training and everyday living.

When teaching your dog, DO:

- Establish rules and limits, beginning on day one.

- Supervise him closely during his early weeks with you. Confine him to a crate or a gated room when you are not at home.

- Have realistic expectations. Your dog will not learn overnight or in a week or two or three. He has much to learn, and the two of you speak different languages.

- Practice patience. Your dog will not know what you want until you show him—over and over and over again.

- Be consistent. Don't laugh at your dog for jumping on you today and reprimand him tomorrow for doing the same thing.

- Make certain that all of the humans in the household operate from the same page. It is confusing and unfair if Mom lets Tiny sleep on the couch, but Dad gets angry when he finds him there.

- Use positive reinforcement. Praise and reward your dog with treats, pats, games, and toys for "doing the right thing."

- Reward your dog immediately, within a few seconds, after he has "done the right thing."

- Understand your dog's limits. Keep training sessions short (10 to 15 minutes) and fun.

- Throughout his life, reinforce what your dog has already learned with praise, rewards, and practice.

- Be firm. You are not doing your dog any favors if you pamper him instead of training him.

- Use single words or simple, short phrases: "Sit." "Come." "Stay." "Down." "Wait" (or "Pause"). "Off." "Leave it." "Heel."

- Use a normal, firm, and friendly tone of voice to give commands.

- Show disapproval with a negative tone of voice and single word such as "wrong" or "no."

- Build your dog's self-confidence. This may be especially important if you adopt a shelter dog who has been abused or neglected. Pour on the affection, games, and praise.

- Learn about canine instincts, motivations, and behavior to better understand your dog.

When teaching your dog, DON'T:

- Decide that he needs to "settle in" for a few days before you start to train him.

- Give your new dog or puppy the run of the house as soon as you bring him home.

- Expect your dog or puppy to understand the rules before you train him.

- Look for a "quick fix" to train your dog, such as an electric shock collar. These devices are inhumane and often counterproductive.

- Forget to decide ahead of time what your dog's limits will be and to reach a consensus within the household on those limits. Is Tiny allowed to sleep on the bed? To climb on other furniture? To bark at the mail carrier?

- Yell at your dog. The anger in your voice will overwhelm the message you are trying to give. Teach your dog to trust you, not fear you.

- Use violence, pain, fear, or physical intimidation to "train" your dog by punishing him.

- Use choke or prong collars.

- Hit, shake, or smack your dog.

- Try to intimidate or "dominate" your dog by force or by pinning him to the ground or using an alpha roll. When you force a dog to bend to your will by using tactics like these you cause him stress, which only makes it more difficult for him to pay attention and learn.

- Use the crate to punish your dog.

- Work with your dog when you are angry, frustrated, or tired.

- Subject your dog to lengthy, rigorous training sessions.

- Give commands in either a questioning or an angry tone of voice.

- Repeat a command over and over or give a string of words and commands: "Come here, Rex. No! Don't do that! Bad dog. Come. Now. I said to come!"

- Feel guilty for training your dog and asking him to learn the rules and respond to commands.

- Give up on your dog if he is slow to learn. Dogs learn in different ways, and some catch on faster than others. A method that works for Tiny may not work for Mabel.

- Forget to have fun with and enjoy your dog before, during, and after a training session.

Puppies need housetraining, and so do some adult dogs whose previous owners failed to train them. This process takes time, commitment, consistency, and patience.

Step One: Say the Magic Words

The moment that you arrive home with your new dog or puppy, put him on a leash and take him to the yard or on a brief walk to allow him to eliminate. As soon as he begins to do so, encourage him in a positive voice using a word or phrase you have decided to use to describe what he is doing. For example:

"Go potty" or "Do your business." This is the way you begin to teach your dog to associate that word with the action. Eventually, your dog will make the connection. As soon as he is finished, lavish praise on him.

Some trainers recommend that you teach your dog to use a certain area of your yard for a bathroom area. To do this, take your dog first to that area, say the "magic words," and wait—patiently—for him to take care of business there before going for a walk or unleashing him in the yard. Don't forget the praise!

Even if you've adopted a fully housetrained dog, you should still supervise him closely for the first few days.

Step Two: Schedule

Create a regular schedule of feeding and walking your dog. This will help regulate his need to eliminate and make it easier for you to predict when he needs to go. Do not free-feed (leave food out all day for your dog to nibble), especially with puppies.

Adult dogs usually need to urinate at least three times a day: once in the morning, once during the day, and once at night. Some may defecate once a day and others more often. Feed your adult dog in the morning either immediately before or immediately after taking him outside for a walk. Do not expect him to "hold it" for more than eight hours after relieving himself in the morning, so give him an afternoon/pre-dinner walk and a final walk at bedtime, a few hours after his second meal of the day.

Puppies are another matter. Not only are they not trained to distinguish between indoors and outdoors, but they do not have the bladder control to "hold it," and they need to relieve themselves more often than an adult dog will. Your challenge is to take your puppy out often and try to anticipate when he will need to go.

Puppies need to eliminate first thing in the morning, when they wake up, before breakfast. They should be taken outside on a leash to relieve themselves about 10 to 20 minutes after each meal, after waking up from a nap, and after playtime. In short, a three- to five-month-old pup will need to be taken outside every three to four hours. You can't take a puppy out too often!

Step Three: Consistency

Stick to the schedule. The more consistent you are in maintaining a routine, the faster your dog will understand, learn, and be trained. One caveat: As your puppy grows, the number of meals and the number of opportunities to eliminate can decrease, but change the schedule gradually, not suddenly.

Always:
- Leash your dog until he relieves himself.
- Repeat your chosen magic word or phrase.
- Praise him lavishly when he finishes relieving himself.
- Feed him and take him outside at the same time every day.

Step Four: Supervision

Establish good habits inside the house. Supervise your dog or puppy at home until he is housetrained. This means keeping him in the same room with you at all times. When you are not at home or cannot keep an eye on him, confine him to a crate or in a single room with a gate across the door. Dogs prefer not to eliminate in their own space, so if your dog or puppy does do this more than once in his crate or room, you are probably leaving him there too long. Do not leave food or water with the puppy, as this will simply create an urge he is trying to learn to contain.

Step Five: Learn the Signs

Learn how to anticipate when your pooch needs to eliminate. Each dog will have a different signal or set of signals, and you won't always be able to catch him every time. Reach for the leash if you see these signs:

Don't punish your dog for housetraining mistakes.

- Your puppy or dog begins to circle around a single spot.
- He suddenly stops what he is doing and stands still.
- He begins to pace back and forth, sometimes but not always in front of the door.
- He stares at the door.
- He looks nervous or uncomfortable.

If you see one or more of these behaviors, quickly take him outside on the leash to the preferred spot and use the phrase or word you are teaching him to associate with "go potty." Always remember to praise.

Step Six: Mistakes

If your puppy or dog makes a mistake, remove the evidence. If he has left a mess in the house, don't punish him for it. He won't understand and won't learn anything if you drag him to it and yell at him. The canine brain does not make cause-and-effect connections if there is any time lapse between the action and the correction. Clean up the mess using an odor-removing cleaner. Odors that are left behind are an open invitation for a return visit to the same spot.

If you do catch your pooch in the act, startle him by clapping your hands or giving a loud yelp. Grab the leash, which you of course keep handy for emergencies like this, or pick up your dog or pup and take him outside immediately to your chosen potty area and say the magic words.

Step Seven: Patience

Hang in there. Be patient and consistent. As your dog or puppy learns and is able to follow the schedule, he can have more freedom inside the house, less confinement, and less supervision.

OBEDIENCE TRAINING

Obedience training is not optional—it is mandatory. There are important commands that you should teach your dog to obey—for your safety as well as his. A rambunctious dog can knock you down as he tears out the front door or bolts down the stairs in front of you. He can pull you over when he strains at the leash or be hit by a car when he chases a squirrel into the street.

Training helps create a bond and a mutual relationship of understanding and trust. It enables you to take your dog with you to many places without worry and stress. A well-trained dog is a joy to walk with and easy to live with.

An obedience-trained dog will respond to these commands:

- **Come.** This is critical if your dog

"Apartment" Training

If you live in a high-rise building, and especially if you have mobility problems or a security issue if you go out after dark, you may have heard about what is sometimes referred to as "indoor," "paper," "high-rise," or "apartment" training. This means teaching your dog or puppy to use a canine litter box, papers, or pads to eliminate inside the home. I don't recommend it unless it's unavoidably your best option. Important cautions to take to heart before you proceed along this line:

- Your dog or puppy will find it confusing to learn that it is okay to go indoors in a certain area and just as good or better to go outdoors. If you succeed with indoor training, he may refuse to go outdoors.
- Indoor training usually takes longer than outdoor training.
- Strong odors inside your home are inevitable unless you have a balcony to use for a dog bathroom area.
- You will need to pay for piddle pads or a PETaPOTTY or other equipment.
- You will need to frequently clean or change trays, replace pads, etc.
- If your dog does become used to using an indoor bathroom, he still must be taken outdoors for exercise.

is running toward danger. And knowing that your dog will come when called allows you to let him run free in the woods or on a beach.

- **Down.** When you ask your dog to lie down, you are "inactivating" him. This can help with grooming and veterinary checkups and visits to outdoor restaurants, hotels, shops, the office, etc.
- **Heel.** This tells your dog to walk quietly by your side without pulling or tugging on the leash.
- **Leave it or Drop it.** Not just for games of fetch, this command can be helpful if your dog picks up or tries to eat forbidden things.
- **Sit.** This command can be used to prevent your dog from jumping on people or engaging in other

unacceptable behavior.
- **Stay.** Best used with *sit* or *down*, this command tells your dog to remain in that position, even if you walk away.
- **Wait or Pause.** This tells your dog to stop—at the bottom or top of the stairs or at an open door—and let you go first.

Going Pro

When someone asks me "What is the best book to read about training a dog?" I usually reply "The phone book." Look up "pet training" or "dog training" on the computer, or ask your veterinarian, breeder, fellow dog owners, local humane society, or the National Association of Dog Obedience Instructors (NADOI) or Association of Pet Dog Trainers (APDT) for a reference. (These last two have websites, as do local humane societies and some breeders.) I strongly recommend working with a professional trainer.

Some excellent "how to train your dog" books have been written, but I believe that working alone from a book is more difficult, less fun, and less effective than working with a professional trainer. I do recommend buying or borrowing a good book to help you learn to understand your canine friend and to supplement what you learn from a trainer. A training DVD or video can be even more helpful than a book.

The best trainers will train you to train your dog. There is more than one proven method of training, and some dogs and owners do better with one method than another. A good trainer will know this, and if her preferred approach isn't working well for you and your pup, she can help you try something different. Unlike a book, a good trainer can answer your questions, evaluate how you and your dog are learning, and offer advice tailored to one or both of you.

Group Training, Private Sessions, Consultations, and More

The world of dog training has advanced greatly in the past few decades, both in methods and in the variety of services that are offered. In many localities, you can choose from:

- puppy classes
- indoor obedience classes (beginner, intermediate, advanced)
- outdoor obedience classes (beginner, intermediate, advanced)
- individual training sessions for puppies and dogs
- in-home individual training sessions
- individual problem behavior modification sessions
- advanced obedience classes
- agility training
- refresher classes

The cost of training varies from

Training your dog should not be optional—it's mandatory.

school to school and from one area to another. Some local shelters offer free or reduced-rate classes and one-on-one consultations by telephone or in person. The cost at private training schools can range from about $100 to $200 for six or eight classes. Individual sessions with a trainer or behavioral specialist can begin at $55 and run as high as $150.

Group Classes

Group classes can be great fun, especially for puppies and their humans. They give your pup the chance to socialize during breaks and offer you the opportunity to meet other owners and swap information about veterinarians, groomers, day cares, dog parks, and pet sitters. It can be enlightening to watch other owners with their dogs and learn from their mistakes and successes.

When I recently went to observe an indoor puppy training class, I expected bedlam but instead found relative peace and quiet among the eight assorted puppies in the oversized room. Pups and owners all seemed to be having a good time. Trainer Debbie Tolstoi worked her class for 15 minutes at a time and then gave play breaks. Thirty minutes into the session, she invited interested parties to go outside for a bathroom break, and as a result there was not a single housetraining accident during the hour-long session. Debbie gave useful extracurricular advice to owners about preventing and correcting problem behavior at home and answered questions. These are hallmarks of a successful class.

Private Trainers

Private instruction is more expensive than a class but offers a number of advantages. Some dogs learn more easily when not distracted by other dogs. If you have concerns about physically keeping up with a group, the one-on-one session is a solution. You have the trainer's undivided attention, the ability to focus on your dog's particular problems or quirks, and the opportunity to ask as many questions as you wish. You and the trainer can work on problem behaviors where they occur: on the hike-and-bike trail if your dog is given to chasing joggers and bikes or at your home if your dog lunges out the front door as soon as it is opened.

Boarding School

A final option is send your dog away to "boarding school"—to stay at a kennel for a week or two and be trained. Some schools offer day boarding. In both situations, the dog is trained without your being there and then you receive one or two lessons in handling him.

Although this is a convenient option, it is usually not ideal. Dogs may be stressed in a boarding environment. Both dog and owner have missed the experience of learning together, which can help cement their relationship. The owner has not been trained and may not be able to "catch up" and step into the trainer's shoes. As a result, the dog may

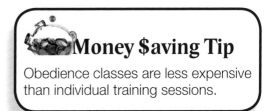

Money $aving Tip

Obedience classes are less expensive than individual training sessions.

be confused and some or much of the training may be lost.

Choosing a Trainer

After you have obtained recommendations, do some preliminary research by looking at local obedience school websites on the Internet and/or by calling the school with your questions. Ask for references and check them out. Before you make a decision, meet and talk to the trainer. It is important that you like and feel comfortable with her. Ask the trainer:

- what method or training philosophy she relies on and why
- if she is willing to try other techniques
- how long she has been training (minimum should be two or three years)
- where and how she learned to train
- what professional associations she belongs to
- the number of dogs or puppies in a class (should be no more than 10 or 12)

Observe a class before you sign up. Some private trainers also lead classes, which would enable you to watch her work. A good trainer:

- uses humane methods—this excludes yelling, physical force, and

Choose a trainer with whom you are comfortable.

electric, prong, and choke collars
- uses positive reinforcement, teaching owners to train dogs with rewards of praise and/or treats rather than punishment or harsh corrections
- will be flexible about trying different techniques
- is patient and friendly toward dogs and people alike
- requires dogs to be fully vaccinated
- explains and demonstrates before

Dogs Behaving Well 203

- asking students to practice
- offers advice, not criticism
- answers questions
- keeps the mood upbeat and pleasant

PROBLEM BEHAVIORS

Dogs have individual personalities that often include quirks or habits. Many quirks are funny and harmless. My mother's Basset Hound loved to eat cherries and spit the pit out between her teeth. An extremely modest Collie of ours always hid behind a bush to take care of business. Some dogs like to sleep in closets, bay at the moon, or sniff flowers.

However, some habits are much less appealing. A dog who jumps on people can seriously hurt your 90-year-old mother or badly frighten your young grandson. An incessantly barking dog can get you evicted. A dog who chews destructively can cost you a lot of money and peace of mind. A dog who pulls on the leash can cause you to fall and break your arm. Early attention and a consistent response to problem behaviors can often resolve them.

Where to begin? Always start with basic training. A dog who has learned to obey basic commands such as *sit*, *stay*, and *come* will pay attention to you and be able to follow commands that will train him out of bad habits.

Barking

All dogs bark, and some bark more than others. Relentless barking can drive you and your neighbors crazy. This behavior often occurs due to extreme boredom and lack of exercise and is likely to take place when you are not at home. If your dog is developing a barking habit:

- Add to his physical and mental exercise. Play games of fetch and practice obedience training in addition to lengthening his walks. If you can, take him to doggy day care once or twice a week where he can wear himself out playing, or hire a dog walker to take him out during the day when you cannot.
- When your dog is left alone, try to liven up his environment with a few toys and by turning on the radio or television.
- When your dog begins to bark—because the doorbell rings or a dog is passing by the front yard—go to him (don't yell from across the room), say "Quiet," and immediately reward him with praise and a treat. If your dog does not hear you, startle him into paying attention with a yelp or by shaking a can filled with pennies. Then tell him "Quiet" and reward him when he is quiet. Practice this by asking friends to come to the door or walk by the front yard.

Tips for Successful Training

Whether you are working alone with a trainer or participating in a class, there are a few things you can do to maximize your success:

- Keep your voice friendly and firm when giving commands.
- Practice at home several times a day every day for about 10 to 15 minutes at a time.
- Make a written note of the equipment your trainer recommends, and remember to bring it to class. There is a reason that trainers recommend head halters for some dogs and want you to use a 6-foot (2-m) leash.
- Have everyone in your household come to class or the training session to watch, learn, and take a turn at handling.
- Do not bring your adorable five-year-old granddaughter to class or to the training session to distract you and the dog.

Destructive Chewing

Teething puppies need to chew. Baby teeth fall out, and the gums itch and hurt as new teeth come in. Chewing helps to relieve the discomfort and pain. Chewing is a normal, innate activity for adult dogs as well. It can have a calming effect for anxious dogs. The challenge is to teach your dog to chew on acceptable objects.

- Remove as many potentially desirable chewable objects, such as shoes and slippers, as possible from your dog or puppy's reach.
- Supervise and spy on your pooch. If he begins to mouth or chew on a forbidden object, give a yelp (not a yell) to startle him, take it away, and give him an acceptable chew toy, such as a hollow chew stuffed

with treats or a Nylabone. Praise him if he begins to chew on what you give him.

- When you can't supervise, confine your pooch behind a gate to a room that does not offer wood to chew, such as a bathroom or kitchen. Give him one or two safe doggy chew toys while he is there. Turn on a radio or television to relieve a sense of isolation.
- Give teething puppies safe chew toys that you have chilled in the freezer. The cold will help soothe their aching gums.
- Give your dog lots of exercise (remember, a good dog is a tired dog) and mental stimulation. My dogs love lying in front of French doors watching street activity. Is

It's natural for teething puppies to chew.

there a way that you can give your dog a view? When you are not at home, leave him with a chew toy or food puzzle.

- Rotate your dog's toys, leaving out just two or three at a time.
- If it is within your means, consider treating your dog to day care once or twice a week. Destructive chewing is often the result of boredom. The more that you can interact with your dog, play with him, and practice obedience training, the less likely he is to chew out of boredom.

Jumping

Dogs jump on people as a greeting, to show excitement, and to get attention. If people respond with a pat or a laugh, it is pure encouragement. Instead:

1. As your dog begins to jump on you, cross your arms over your chest and turn your back on him, ignoring him completely. Repeat until he realizes that jumping results in no attention at all.

2. Ask some good (dog-loving) friends to come to your home and ring the doorbell after you have shown them how to respond (see Step 1, above) when Max tries to jump on them in

greeting. Repeat.

3. After Steps 1 and 2, when Max's four feet are all on the ground, tell him to sit and reward him with praise and a treat.

Leash Pulling

If you use a retractable leash, you are allowing your dog to lunge and run back and forth *while on a leash*. I recommend that you always walk your dog using a 6-foot (2-m) leash. He needs to understand that while walking on a leash, he is to walk quietly at your left side. If your dog is stronger than you are, consider using a head halter or harness instead of a collar to give you more control.

If your dog pulls on the leash, do one of two things:

- Stop in your tracks. When he stops pulling you, start walking again. Repeat as often as necessary until he realizes that if he wants to walk, he must stop pulling.
- Turn and walk in the opposite direction, or randomly walk to the right or the left. Repeat as often as necessary until your dog realizes that his pulling won't get him where he wants to go.

Nipping

Puppies nip, mouth, and bite as they play with their littermates, and they may try this with you. Some dogs nip to play or to get your attention. Don't let them. If your puppy or dog nips you:

- Give a yelp or "Ouch!" and immediately stop playing or patting him. Get up and walk away. Repeat every time your puppy tries to play in this way. Make certain that any visitors who play with the puppy do the same.
- Always supervise young children when they play with your dog or puppy. Do not allow nipping or mouthing.

Serious Problem Behaviors

Some dogs develop serious problem behaviors that are beyond the ability of most owners to cope with. While training can usually help resolve pulling, jumping, nipping, barking, and chewing, it may not be effective with problems such as aggression, separation anxiety, and noise phobias.

Although some professional trainers describe themselves as "behaviorists," only a handful of behavior specialists have received advanced degrees in animal behavior and been certified by the Animal Behavior Society (ABS). They have completed veterinary training and a program in behavior medicine.

Some, but not all, trainers may be able to help diagnose

Don't let your dog pull on his leash—teach him to walk nicely.

and resolve the most serious problem behaviors. Whether you turn to a trainer or a behaviorist, follow guidelines similar to those you would employ in finding a trainer. Look for a professional who tries to understand the underlying causes of your dog's behavior (usually fear or anxiety) and relies on positive reinforcement rather than punishment or intimidation. In some cases, medication prescribed by a veterinary health professional can be helpful.

DON'T GIVE UP

Don't give up if you find yourself in a rough patch with your dog. Think back for a moment. It's very possible that one of your children or a sibling or friend (or even you yourself) created a problem or two for those who loved you. But someone, probably a parent, stood by you and helped you get straightened out. You loved them all the more for it. And look how well you turned out!

RESOURCES MADE EASY

Books About Dog and Puppy Training

- Anderson, Teoti. *Puppy Care & Training*. Neptune, NJ: TFH Publications, Inc., 2008.

- Dodman, Dr. Nicholas (ed). *Best Behavior: Unleashing Your Dog's Instinct to Obey*. Medford, MA: Tufts Media, 2004.

- Dunbar, Ian. *Before and After Getting Your Puppy: The Positive Approach to Raising a Happy, Healthy, and Well-Behaved Dog*. Novato, CA: New World Publishing, 2004.

- Geller, Tamar. *The Loved Dog*. New York: Simon Spotlight Entertainment, 2007.

- Greye, Jan, and Gail Smith. *Puppy Parenting: Everything You Need to Know About Your Puppy's First Year*. New York: Regan Books, 2002.

- King, Trish. *Parenting Your Dog*. Neptune City, NJ: TFH Publications, Inc., 2004.

- McConnell, Patricia. *The Other End of the Leash*. New York: Ballantine Books, 2003.

- St. Hubert's Animal Welfare Center. *Dog Will Be Dogs*. (audio) Roseland, NJ: Listen & Live Audio, Inc., 2003.

Finding Trainers or Behaviorists

- Association of Pet Dog Trainers (APDT): www.apdt.com; 800-738-3647

- International Association of Animal Behavior Consultants (IAABC): www.iaabc.org

- International Association of Canine Professionals (IACP): www.dogpro.org

- National Association of Dog Obedience Instructors (NADOI): www.nadoi.org

- Truly Dog Friendly: www.trulydogfriendly.com

- Look in the Yellow Pages or search online under "pets" or "dog obedience" or "dog trainers."

Training Information

- American Animal Hospital Association (AAHA): www.healthypet.com

- American Society for the Prevention of Cruelty to Animals (ASPCA): www.aspca.org

- Animal Behavior Clinic, Cummings Veterinary School, Tufts University: www.tufts.edu/vet/behavior

- Humane Society of the United States (HSUS): www.hsus.org/pets

Chapter 11

Fido on the Go?
Traveling With—or Without—Your Dog

Frequent travel is a goal of many in our age group, achievable because of retirement or semi-retirement. Those of us who are still working may be sitting on an empty nest, with several weeks per year of vacation time accumulated through seniority.

It is time to book those "nonfamily" vacations or to visit children and grandchildren living in other states or other countries. As we plan these trips, a question looms: "What about Fido?" You have two options. You can take Fido with you by land or air (rarely by sea) or leave Fido behind in good hands.

Fortunately, traveling with a dog is easier than ever before, thanks to the wide and growing availability of pet-friendly hotels and motels. Or if you choose to travel without your dog, you have more options to choose from than in the past: pet sitters, dog walkers, kennels, pet hotels, and resorts. But more than half of all pet owners report traveling with their pet.

CHOOSING THE BEST OPTION

Deciding which option is right for you will depend on your preferences and resources, how far you will travel, how long you will be gone, and your dog. Many travelers love the open road and would prefer to drive almost anywhere rather than travel by train, bus, or plane. Even before gas prices doubled, I did not like to drive long distances. I would prefer to take the train or bus for the four-hour trip from Washington, D.C., to New York, but major train and bus companies do not allow dogs (except for service dogs). For those of you who like the open sea, few cruises allow pets. Very small dogs can often travel in the cabin of an airplane with an owner, but medium and large dogs must travel as cargo, which is not always safe for them.

Dogs have preferences too. Some do not adapt well to travel or unfamiliar surroundings and are better off at home. Canine travel issues to consider:

- Does your dog get carsick?
- Will he fit comfortably in your car along with luggage or other travel items?
- Is your dog too old or frail to travel well? Too young or pregnant?
- How will he handle the stress of travel, whether by car or plane?
- Would flying in the cargo hold of a plane be traumatic for your dog?
- If you are visiting friends or relatives, how do they feel about having a canine houseguest?
- Will the campgrounds, hotels, or motels that you plan to stay in accept dogs?

Traveling with a dog is easier than ever before.

FIDO ON THE GO

If you have decided to take Fido with you, you have two main options: drive or fly. Basic preparations are the same for both:

- Have Fido wear ID tags with home information and a cell phone number or vacation contact number.
- Consider having him microchipped.
- Take a photo of your dog to bring with you in case he gets lost.

- Make certain that your dog's vaccinations and monthly preventive medications are current.
- Take your dog's health certificate documenting current vaccinations.
- Gather and take information with you about animal clinics and dog parks in the places you will be visiting.

Whether or not Fido has his own set of matched luggage, he needs to take certain key items:

- crate, if your dog is used to one, or travel kennel for air travel
- dog bed (if there is room) or blanket
- food and water bowls

- grooming tools if Fido is off for an extended trip
- his regular dog food—kibble can be packed in plastic baggies or plastic containers (remember a can opener and spoon if you use wet food)
- leash
- medication (if any)
- poop-scoop bags
- toys

FLYING WITH FIDO

If you are traveling a long distance, you may decide to fly and take your pooch with you. If you are fortunate enough to be able to charter a jet or own a share of a private plane, your dog can travel safely and comfortably alongside you in the cabin. Most of us, though, rely on commercial airlines. Depending on the airline you select and the size of your dog, he will either be allowed to travel with you in the cabin or be placed in his travel kennel in the cargo hold.

Be informed—be very informed. The first rule of traveling by air with your dog is to do your homework. Check with individual airlines that fly to the destinations on your itinerary. Each airline has different rules about:

- whether small dogs can travel in the cabin
- whether medium and large dogs will be transported in the cargo hold
- the size of dogs who can travel in the cabin
- the size of dogs who can travel as checked baggage or cargo
- the number of dogs allowed to travel in the cabin on a flight
- the cost of transporting dogs in the cabin or hold
- breeds or types of dogs the airline will not transport as cargo
- weather/temperature restrictions for accepting dogs as baggage or cargo
- minimum age of dogs the airline will transport as cargo
- whether a health certificate will be required, type of certificate, and how recent it must be

Some airlines do not transport pets in the hold. A few do not accept pets, even small ones, in the cabin. Some place a maximum weight and size on dogs being transported in the hold. Some refuse to transport certain breeds (snub- or short-nosed brachycephalic dogs, such as Chow Chows, Pugs, and Bulldogs) in the cargo hold during hot weather. These brachycephalic dogs are more likely than other dogs to have breathing problems during flights. To keep matters interesting, airlines frequently revise their prices and guidelines for transporting pets.

Cabin Dog

A few local "puddle jumper" airlines have begun offering cabin travel for medium to large dogs. But almost all airlines limit cabin dogs to toys and miniatures. If your dog is small enough to fit into a carrier that will fit under the seat in front of you, he may be able to travel with you in the cabin. The definition of "small" varies from one airline to another. Small is usually 15 pounds (7 kg) and under, but it may be less. Whatever you do, do not cram your dog into a carrier so tiny that he cannot move. You will probably find that a soft traveling carrier is preferable to a hard kennel. But with a soft carrier, you need to be especially careful that Tiny, in his carrier, is not stepped on or banged about.

Smaller dogs may be able to fly with you in a carrier that fits under the seat.

If Tiny can indeed travel with you in the cabin, make a reservation for him at the same time that you make reservations for yourself. Double-check and confirm his reservation as well as your own as the day of your departure approaches.

Cabin Dog: Before Takeoff

- Do not feed your dog for at least two to three hours prior to your planned departure.
- Even if your dog is the nervous type, do not give him sedatives or tranquilizers, which can affect his ability to balance himself. For brachycephalic dogs, sedatives or tranquilizers can worsen respiratory problems.
- Give your dog a good walk before heading to the airport so that he can relieve himself, get some exercise, and hopefully get tired. A few airports now thoughtfully provide "pet parks," also known as "bone yards" or "paw pads," where dogs can relieve themselves and stretch their legs.

Cargo Dog

I share the trepidation and concerns of animal welfare advocates about the safety of dogs transported as cargo. Airlines that transport animals in the cargo hold maintain temperatures and air pressure that should be safe. However, in addition to the stress of darkness, noise, motion, and strange surroundings, there is some danger to pets of hypothermia, hyperthermia, and oxygen deprivation, largely due to runway delays. In addition, every year a few pets somehow escape from their travel kennels and are lost.

If your dog will travel in the hold, there are steps that you can take to ensure his safety and comfort:

- Choose a major airline. If you have a choice, select an airline with the best on-time record.
- Search for and book a nonstop flight, which will be safer and less stressful for your dog. If necessary, be prepared to drive some distance to and from an airport to find the shortest nonstop flight.
- Book your dog on the same flight that you will travel on.
- During warm weather, book night flights, when it is cooler.
- During cold weather, book day flights, when it is warmer.

As you research airlines and flights, find out whether your cargo dog needs a reservation or whether dogs will be carried on a first come, first served basis. When you decide on a flight, ascertain *all* of the airline's requirements, which typically include a recent health certificate from a veterinarian, including evidence of up-to-date vaccinations.

The airline will require that your dog travel in a kennel. Determine your airline's kennel requirements as soon as you make the reservation. The crate that your dog is using at home may not be the type of travel kennel that airlines require. Travel kennels must meet size, strength, ventilation, and sanitation

Large dogs can't travel in the cabin; they must fly in the cargo hold.

Only fly with your dog if he is healthy.

standards approved by the United States Department of Agriculture (USDA), and the airline may have additional standards. Whether you shop for a kennel from a catalog, on the Internet, or at a pet store, make certain that it is USDA approved for airplane travel. Minimum standards for a safe traveling kennel include:

- room for your dog to stand, sit, and lie down
- strong enough to withstand the bumps and thumps of transportation
- a door that is easy for human hands to open but not likely to spring open
- leak-proof floor
- well ventilated, with openings on the top as well as both sides
- grips or handles for lifting

Purchase the travel kennel as far in advance of the trip as possible so that you can help Fido become accustomed to it and feel safe inside it. If he has been using a crate at home, place the kennel next to it and help him make the transition from one to the other. Whether or not you have been using a crate at home, leave the kennel door open and lure Fido inside with treats and toys. Let him enter and leave at his own pace, as often as he likes, for several days, and then close the door and let him get used to being inside it. If you can pick it up (or get someone to help you), put it in your car and take Fido out for a spin so that he can get used to traveling in the kennel. As your travel day approaches, prepare the kennel:

- Attach prominent "LIVE ANIMAL" signs to the outside of the kennel.
- Attach a label to the outside of the kennel with your name, address, destination address, and phone numbers where you can be reached.
- Place absorbent material in the bottom of the crate.
- Attach instructions for feeding and watering your dog to the outside of the kennel (in case the kennel is diverted or lost).
- Attach some dry food in a pouch and attach food and water bowls (the collapsible traveling kind are best) to the outside of the kennel (in case it is lost or diverted).
- Attach a leash to the outside (not inside) of the kennel.

Cargo Dog: Before Takeoff

A few days before departure:

- Confirm your flight and pet travel arrangements with the airline.
- Find out whether you will take Fido and his kennel to the regular baggage check-in or the cargo desk.
- Find out the pre-departure acceptance cutoff time for your dog.
- Double-check the ID that Fido

will wear—it should have home and travel contact information. He should not wear a choke collar of any kind.

On the day of departure:

- Give Fido his final pre-travel meal or treat, as well as water, at least two hours but no more than four hours before departure time. If your dog is traveling in the hold, the USDA requires documentation that he was offered food and water within four hours of transport.
- Give him a good walk at the last possible moment.
- Do not give him sedatives or tranquilizers, which can affect his ability to balance himself, which is especially important if he is in a kennel in the cargo hold.

At the airport:

- Tip the baggage or cargo handlers when you hand Fido and his kennel over to them.
- When you board the plane, tell the pilot and flight attendant that your dog is in the cargo hold.

When you arrive:

- Retrieve the kennel as quickly as you can, leash Fido, and take him to a safe outdoor area where he can relieve himself. Give him some water and check him over to make certain that he is healthy and uninjured.

International Flights

Long international flights can be dangerous for dogs in cargo holds. If you are considering this option, be certain to fully discuss with your veterinarian and airline officials or travel agent how to safeguard your dog's health and safety. It is possible that you may need to consider leaving him behind for his own good. If you plan to fly internationally with a dog in the cabin with you, check and double-check airline policies. It is also necessary for you to investigate well ahead of time the pet entry guidelines (usually related to proof of health and vaccinations) for the countries that you plan to visit with him.

ON THE ROAD WITH FIDO

Taking a road trip with a dog has become easier, more fun, and more popular than ever before. Hotels, motels, inns, bed-and-breakfasts, campgrounds, and recreational vehicle parks are more likely to welcome your pooch than just a decade ago. Dog-related travel accessories and equipment make long car trips safer and more comfortable for humans and dogs. Nearly 50 percent of dog owners reportedly take their four-legged passengers into account when buying a car.

Getting Ready

I'm assuming that your dog enjoys car trips as much as you do, or he would not be coming with you. If your dog is a reluctant passenger, make an effort to change his mind.

Begin by luring him into the car with a treat. Praise him for even getting into the car, give him another treat, and let him sit in an unmoving car. Repeat this exercise several times over several days and then take him for a short drive. It is helpful if someone can sit in the backseat with your dog for his first rides, to help him remain calm. Gradually take him on longer drives.

Decreasing an animal's anxiety can help overcome motion sickness, but even a seasoned rider can get carsick on lengthy road trips. Consult with your veterinarian before you leave, as new medications are available to counter motion sickness in pets.

Ensure your dog's safety and your own by choosing a restraint system for him: crate, seat belt harness, canine car seat, or barrier. Do not attach a dog to your car's seat belts or a tether by a leash and collar, as this can result in serious injury to the neck.

Travel Gear

In addition to basic travel gear, add towels for wiping down dirty paws, bottled water for stops along the way, and a flashlight for walking your dog at night in strange surroundings. Planning a road trip with your dog can be fun, thanks to an extensive, even glamorous, assortment of canine travel gear—and some of it is even practical. Here's how to decide what you *really* need.

Barriers

Made of mesh, metal, or plastic, these can easily be installed to keep Fido in the cargo hold of an SUV, van, or station wagon. A mesh barrier is also available for installation between the back and front seat. Barriers prevent Fido from distracting the driver or from being thrown around the car's interior in case of an accident.

Booster Seat

Padded, comfortable booster seats for small dogs are attached by the car seat belts. Some dogs really like them because they allow a small dog to see out the window or curl up inside and go to sleep. Choose one that has a restraint system (harness and strap) to keep your dog from roaming in the car and for added safety in case of an accident.

Car Seat Covers

Covers can protect your car's upholstery and create a more comfortable ride for Fido. They come in many sizes, colors, fabrics, designs, and prices. Luxuriously padded or made more simply of heavy-duty nylon or cotton, covers can be purchased for the backseat, cargo area, or individually for front seats. A new twist is a "hammock" that hangs over the backseat.

Crate or Kennel

Some dogs are happier and some drivers less nervous if the canine traveler is confined to a crate in the car. Small crates in the front or backseat should be secured with seat belts. A large crate in the cargo hold should also be secured. Choose a crate with plenty of ventilation and room for your dog to stand up, turn around, and comfortably lie down. Put Fido's favorite blanket or bed on the bottom for comfort. For your convenience, choose a model that can easily be folded or disassembled. A crate can also come in handy when you reach your destination or for overnight stays at hotels and motels.

First-Aid Kit

You can purchase a kit for humans as well as dogs, or assemble your own supplies, which should include:

- antibiotic ointment
- eye wash

- gauze bandage, adhesive tape
- scissors to cut out burrs
- tweezers to remove ticks

Portable Bowls and Feeders

These come in all sizes and styles and some are ingenious, such as a folding travel bowl that will fit into your pocket or clip onto your belt; a plastic bowl and bottle combo that can also clip on; a travel kit that holds a supply of food and water and doubles as food and water bowls; and a portable, airtight nylon pet food container with carry strap. Of course, you can just as easily pack your dog's regular water and food bowls and pack dry food in plastic bags. It just might not be as much fun.

Restraint System

A minor accident or sudden stop can hurl your dog onto the car floor. If he is too big for a booster seat with its built-in restraint, a seat belt restraint system will help keep him safe on long trips. In some states, they are mandatory. A restraint system has the added advantage of keeping Fido where you put him and preventing him from distracting you as you drive.

Hitting the Road

Feed Fido two hours or more before your planned departure time, and give him a long walk before you set off. It is definitely all right to keep the car

Money $aving Tip

Old blankets or towels make good car seat covers when your dog travels with you.

windows partially open while you are driving—fresh air can help counter motion sickness. Do not let your dog hang his head out the window. Although it looks like fun, the wind can blow debris into his eye. In hot weather, make certain that the car's air-conditioning is reaching the backseat or cargo area if that is where your dog is traveling.

Make frequent rest stops—every two or three hours—to allow your dog to eliminate, walk around, drink some water, stretch, and even play for a few minutes. Keep Fido on a leash, do not leave him unattended in the car or rest area, and remember to clean up after him.

CHECKING IN

Your destination or a stop along the way may be the home of friends or family; a hotel, motel, inn, or bed-and-breakfast; or campground. Whatever your destination, the key to a successful trip depends on planning ahead.

Houseguests

If you are planning to stay overnight with friends or family, make certain that they know about Fido ahead of time and that he is welcome to stay in their home. "Make certain" means that you disclose ahead of time pertinent facts, such as that Fido is a 150-pound (68-kg) Great Dane. It could be that the folks you are visiting live in a pet-free building, or that one or more of them are allergic to dogs, or that they have a tiny apartment full of fragile antiques, or that they have a dog or cat who simply can't and won't abide an interloper. Don't assume that because you love Fido, everyone in your extended family or circle of friends will feel the same.

If you will be staying in someone's home where your dog is not welcome and if you do not want to leave him behind, make arrangements ahead of time to board him at a pet hotel or kennel near where you will stay.

Hotels, Motels

In the "old days," it was difficult to find a hotel or motel that happily accepted pets. Some motels would allow pets but require that they stay in an outdoor kennel area, not a guest room. Times have changed for the better. Quite a few hotel and motel chains, ranging from budget motels to the most luxurious of luxury hotels, as well as "extended stay"

residence hotels and individually owned inns and bed-and-breakfasts now accept pets. These changes are reflected in the fact that more than 40 percent of dog owners who stay in hotels bring their dogs with them.

Some lodgings that cater to pets *really* cater to them, with canine cocktail hours, canine room service menus, and daily in-room treats. Some innkeepers provide information about local dog walkers, doggy day care options, and pet sitters— or even make those arrangements, sometimes for a fee.

A harness is a great way to keep a dog safe in the car.

Finding Pet-Friendly Lodging

The key to a good lodging experience with your dog is planning. Many lodgings set aside a limited number of rooms for rental to guests with pets. During busy travel seasons, these rooms can fill up quickly.

Many resources for locating pet-friendly lodging are found on the Internet, and some are available in book form. A book is a convenience if you do not travel with a laptop computer and want to bring it along as a security blanket should some plans fall through or change. Take a good look at print travel guides before you buy because some of them have print so tiny they are hard to read, and some portions may be outdated.

In addition to nationwide pet travel guides, guides are available for many cities, states, and geographic regions of the country. Availability of pet-friendly lodging varies from one region, city, and state to another, which can make these geographically specific guides very useful. Some guides focus on camping and hiking; some focus on lodging only, including time-shares, cabins, cottages, vacation rental houses, and apartments, in addition to hotels, motels, inns, and bed-and-breakfasts; and others are comprehensive and include information about local dog parks, pet-friendly restaurants, malls, emergency veterinary clinics, and other dog-related locations.

Pet Policies

Internet or published guides can help you discover which lodgings fit your needs. When you have narrowed your search, follow up with phone calls, not only to make reservations but to ask questions about pet policies, which vary from place to place and can change from one month to the next. Pet policies may:

- prohibit dogs over 25 pounds (11 kg)
- prohibit dogs over 50 pounds (23 kg)
- prohibit dogs over 100 pounds (45 kg)
- have no weight limit for dogs
- prohibit certain breeds
- limit number of pets
- require an up-front refundable deposit to cover potential damage to the room
- require an up-front nonrefundable fee
- charge an extra nightly fee
- place guests with dogs in smoking rooms
- place guests with dogs only on

certain floors or only on certain corridors

- require that dogs be kept in crates when the owner is not in the room
- prohibit dogs from being left unsupervised in the room

Some lodgings may have policies unacceptable to you. For instance, I am not comfortable in a room used by smokers. Plus, I do not have crates for my dogs—and if I did, I could not fit them in my car.

Cost

Pet stay fees may put an additional strain on your travel budget, so it is important to learn about them ahead of time and to confirm, by phone, fee information provided in pet travel guides. Nightly fees for a dog in the room typically range from a low of $10 to a high of $25 to $35. Some hotels charge a one-time fee of $75 to $125. Some charge no fee at all. Deposits can range from $50 on up.

Amenities

In addition to asking about policies, ask about amenities that can make combined dog–human hotel stays fun and easy. Ask the innkeeper or concierge about nearby dog parks and walking trails. How easy will it be for you to walk your dog nearby? A few lodgings have fenced-in dog play areas.

Canine guests are becoming so popular that some hotels are competing for

Find out the pet polices of your lodging before you stay.

their patronage. When I checked into a chain hotel in Annapolis with my two Collies, we were greeted warmly by every employee. I was a bit jealous—I felt that the dogs received a lot more attention than I did. They received dog food and water bowls, treats, and an expensive brand of bottled water—all free. The water bottle in the room, presumably for my use, came with a price tag. We were given a nonsmoking room. There were no crating requirements and no prohibition against dogs being left in the room. Instead, we received a pet sign for the door that I used

Rules about dogs in camping areas are more relaxed than for hotels and motels.

to let the housekeepers know when we were out so that they could make up the room. I did not want to leave my dogs alone in the room and was able to take them with me on errands and to a terrific dog park recommended by the hotel concierge. Management of this hotel, like some others, contributes a portion of the pet fee to local animal welfare charities.

Make Your Reservation

When you decide which lodging you want to book, be sure to include your dog in the reservation. Call back a few days before you embark on your trip to confirm the reservation for both your family and Fido.

While on the premises, both inside and out:

- Keep your dog leashed in common areas.
- Always pick up after him.
- Follow the hotel rules about supervision and crating.
- Do not leave him alone in the room if he will bark.

Campgrounds and Recreational Vehicle Parks

I confess to never having gone camping with my dogs, but camping and dogs seem to go together. Nearly 60 percent of all campers or RVers take their dogs with them, while 40 percent bring their children. People between the ages of 55 and 64 are the largest group of campers, representing 42 percent of the total. Camping dogs are not all big hunting dogs. Nearly half are small dogs, and medium dogs outnumber large dogs.

Finding a Campground

Rules about dogs in camping areas are more relaxed than for hotels and motels. There are more than 16,000 publicly and privately owned campgrounds in the United States, with a wide range of amenities—from spare and relatively spartan campgrounds to comfortable cabins to luxury privately owned RV "resorts." Many of these sites welcome dogs.

As is the case with hotel or motel travel, it is important to research, plan, and reserve ahead of time; you will find that resources for your research are comparable to those available for hotels and motels.

Pet Policies

Once your research yields a site or sites that you want to visit, call ahead to verify pet policies and inform the management that you plan to bring your dog. Ask about policies, which may include:

- additional fees for a dog
- limitation on the number or size of dogs allowed
- restriction on "aggressive" dogs, sometimes by breed
- regulations about keeping dogs leashed

Some sites require pet owners to provide proof of current vaccinations. Leaving dogs (especially barking dogs) alone in tents or RVs for long periods is frowned upon.

A few campgrounds now provide "pet playgrounds"—fenced-in play areas for dogs.

Be doubly certain that your dog is wearing current identification or is microchipped and that his protection against fleas, ticks, mosquitoes, and rabies is current. Keep him leashed in populated areas, clean up after him, and supervise him on longer hikes—you both want to avoid confrontations with skunks, porcupines, and snakes.

LEAVING FIDO BEHIND BUT NOT ALONE

Some dogs are not meant to travel. They are too young, too old, too anxious, sick, or frail. They get carsick and are terrified of flying. Even healthy dogs who enjoy a short car ride can be stressed by travel. Some trips and vacations, whether by train, bus, or ship, cannot accommodate dogs. Some involve too many hours of driving, long plane rides and connecting flights, international travel, travel to locations where it is difficult to find pet-friendly accommodations, etc. Don't feel guilty!

A few years ago, the options for leaving your dog behind while the family traveled were limited to boarding at a kennel or veterinary clinic or perhaps a helpful neighbor or local teenager who stopped in twice a day to feed your dog and let him roam the yard for a few minutes.

From Fido's point of view, options have certainly improved. In some areas, kennels compete with climate-controlled "suites" in "pet hotels" that can be embellished (for a fee) with music, television sets, play yards, daily playtime with a human playmate, and even daily swims. Other choices include pet sitters, dog walkers, and doggy day care/boarding combinations.

Preparing to Leave

No matter what option you choose, make preparations ahead of time:

- Be certain that your dog's vaccinations are up to date. Boarding facilities should require documentation for immunization against rabies, distemper, and bordetella.
- Be certain that you have a large enough supply of Fido's food and medications to last during your absence, and then a little extra, in case of delay.

Write up instructions and pertinent information, including:

- contact number wherever you will be
- instructions for feeding and walking your dog
- instructions for giving him medication, if any
- description of any of his behavioral or medical quirks
- location and contact number for both regular and emergency veterinary clinics

Boarding

It may be called a kennel, pet hotel, pet motel, or pet resort. These establishments all offer the same service: overnight dog boarding. We've come a long way from the "old days," when kennels were the only commercial alternative to a veterinary clinic. Often located in a rural area, kennels typically offered a caged run with an indoor and outdoor area for each dog. The dog was given food and water and his kennel area was kept clean. That was pretty much it.

Although some basic old-fashioned kennels are still to be found, most now give the upscale hotels and resorts a run for their money. Kennels often offer more outdoor space and activities than hotels, motels, and resorts located in urban areas. Urban and suburban facilities offer convenience to local owners but may shortchange dogs. I recently visited an upscale suburban pet hotel and learned that boarding dogs receive two walks a day in a medium-sized room with no windows and a concrete floor.

My preference is for a boarding dog to have at least some access every day to the outdoors. Many dogs prefer not to eliminate indoors and have been trained not to; it is confusing and a bit unfair to keep them cooped up indoors for days at a time.

A stay in a boarding facility can be boring, stressful, and even traumatic. A dog finds himself confined to a cramped space in a strange, noisy environment filled with the powerful odor of other dogs, disinfectants, and cleaners. Many facilities try to make a dog's stay more pleasant by offering various opportunities for exercise, attention, and activity, often for an additional fee. Options may include:

- daily walk—or two, three, or four
- group playtime (usually 30 minutes) with other dogs
- day care—half or full day with other dogs
- toy stuffed with treats
- individual playtime with an employee
- in-room television
- large "suite"
- room with window
- swimming or wading pool
- bedtime story read to your dog at night (I did not make this up)
- daily brushing
- massage

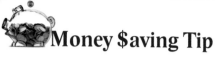

Money $aving Tip

If you are leaving your dog behind, you may be able to swap dog care with a dog-owning neighbor or friend rather than paying for kenneling or a pet sitter.

For the convenience of owners, some facilities offer:

- pet pickup and delivery
- in-room cyber "nanny cam" so that owner can observe pet online
- full grooming
- training sessions

Cost

The cost to board your dog will vary dramatically depending on geographic area, type of facility, and size of your dog (the larger the dog, the higher the fee). Services such as giving medication may involve an extra charge. Boarding a small dog overnight with no extras can cost $15 to $20, and boarding a large dog in a "suite" with extras can cost more than $100 per night. If your small dog is kept healthy and safe and treated kindly by a caring, knowledgeable staff for $15, don't hesitate to make this choice if your budget dictates it. One caveat: If your dog's stay will be more than a few days, try to arrange for some playtime or a treat-filled toy every few days to make his stay less stressful and boring.

Finding a Boarding Establishment

In searching for a boarding establishment, begin by asking friends and your veterinarian or groomer for recommendations. Look at boarding websites to learn about their policies, services, and fees. Call and ask questions. If you are planning to travel during a holiday season, you will need to make reservations well in advance—but first visit in person and consider:

- Does the facility look and smell clean?
- Is it well ventilated?
- Is it temperature controlled?
- Is there a food and water bowl and some type of bed for each dog?
- Are kennels cleaned daily?
- Are outdoor areas secure?
- Will the staff feed on your dog's schedule with his own food?
- If needed, will the staff medicate your dog?
- Are owners required to present proof of vaccinations?

Most importantly:

- How do you feel about the staff?
- Are there enough people on hand?
- Is the exercise or play area supervised when dogs are in it?
- Are your questions answered courteously and fully?
- Do staff members appear to care about their charges?
- Do they seem knowledgeable when you talk with them about the facility and dogs?

Be choosy. During a recent visit to an upscale hotel, I saw a small dog in one of the kennels busily chewing and licking at a hot spot. I reported this to an uncomprehending young woman at the front desk. I explained "hot spot" and said that it could become infected, but she remained unconcerned.

Home Away From Home

In yet another twist on the traditional boarding kennel, "kenneling at home" or "cageless boarding" is growing in some suburban areas. A dog-loving couple, individual, or family opens their home and fenced-in yard to overnight boarders. At a typical home kennel:

- Dogs (and owners) are pre-screened and temperament tested.
- The number of boarders is limited, sometimes to as few as five or six.
- Dogs are fed on their own individual schedules.
- Older dogs and dogs needing medication can be accommodated.
- Proof of current vaccinations is required.

In some homes, boarding dogs are given the run of the house, while in others they are restricted to one or a few rooms. A few accept only small dogs. These facilities usually charge more than their larger counterparts but promise more individual attention to each dog.

The good ones are booked long in advance and may not be open for business on holidays. If you find a "home away from home" for your dog that is clean, safe, and run by dog-loving people, you may have found a fairly stress-free environment for him.

A boarding kennel may offer group playtime with other dogs.

Dog Walker

If your trip is a brief one—overnight or over a weekend—you may feel comfortable relying on a dog walker to exercise and feed your dog, especially if he is already used to someone whom you trust. Your dog needs to be walked at least three times a day and fed on his usual schedule.

Pet Sitter

Many travelers who leave their dogs behind believe that hiring a pet sitter to live in their home with their dog is the best solution. Having a pet sitter ensures:

- less stress for a dog who is happiest in his own home
- one-on-one attention, play, and exercise
- feeding and walking on a regular schedule
- someone is with your dog all night and much or most of the day, so

he will get immediate attention if something goes wrong, such as an injury or illness
- added security to your home, which means less stress for you
- the newspaper and the mail are brought inside, and some sitters will even water the plants and put out the trash cans
- your dog receives any necessary medications, including injections (some charge an extra fee for this service)

Finding a Pet Sitter

To find a pet sitter, begin by asking dog-owning friends for recommendations. Veterinary clinics often yield good pet sitters: veterinary technicians and receptionists who like dogs, know a lot about them, and are interested in making extra money. You can also find pet sitting services on the Internet and in the Yellow Pages.

You cannot be too careful about whom you hire to live in your home and care for your pet. Take time to find someone who is reliable and experienced with dogs. When you have found one or two promising pet sitters, follow through carefully:

- Get and check references. Ask each reference what she liked about this sitter and what problems arose, if any. Ask about the pet who was cared for. It's possible that a good caretaker for a cat or an elderly Chihuahua is not the best caretaker for a headstrong Chow Chow.
- Meet the sitter in person, preferably in your home, before you hire her.
- How does she interact with your dog?
- Does she ask questions about your dog's habits, health, and temperament?
- Does she have a dog of her own?
- What kind of experience has she had working with dogs?
- How much time each day does she expect to be away from your home?
- Does she seem knowledgeable about dogs?

Unless you know the sitter personally (and are willing to assume some risks), ask for documentation that the sitter is bonded and carries commercial

The kennel you choose should be clean and well staffed.

liability insurance (to cover negligence or accidents). Agencies, rather than freelancers, are most likely to have this coverage, as well as a service contract.

Hiring a Pet Sitter

If you find a pet sitter whom you want to hire, make reservations in advance and discuss and resolve details, such as:

- Exactly what time will the pet sitter arrive?
- Will she be at your home when you return from your trip?
- Does she understand and agree to provide the care you expect—number of walks, meals,

medication?

- Does she know where to walk your dog?

Leave detailed written instructions and a backup key with a neighbor. Let your sitter know:

- where you keep dog food and other supplies
- how often and how much to feed your dog
- how often and where to walk your dog
- where you can be reached
- name, location, and phone number of your veterinarian and nearest emergency clinic
- general household information, including security system, trash pickup

Cost

The cost of an overnight pet sitter varies depending on the professionalism and experience of the sitter and geographic location. A fee of $75 for a 24-hour period is not unusual in some areas. The fee may also vary depending on the number of dogs and the number of walks they need.

Veterinary Clinics

Many people feel comfortable leaving their dog with his regular veterinarian. Rapport and trust have already been established. On the downside, your dog may associate the clinic with unpleasant events and may be frightened by the noise made by unhappy dogs and cats. Most clinics can offer only a limited number of large kennels or runs. Ask if you can bring your dog's bed or favorite toy to the kennel.

A boarding dog should receive at least two (preferably three) outdoor walks a day, which may involve an extra charge. Some clinics are associated with next-door doggy day care, which offers a better alternative for your dog than remaining in a cage all day. Day care charges are added on to boarding charges.

A pet sitter will come to your home and care for your dog while you are away.

RESOURCES MADE EASY

Books About Traveling With Dogs

- AAA. *Traveling With Your Pet, 10th Edition: The AAA Petbook*. Heathrow, Florida: AAA Publishing, 2008.
- *Fido Friendly Magazine* (www. FidoFriendlyTravelClub.com; 888-881-5861).
- Gelbert, Doug. *The Canine Hiker's Bible*. Montchanin, Delaware: Cruden Bay Books, 2004.
- Kain, Tara, and Len Kain. *DogFriendly.com's Campground and RV Park Guide*. Pollock Pines, CA: DogFriendly.com, Inc., 2006.
- —. *DogFriendly.com's Lodging Guide for Travelers with Dogs: United States and Canada*. Pollock Pines, CA: DogFriendly.com, Inc., 2008.
- —. *DogFriendly.com's United States and Canada Dog Travel Guide*. Pollock Pines, CA: DogFriendly.com, Inc., 2006.
- Martz, Gayle, and Delilah Smittle. *No Pet Left Behind: The Sherpa Guide for Traveling With Your Best Friends*. Nashville, Tennessee: Thomas Nelson, 2008.
- Meltzer, Julee, and Jack Meltzer. *Camping and RVing with Dogs*. Belfast, Maine: Desert Winds Press, 2006.

Airline Travel

- PetTravel.com: www.pettravel.com
- US Department of Agriculture (USDA): www.aphis.usda.gov (government regulations about air travel with dogs)

Airports With Pet Parks

- Austin, TX: www.ci.austin.tx.us/austinairport
- Denver, CO: www.flydenver.com
- Los Angeles, CA: www.lawa.org
- Minneapolis-St. Paul, MN: www.mspairport.com
- Phoenix, AZ: www.phoenix.gov/aviation
- Portland, OR: www.flypdx.com
- San Diego, CA: www.san.org
- Seattle, WA: www.portseattle.org

Car Safety Products (Including Barriers, Seat Covers, Booster Seats, and Restraint Systems)

- Always check your chain pet store or local pet store first.
- Buckle Up Pup: www.buckleuppup.com; 1-800-571-7972
- EzyDog: www.EzyDog.com
- FidoRido: www.fidorido.com; 1-877-Fido123
- Kurgo: www.kurgo.com; 1-877-847-3868
- PetBuckle: www.petbuckle.com; 1-888-937-4626
- Ruff Rider: www.ruffrider.com; 1-720-249-2986
- SeatKeeper: www.seatkeeper.com; 1-800-600-SEAT
- Snoozer: www.snoozerpetproducts.com; 1-800-635-9755

Kennels

- Humane Society of the United States (HSUS): www.hsus.org/pets

(choosing a boarding kennel)

- Pet Care Services Association: www.petcareservices.org; 1-877-570-7788
- Look in the Yellow Pages or search online for "kennels" or "pet boarding."

Pet Sitters

- Humane Society of the United States (HSUS): www.hsus.org/pets (choosing a pet sitter)
- National Association of Professional Pet Sitters (NAPPS): www.petsitters.org; 1-800-296-7387
- Pet Sitters International (PSI): www.petsit.com; 1-800-268-7487
- Look in the Yellow Pages or online for "pet sitting services."

Travel

- American Veterinary Medical Association (AVMA): www.avma.org (search "traveling with pets")
- Bed and Breakfast Inns Online: www.BBonline.com (search the "Pets Welcome" amenity)
- Bring Fido: www.bringfido.com
- DogFriendly: www.DogFriendly.com
- Dog In My Suitcase: www.doginmysuitcase.com
- Go Camping America: www.gocampingAmerica.com
- Hike With Your Dog: www.hikewithyourdog.com
- Kampgrounds of America (KOA): www.koa.com; 1-406-248-7444

- PetFriendly Travel: www.PetFriendlyTravel.com
- Pets On the Go: www.PetsOnTheGo.com
- PetsWelcome.com: www.PetsWelcome.com
- PetTravel.com: www.PetTravel.com
- PetTravelCenter.com: www.pettravelcenter.com
- RVing With Dogs: www.rvingwithdogs.com
- RV Park Reviews: www.rvparkreviews.com
- Travel Pets: www.TravelPets.com
- TripswithPets.com: www.tripswithpets.com; 1-207-767-1613
- U.S. National Parks: www.nps.gov (rules regarding pets in national parks)
- Woodall's (Campground Directory): www.Woodalls.com; 1-877-680-6155

Travel Crates and Small Dog Carriers

- Always check your chain pet store or local pet store for supplies.
- Nylabone: www.nylabone.com

Travel Water Bowls and Feeders

- Always check your chain pet store or local pet store for supplies.
- Humane Society of the United States (HSUS): www.hsus.petfulfillment.com; 1-212-255-6322
- Water Rover: www.WaterRover.com; 1-866-229-3447s

Part IV
Your Older Dog

Chapter 12

Growing Older Together

She has a bad back. His is worse.

She has a bad knee. He has a bad shoulder.

She sleeps fitfully. He takes long naps.

She doesn't hear so well. His vision is blurry.

This isn't about our dogs, Charlotte and Tony. It is about me and my husband. I am 62 and he is 75. These complaints, typical of people our age, are equally typical of dogs growing older. The four of us have much in common. Not to mention:

We visit bathroom facilities more often than we used to.

We've gained some weight.

We walk instead of jogging, and our walks this year are shorter than last year.

We enjoy life tremendously—all four of us. We object to one of the common assumptions about growing older, that it implies decrepitude and a lessened quality of life.

Not so. Growing older with a dog is largely a positive experience. We've gotten used to each other. We know each other's routines and have comfortably adjusted. We have mellowed, have learned how to take life easy and appreciate it.

AGE IS RELATIVE

These days we humans like to assure each other that "Fifty is the new 40!" and "Sixty is the new 50!" This is not all hyperbole, especially in the United States, where people are living longer, healthier lives. What is true for people is also true for dogs. Dogs are living much longer than they did a few decades ago, with a much higher quality of life. This is largely explained by:

- better nutrition

Growing older with a dog is a positive experience.

- advances in preventive care (against disease, parasites)
- greater safety (leash laws, indoor living, less roaming)
- advances in veterinary care
- more spaying and neutering
- increased understanding of canine behavior and improved training

As with humans, an individual dog's genes, environment, and lifestyle (not to mention just plain luck) affect longevity and the potential for illness or disability in old age.

Aging Gracefully

As he grows older, your dog will change. He will begin to show white or gray on his muzzle. He may sleep more. He may have less energy and be less active. One or more of his senses—smell, taste, hearing, or vision—may decline.

There are important actions that you can take to keep your dog at his healthy best:

- Maintain a good weight. Too many dogs are allowed to gain weight as they grow older, as their metabolism slows and they exercise less. Studies show that dogs who are lean live longer than dogs who are overweight, and the extra pounds (kg) contribute to arthritis and heart disease. Ask your veterinarian for recommendations for a new senior weight-control diet to gradually replace an active adult dog diet.

Senior diets are lower in salt, fat, protein, and minerals and may contain helpful supplements.

- Some dogs, when they reach old age, lose an alarming amount of weight. If yours is losing weight, take him to a veterinarian to rule out underlying illnesses or conditions, such as diabetes, kidney disease, or an infected tooth or abscess in the mouth, and then consult with your veterinarian about switching to a high-calorie, easily digested food. Add a touch of beef or chicken broth for flavor and aroma, and serve four or more small meals a day rather than one or two larger meals. Feel free to offer tasty, healthy treats!

- Keep him active. Even though your dog may no longer leap into the creek or dash through the bushes, it is important to keep him moving. Your walks with him may be shorter and slower, but don't give them up! Continue to play with him and keep him mentally stimulated as well as physically active.

- As he grows older, your dog may need protection against cold weather that he did not need before, so think about providing him with a sweater or jacket. Avoid long walks during extremes of hot or cold weather.

- Pay special attention to preventive care. Now more than ever, it is important to remain current with vaccinations and parasite prevention.

- Add another annual veterinary checkup. Older dogs should receive at least two exams a year.

- Be alert to behavioral and physical changes, and report them to your veterinarian.

- Keep grooming. If your dog's coat has changed—if it becomes very dry or begins to fall out—take him to a veterinarian to rule out underlying conditions. A dry coat or skin can be improved with supplements recommended by a veterinarian. Calluses may develop on the elbows and hocks of older dogs. Rubbing some scent-free moisturizer into the area will help prevent cracks in the skin from becoming infected. Keep nails trimmed and ears clean. Gum disease and tooth loss become more of a problem as a dog ages. You can help prevent both by frequent cleaning.

POTENTIAL PROBLEMS

As your dog enters his golden years, he may experience some problems. I would caution you not to diagnose your dog based on observed symptoms but to take him to the veterinarian for a diagnosis. There is no need to panic if you do observe a symptom. Most conditions are manageable.

Arthritis

Arthritis, also known as degenerative joint disease, afflicts one out of five adult dogs and the ratio grows higher with added years. Arthritis is a chronic condition that can be painful and limit movement. It results from breakdown of the cartilage that cushions bones and prevents them from rubbing against each other at a joint. It may result from wear and tear, be secondary to an injury, or be a developmental or degenerative disease.

A dog may reveal symptoms of arthritis when he:

- limps
- is stiff, has trouble getting up or lying down
- is unwilling to run, walk, play
- has difficulty on stairs, getting into and out of a car, climbing on furniture

Be alert to any physical or behavioral chances with your older dog.

What You Can Do

Arthritis is not curable but it is manageable, and there are steps you can take to keep your dog comfortable.

- Prevent weight gain. The importance of not allowing your dog to gain weight cannot be overemphasized. Excess weight is a major factor in causing arthritis and continuing damage to joints.
- Keep him moving. Although your dog should avoid overexertion and extreme activity, daily exercise is necessary and helpful. Make your walks shorter but more frequent.

Avoid steep hills. Stick to level paths, and walk your dog on soft surfaces such as dirt or grass rather than asphalt or pavement whenever possible.

- Keep nails clipped. A dog who is unsteady on his feet is more likely to slip if his nails are too long.
- Provide a comfortable bed. Orthopedic and heated beds are available but not necessary. Some veterinarians prescribe heat therapy, but some dogs do not like lying on a heated bed. Do not let your arthritic dog sleep on a cold, hard floor or lie down in damp areas.

- Consult your veterinarian. Some dogs get pain relief from nonsteroidal anti-inflammatory drugs (NSAIDs) or from supplements such as glucosamine, but follow your veterinarian's recommendations because not all medications or supplements are safe for all dogs.
- Provide safety at home. Close off stairs with pet gates, and cover slippery floors with nonskid mats.
- Provide accessibility. Portable pet ramps make it possible for your dog to get in and out of a car and can be used to provide access to a front or back door if stairs are involved. Ramps fold or are collapsible so that they can be stored in a car, weigh from about 15 to 20 pounds (7 to 23 kg), usually have a nonskid surface, and typically will bear as much as 200 pounds (91 kg). Depending on the material and weight-bearing ability, a ramp can cost from $50 (for a small "half" ramp) to more than $250.
- Make accommodations. A stiff dog might appreciate a raised feeding station and raised water bowl. "Puppy stairs" or "dog stairs" allow a stiff dog to climb onto and off of furniture and are especially helpful to small dogs. Stairs are available in varying materials (plastic, wood, carpeted), strengths, and heights to accommodate dogs of different sizes and weights, and they vary in price from $50 to more than $100. Measure the height of the furniture that you want your dog to reach, and consider his height in selecting the appropriate step interval.
- Provide physical support. Some dogs may not be able to climb stairs or navigate a ramp. A supportive or "lifting" harness can be used on the dog's rear end or middle section, which allows an owner to help the dog climb or walk. These cost from $25 to $100 depending on size and material.

A stiff dog might appreciate raised food bowls.

Canine Cognitive Dysfunction (CCD)

Canine cognitive dysfunction (CCD), also known as cognitive dysfunction syndrome (CDS) and sometimes called canine Alzheimer's, is a condition caused by physical and chemical changes in the brain. Reports vary as to the prevalence of the disease, but it is likely that the majority of dogs over the age of ten display at least one of these symptoms:

- appears confused, disoriented
- becomes nervous, agitated, or restless
- experiences disruption in sleep pattern
- forgets training, does not understand or respond to commands
- forgets familiar places, people
- has soiling accidents in the house
- paces
- shows less affection
- stares off into space
- wanders aimlessly

What You Can Do

- If your dog displays one or more symptoms, report them to your veterinarian and take him in for a thorough checkup, including a neurological examination and blood and urine tests. It is possible that your dog's symptoms are due to a curable or treatable condition, such as kidney disease, hypothyroidism, or hearing or vision loss. If these possibilities are ruled out, your veterinarian may prescribe one of the newer drugs available to treat dogs with CCD. The drugs are promising and are helpful to some (but not all) dogs, but they can have unpleasant side effects.
- Refocus on your dog's nutrition, make certain that it is excellent and appropriate to his age and weight, and discuss with your veterinarian whether dietary supplements are called for.
- Keep your dog active with outdoor walks and indoor play and attention.
- If house soiling is a problem, increase the number of outdoor walks.
- Take safety precautions so that your dog cannot wander off or leave the yard or house.

Help for the Senior Dog

Ramps, stairs, feeding platforms, indoor barriers, and lifting harnesses can be purchased in pet stores and through catalogs and websites.

Deafness

Most dogs who live into their golden years suffer at least some gradual loss of hearing, although total deafness is not nearly as common. If your dog does not respond or rouse when you stand behind him and call him, you are right to be concerned about loss of hearing.

What You Can Do

- Take your dog to the veterinarian to be examined. If the problem is due to wax buildup, a tumor, or an infection caught at an early stage, treatment can save his hearing.
- Approach a hearing-impaired dog from the front whenever possible so as not to startle him. Stamp on the floor to attract his attention, especially if he is sleeping.
- Keep him on a leash except in an enclosed space, such as a fenced-in yard.
- Determine whether your dog can still hear a dog whistle, which you can purchase at a pet shop or through a catalog. Dogs who lose their hearing with age are often able to high these high-pitched sounds. You can use the whistle as a way to get his attention. You may also be able to train him to respond to a whistle and hand signals.
- Maintain his exercise, nutrition, and mental stimulation at optimum levels so that he can still enjoy an excellent quality of life.

Decreased Vision

It is not unusual for a dog's eyesight to diminish after he passes middle age. In some dogs, the lens of the eye thickens with age and the eyes may appear cloudy with a bluish-gray film, a condition that does not interfere with vision.

Older dogs should be taken for veterinary checkups twice a year.

Cataracts are a different matter. A cataract is the clouding over of the lens. Although it may begin in a small area, impairing vision slightly, a cataract will continue to grow until the lens becomes opaque and vision is completely lost. Cataracts are often hereditary, are particularly common in certain breeds, and may appear at a young age if genetically transmitted. They may also be caused by injury or an illness such as diabetes. So-called "senile" cataracts are a major cause of blindness in dogs over six years of age and tend to afflict both eyes, although the cataract may spread more rapidly in one eye than the other.

Surgery can successfully treat a cataract if performed at an early enough stage. If only one eye is affected or if vision is not unduly impaired, surgery may not be indicated for an older dog who is frail or suffering from other health problems.

What You Can Do

- Take your dog to the veterinarian if one or both of his eyes appear cloudy.
- Take your dog to the veterinarian if he shows signs of impaired vision, such as personality changes, bumping into or stepping on objects, or moving slowly or cautiously.
- If your dog suffers from impaired vision that cannot be corrected, take steps to keep him safe. Keep him on a leash except in an enclosed yard. Remove dangerous objects from the yard (shovels, rakes, other implements). Fill in holes in the yard. Keep "surprise" objects that he might trip on off of the floor (shoes, suitcase, books).

Diabetes

Diabetes mellitus is a type of diabetes that often affects older dogs; the average age of diagnosis is about ten years. Twice as many females as males are affected, and excess weight is a major risk factor. Untreated diabetes can cause cataracts, blindness, liver and neurological problems, and death.

Diabetes is a metabolic disorder. The pancreas fails to produce sufficient insulin, or the body is unable to use the insulin that is produced. As a result, sugar in the blood cannot be absorbed and used by cells to produce energy. Excess sugar in the urine causes the dog to urinate frequently, which in turn causes dehydration.

Symptoms include:

- drinking more water than usual
- urinating more frequently than usual
- weight loss
- increased appetite
- dehydration
- vomiting
- fatigue, listlessness
- weakness

What You Can Do

- Report symptoms to your veterinarian and take your dog for a complete examination, including urine and blood tests. The sooner that a diabetic dog is diagnosed and treatment begins, the better and longer his life will be.
- Carefully follow your veterinarian's recommended guidelines for your dog's diet, which may include supplements and oral medication as well as glucose-control/high-fiber food.
- Follow veterinary guidelines for when and how often to feed your

Diabetes mellitus is a type of diabetes that often affects older dogs.

Heart Disease

Heart disease occurs in about 10 percent of dogs. Many dogs with heart disease are symptom- and trouble-free through most of their lives, but heart problems can become serious during their senior years. Diseases include chronic valvular disease (degenerative changes in the heart valves); dilated cardiomyopathy (chambers of the heart enlarge, heart muscle weakens); congenital defects that worsen with age; arrhythmias (irregular or erratic heartbeat); inflammation or infection; and infestation by heartworms (preventable with medication). An older dog's heart problem may be detected by a veterinarian before symptoms appear or go undetected and gradually worsen over time. Symptoms may include:

- coughing
- shortness of breath, trouble breathing, rapid breathing
- lethargy, loss of energy
- loss of appetite
- weight loss
- abdominal swelling

dog (usually four times a day in small amounts). It is important to follow a regular schedule.

- Follow veterinary guidelines for how often and how much to exercise your dog.
- Follow veterinary instructions for giving insulin injections (almost always necessary, usually twice a day). Owners can quickly learn from a veterinarian how to give injections.
- Owners can also monitor a dog's glucose level at home by using a portable monitor to test either urine or blood.

Your dog is likely to be in distress by the time one or more of these symptoms appear.

What You Can Do

Proper care can manage the condition, help him feel better, and prolong his life.

- Take your dog to the veterinarian if any of these symptoms appears. Depending on the problem, your veterinarian may refer you to a specialist. In a small percentage of cases, surgery may be recommended. In many more cases, one or several medications will be prescribed that can help keep your dog comfortable and assure him a good quality of life. If heartworms are present, treatment is more difficult but necessary.
- Ask your veterinarian about the advisability of (gradually) switching to a therapeutic diet. It may also be advisable to divide his daily meals

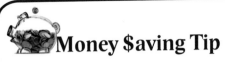

Money $aving Tip

In consultation with your dogs veterinarian, make adjustments to his diet, exercise, and grooming to help him maintain good health and prevent costly veterinary interventions.

into several smaller meals.
- Maintain your dog at a healthy weight. Extra weight puts extra strain on the heart.
- Continue a good exercise program but avoid overexertion. If you have concerns about how much exercise is too much for a dog who seems to tire easily, discuss this with your veterinarian.

Incontinence

Incontinence (involuntary urination) or the need to urinate frequently can be a problem for older dogs, especially females.

What You Can Do

- Because incontinence can be a symptom of a urinary infection or underlying illness, such as diabetes or kidney disease, have your dog examined by a veterinarian. Incontinence in some older spayed females and neutered males results from a hormone deficiency that can

Wee-Wee pads can be helpful for an incontinent senior dog.

be treated with drugs.

- At home, continue to give your dog access to plenty of fresh, clean drinking water.
- Maintain a healthy weight. Obesity can make the problem worse.
- Take him outside to potty as often as you conveniently can.
- Consider training your small dog to use an indoor canine potty or piddle pads if this is more convenient.
- Blot up as much urine as possible where the accident occurred, and use a pet stain and odor remover on the spot. Lingering odor can invite your dog to return—and urinate again—on the same location.
- If all else fails and the condition worsens, you can turn to doggy diapers or "bloomers," which will need to be changed when they become wet or soiled.

Kidney Disease

The type of kidney disease that most often strikes older dogs, chronic interstitial nephritis (CIN), has no known cause. Acute kidney disease can also result from an infection, ingestion of a toxin such as antifreeze, and other problems such as blood clots. Kidney disease, whether chronic or acute, occurs when the kidneys lose the necessary ability to remove waste products from the blood and channel them into urine so that they can be eliminated from the body. The result is uremic poisoning, which is fatal.

Symptoms of kidney disease include:

- more water intake
- more frequent urination
- weight loss, loss of appetite
- decreased energy, listlessness
- weakness
- diarrhea
- bloody urine
- vomiting

What You Can Do

- Kidney disease is not always easily diagnosed, and a dog may live with developing kidney disease for some time before showing any symptoms. If you have suspicions along this line, ask your veterinarian to not only check your dog's urine and blood but to take X-rays or perform an ultrasound.
- Your veterinarian will probably prescribe a special diet. Historically, this was a dog food low in protein. More recently, this aspect of the diet has been questioned and refined, so your veterinarian may prescribe a food with an easily digestible form of protein.
- Your veterinarian will ask you to restrict phosphorus intake by your dog, either through a special diet or medication or both. Vitamin B and other supplements will probably be prescribed as well.

- Make certain that fresh drinking water is available to your dog around the clock. He will drink more than he used to, so it is helpful to put down a water bowl in more than one room.
- Take your dog outside frequently to urinate.
- Monitor your dog for signs of dehydration (vomiting, diarrhea, loss of skin elasticity) and take immediate steps to rehydrate him if he shows one or more of these symptoms. Many owners learn to do this at home by giving subcutaneous fluids, or it can be done at the clinic.
- Kidney dialysis is also available in limited areas of the country. It is very expensive and time consuming (three to four hours, two to three times a week) and usually makes sense only for short-term problems, such as poisoning.

Keeping your dog at a healthy weight is one of the best things you can do for him.

The "ultimate" solution of a kidney transplant is also available for dogs but is extremely expensive and only available at limited specialized clinics. A compatible shelter dog is used as the donor but only if the owners of the recipient dog agree to adopt the donor and give him a good home for life. The dog receiving the kidney must be maintained on post-transplant medications.

As is usually the case in writings about older dogs, much space is taken up with problems, illness, and conditions. But taking care of and living with an older dog is so much more than that. There is joyful satisfaction in hanging out with a dog who has known you for 10 or 15 years. Who is going to begrudge him his eccentricities, quirks, mistakes, or need for special care? After all, isn't that what we hope and expect for ourselves from our loved ones? As we grow old together, this is a time to revel in the mutual acceptance, devotion, and love that we share with our dogs.

RESOURCES MADE EASY

Books About Senior Dogs

- Alderton, David. *Young at Heart: 120 Things You Can Do Right Now to Give Your Older Dog a Longer, Healthier Life.* Pleasantville, NY: Reader's Digest Association, 2007.
- Becker, Susan. *Living With a Deaf Dog: A Book of Advice, Facts and Experiences About Canine Deafness.* Published by Susan Becker, 1997.
- Levin, Caroline. *Living With Blind Dogs: A Resource Book and Training Guide for the Owners of Blind and Low-Vision Dogs.* Oregon City, OR: Lantern, 2004.
- Morgan, Diane. *The Living Well Guide for Senior Dogs: Everything You Need to Know for a Happy & Healthy Companion.* Neptune City, NJ: TFH Publications, Inc., 2007.
- Schmidt-Roger, Heike and Susanne Blank. *The Senior Dog.* New York, NY: Dorling Kindersley, 2007.
- Shojai, Amy D. *Complete Care For Your Aging Dog.* New York, NY: New American Library, 2003.

Deaf Dogs

- Signs of Love for Our Deaf Dogs: www.deafdogs.com

Diabetes

- Canine Diabetes: www.caninediabetes.org

Ramps, Stairs, and Other Supplies

- Always check your chain pet store or local pet stores for supplies.
- Doggy Steps: www.doggysteps.com
- Draper Equine Therapy (therapeutic dog bed): www.draperequinetherapy.com; 781-8280-0029
- HandicappedPets.com: www.handicappedpets.com
- HelpYourPets.com: www.helpyourpets.com
- Paw Steps: www.pawsteps.com
- Puppy Stairs: www.puppystairs.com
- Ramp4Paws: www.Ramp4Paws.com; 800-654-PAWS
- Search online for "senior pet products" or "senior pet supplies."

Senior Dogs

- American Animal Hospital Association Pet Care Library: www.healthypet.com

Chapter 13

Parting

Some years ago, a neighbor and friend of mine lost her elderly dog to cancer. Sarah was only 65, but she swore she would never get another dog "Because I won't live long enough to take care of him. And I simply can't go through that pain again."

I am happy to report that Sarah changed her mind. It was a long time before she was able to grapple with and move past the trauma of losing Banjo. Once she did, she adopted a middle-aged dog from our local shelter. That was five years ago. The two of them are devoted to each other and going strong health-wise and in every other way.

Whether you live alone, like Sarah, or are living with a spouse, friend, or relative, the death of a beloved pet can be devastating. Grief is the normal and natural reaction to the end of the strong emotional and psychological bond that we forge with our dogs. With the loss of a dog, we lose unconditional love, comfort, companionship, and part of our lifestyle. We have arranged our day around that early-morning walk, that pre-dinner and bedtime walk.

GRIEF

Every individual reacts to the death of a loved one in a different way. Many years ago, in her groundbreaking book On Death and Dying, Elizabeth Kubler-Ross identified at least five stages of grief over the loss of a loved person, and subsequent research has shown that the grieving process is similar when a pet dies. These stages can include:

1. Denial, possibly accompanied by shock: inability to accept that the pet is dead.
2. Bargaining with God or another power. If death of a pet is expected, this is an attempt to forestall it.
3. Anger, possibly accompanied by guilt. Anger may be directed at the pet for abandoning us or at the veterinarian for failing to "save" the pet.

4. Acceptance of the reality of loss and feeling the sadness that accompanies it.
5. Resolution as pain diminishes and we are able to enjoy memories of our pet.

Individuals do not necessarily move through these stages in order, may skip one or more stages entirely, or experience them in varying degrees of intensity. Depending on the individual and circumstances, the death of a pet may cause crying, fatigue, depression, sleeplessness, confusion, anxiety, withdrawal, loss of appetite, relief, loneliness, disorganization, and absentmindedness.

For some of us, the death of a pet brings forth powerful emotions that complicate our grief:

- The pet may be the last link to a deceased spouse or other family member.
- Issues of our own mortality are brought to the fore.
- Like Sarah, we may question whether we are able to have another pet or whether we want one.
- If living alone, we may lose a sense of purpose, of being needed on a daily basis.

There is no "right" or "wrong" way to grieve, and grief has no schedule. It may last for weeks, months, or years.

Grief is the normal reaction to the end of the strong bond that we forge with our dogs.

A few decades ago, the painful emotions involved with the loss of a pet were usually minimized or ignored. Bereaved pet owners were told "It's just a dog" or "You can always get another one." Often, we were embarrassed to talk to others about our sadness or to reveal how badly we felt. Emotional isolation of this kind prolongs grief and can even intensify it.

Fortunately, today there is more understanding and broader acceptance of the importance of pets in our lives and the painful void left behind when they die. When you experience this pain:

- Talk to a sympathetic person about your feelings. This may be a friend, relative, veterinarian, fellow dog owner, counselor, or therapist.
- Seek help and understanding from a pet loss support center. Many local humane societies offer pet loss support groups, also called pet bereavement seminars, and many pet loss support centers have hotlines that you can call. Mental health professionals have become more attuned to the importance of pets in our lives, and some specialize in pet bereavement counseling.
- Consider writing about your feelings. You might share a letter to your pet or an essay about him with friends and relatives—or with no one.
- Plan a ritual to help you accept this loss.

FAREWELLS

The death of a pet may be sudden and unexpected, leaving us emotionally unprepared, or it may occur after an illness. If you receive a terminal diagnosis for your dog, you have time to say good-bye. Savor this time and spoil him like you've never spoiled him before. Give him special treats, take him on his favorite walks, or just sit with him. A few pet loss support centers wisely offer support for people facing the approaching death of an ill or aging pet. Upsetting as the prospect is, it is advisable to make decisions about cremation or burial ahead of time.

Hospice Care

Many veterinarians and dog owners have practiced hospice care for years without using the term "hospice." The goal of hospice for pets, which today is being taught, studied, written about, and discussed, is to enable a terminally ill pet to spend his final days, weeks, or months pain-free at home in a loving and familiar environment.

Hospice becomes an option when owners determine that their dog's life cannot be saved through veterinary measures. They have concluded that treatments such as surgery, chemotherapy, and radiation offer too little promise of prolonging life and that the price paid by the dog in pain and discomfort is too high. In choosing hospice care, owners give up all treatment except palliative (pain-reducing) care. They have decided that preserving the pet's quality of life in his remaining days is more desirable than trying to add to the quantity of his

Money $aving Tip

Many local animal shelters offer free pet loss support groups, also known as pet bereavement groups.

remaining days. In deciding whether to choose hospice care over continued treatment, it is useful to ask:

- What are your dog's chances of survival with treatment or surgery?
- If treatment or surgery is successful, how long might he survive?
- What will his quality of life be after such treatment?

Being cared for at home can be comforting for a sick dog and comforting for the family as well, but it can be time consuming, stressful, and physically and emotionally demanding as the family takes responsibility for the dog's daily care. This involves careful monitoring of the dog's condition and administering pain medication. Caretakers may need to learn how to give injections, handle intravenous medications, and deal with incontinence.

Before deciding to undertake hospice care, owners must first meet with their veterinarian to learn what their caretaking tasks will be, learn how to carry them out, and understand what to expect in terms of their dog's behavior and physical condition. Caring for a failing dog at home can be rewarding and provide owners with time for a long good-bye, but it is not for everyone.

Euthanasia

The word "euthanasia" means "easy or painless death." This is a gift that we can choose to give to a dog who is suffering

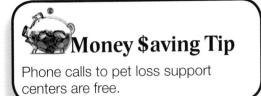

Money $aving Tip

Phone calls to pet loss support centers are free.

from a terminal illness or irreparable, serious injury. Making this choice is neither easy nor painless. Part of the decision is emotional—our love and protective feelings toward a pet. This part you can discuss with family and friends. Although it feels counterintuitive, love for a pet can lead us to end his suffering with a painless death. The second component of the decision is rational—the reality of the dog's condition and prognosis. This part depends on acquiring all the facts that you can. Ask your veterinarian questions until you can't think of any to ask. Seek a second opinion, if you wish, from a specialist or another veterinarian. Research your dog's condition to your heart's content in books and on the Internet. In the end, you will make the decision that is best for your dog after weighing his potential for suffering against his potential for recovery.

Whether you seek continued treatment to try to save or extend your dog's life or choose hospice, euthanasia may still need to be considered. Some pets are able to die comfortably and "naturally" at home with proper pain management, but this is not always the case. If your dog is seriously injured or ill, it is helpful to establish a bottom line about his quality of life ahead of time, before it is necessary to make a decision about euthanasia. Possible benchmarks:

- Your dog cannot stand.
- He is unable or unwilling to eat.
- He no longer recognizes you.
- He is disoriented and unaware of his surroundings.
- Pain management is possible only by rendering him unconscious.

These questions are upsetting to ponder. But making this decision ahead of time enables you to make it with a clearer head.

If you have decided upon euthanasia, discuss it with your veterinarian so that you understand exactly what is involved, and then make an appointment. Some veterinarians will make a home visit for this purpose, and I recommend that you request it. My experience is that this is less stressful for both the dog and the family. If you live alone, ask a good friend or relative to be with you at this time. If a home visit does not feel right to you or if your veterinarian will not come to your home, make an appointment at the clinic. Whether at home or at the clinic, make arrangements ahead of time for payment and for removal of your dog's body.

When the time comes, ask a friend or family member to go with you to the clinic. Most clinics will give you time alone in a private room to say a last good-bye. Contrary to years past, when veterinarians routinely barred owners from being present during a pet's final moments, today almost all veterinarians will invite you to be present. I have found it comforting, both to me and to my dog, to be present. You may reach the same conclusion. If you do, you will see your friend slip away peacefully, and you will be there to hold and comfort him to the very end. Most veterinarians will administer a sedative that causes your dog to quickly fall into a deep and peaceful sleep. The veterinarian will next inject a drug that stops the heart from beating. This will complete your final brave, loving gift.

FINAL ARRANGEMENTS

When your dog passes away, you can arrange for burial or cremation or ask your veterinarian to make the arrangements for handling and disposing of his body.

Burial

A majority of pet owners choose to bury their deceased pets, almost always on their own property. This is possible in rural areas, but many local governments in urban and suburban areas prohibit such burials for public health reasons. If you make this choice, purchase a nonbiodegradable container for your dog, available at pet cemeteries. Prices start at approximately $100 for a small,

"You Will Know"

"You will know," I've been told.

"You will know" when to make the heartbreaking decision to end your dog's life.

"You will know" when the time has come. Maybe, but that doesn't make it easier.

Sunshine was a found dog, a mutt. Without exaggeration, she was one of the most beautiful and intelligent dogs I've ever known and she was mine. Huge brown eyes, golden brown hair, plumed tail. She was wandering the neighborhood streets. A cloud of fleas rose from her fur when I patted her. The vet put her age at 12 to 18 months.

I have never had a healthier dog—not a single illness or injury. When she was 12, she suddenly began to limp on a front leg. Not unduly worried, I waited a day or two to take her to the vet. This was back in 1998.

Our vet examined Sunshine and took X-rays. As gently as she could, she told me that the X-ray revealed that bone cancer had spread throughout the afflicted leg. Horror, shock, and sadness wilted me. I clung to Sunny's mane and cried. When I pulled myself together, I asked the vet, "What can we do?"

"The only thing you could do is amputate and then try chemotherapy and radiation. We had a young Doberman in here. She was three years old with the same situation. The owners asked us to amputate her leg. She lived six more months, but she was going through treatment much of that time."

I knew then that even though I could not admit it until later, I would not do that to Sunshine. Did I want her to live another six months? Of course. But to go through the inevitable postoperative pain? To be afraid and alone when she woke up at the veterinary clinic? To feel the discomfort of radiation and chemotherapy? And maybe live six more months—but at her age, maybe not? To me, this meant that those last six months would be hellish, and I wanted her remaining time to be heavenly.

I took Sunshine home. Together we went and sat on a hillside most afternoons. I cried and she turned her face into the sun. We gave her painkillers and steroids, but then the side effects began to kick in and they were bad.

She was still gorgeous when we called the vet to ask her to come and put Sunny down. The only comfort we—my husband and I—felt was in the thought that she had had a wonderful life with us and that up until the very end she did not suffer.

"You will know." Yes, I did know what to do. But the decision is never easy, simple, or uncomplicated. The one sure thing: It will hurt.

simple container and increase depending on the size needed and the type of material.

Clearly, burial becomes a less desirable or impossible option if you live in an elevator building in the city or have a very large dog. An alternative is burial in a pet cemetery.

There are about 600 pet cemeteries throughout the country, and fewer than 10 percent of pet owners arrange for burial in one of them. The cost of doing so varies with geographic location, the cemetery itself, and the size of your dog. A plot for a small dog may be in the $100 range. Owners are charged additionally for a casket (usually at least $100); for continuing maintenance of the plot; for a commemorative plaque, headstone, or marker; and possibly for picking up the dog's body. For a smaller fee, your dog can be buried in a communal area. Pet cemeteries will also arrange a funeral for your dog—again, for a fee, which may be several hundred dollars.

If you are considering using a pet cemetery, ask your veterinarian for a recommendation. These cemeteries vary in quality, and a few have been revealed to operate at a very substandard level. I have found limited information available on pet cemetery websites. Phone calls are necessary to learn about fees, and an actual visit is needed to learn about the physical appearance and maintenance of the property.

If your pet has only recently passed away and you have not been able to make arrangements ahead of time, I recommend that you ask a friend or relative to investigate and advise you about pet cemetery options. You are in a vulnerable situation, when it is hard to think straight and difficult to make good decisions.

Cremation

One-fourth of pet owners have their deceased pets cremated, a service performed by pet cemeteries. Many people choose communal cremation of the pet. Or you can choose to have your pet cremated individually and ask to have his ashes returned to you.

Cremation costs increase with the size of your dog, ranging from $100 to as high as $350. Individual cremation is more expensive than communal. Ashes can be returned to you in a simple cardboard box, for which there is usually no charge. A carved wooden box or an urn will cost more, beginning at about $50. A cemetery may charge for picking up your pet's body and delivering his ashes to you.

Like many others, I have arranged to have my deceased dogs individually cremated and the ashes returned to me. I have scattered the ashes in favorite places where I walked with them, usually in the woods. Others have buried the ashes in the yard, and some prefer to keep them inside in a decorative urn.

Your Veterinarian

Nearly one-third of pet owners do not choose cremation or burial. They ask their veterinarian to handle disposal of their pet's body and prefer not to know what these arrangements are. There is nothing wrong with choosing this option. But if you do have an interest in how your pet's body is handled, ask your veterinarian ahead of time what the normal arrangements are and decide whether you are comfortable with them.

Memorials and Rituals

Rituals that we turn to upon the death of beloved dog can help us deal with grief. A ritual can be as simple as a moment of silence or prayer as you stand over your pet's grave or scatter his ashes or a ceremony that includes other people.

Thinking about ways to memorialize a pet can help us work through grief, and memorials can help us remember the good times. Whether or not you choose to bury your dog or his ashes on your property, you can plant a tree, bush, or garden in his memory or install a bench or an inscribed plaque. Consider making a scrapbook or framing a favorite photograph to capture happy memories. A wonderful way to honor a canine companion is to reach out and help pets in need by making a contribution to an animal welfare group in his name.

ANOTHER DOG?

In years past, a bereaved dog owner was commonly advised, "Go out and get yourself another dog!" This advice sprang from the mistaken assumption that dogs are interchangeable: a new Mabel can substitute for the old Mabel and quickly heal the owner's pain.

But coming to terms with the loss of a beloved canine companion will take time. Grief over the "old dog" needs to run its course before a new dog is brought in. This process may be months for Mrs. Jones and perhaps a year for the Smiths. How long will it take for you to be ready? You will not know until you get there. Perhaps it will be the moment when you meet a dog who is very unlike "old Mabel" and you realize that you are ready to think about a new companion "from the bottom up," beginning with Chapter 1 of this book. You will be ready when you truly feel that your new dog is not a replacement or substitute for the dog who has died but a new friend whom you will get to know.

PEACE OF MIND

My friend Sarah hesitated to adopt a dog because she feared that her dog would outlive her. She worried about what would become of the dog if she were disabled and not able to care for him—or worse.

This kind of fear is neither uncommon nor irrational and springs out of a sense of responsibility toward a loved companion animal and awareness of our human fragility and mortality. It brings to mind a dilemma that pet owners of all ages should address: "What will happen to my dog if something happens to me?"

Unfortunately, because the question reminds us that we too have a limited time on earth, we often prefer to avoid it entirely, leaving no plan for the care of a canine family member who may be left behind after our own death or hospitalization. Too often, a beloved dog is consigned to a shelter because no provision has been made for his care, and yet this result is surely not what his owner would have wanted.

Fortunately, there are practical solutions.

You'll know if and when you are ready for a new companion.

Temporary Caregivers

We all face unexpected emergencies: a car accident, a fall, a sudden illness. If we live alone, the dog is left without a caretaker. If we live with a spouse or partner, he or she may also be injured or not able to walk a dog because of a pre-existing condition or be fully occupied caring for us.

Plan ahead in anticipation that you may face a problem of this nature. Ask at least one person whom you know and who likes dogs if she is willing to commit to being a temporary caregiver to your dog in case of emergency. Ideally, this would be someone who has or has had a dog and also knows and is comfortable with your dog, someone whom you trust. Discuss what the care of your dog involves. Give your emergency helper a key to your home, written instructions, and contact information for your dog's veterinarian. I recommend recruiting a backup helper as well and putting these two good Samaritans in touch with each other.

Long-Term Caregivers

The arrangement that dog owners make most frequently for the care of a dog who might outlive them is to ask another person to commit to becoming the dog's new owner and permanent caretaker. Usually, this is a family member, such as a sibling or adult child, but it can also be a friend or neighbor who knows and is fond of the dog. Any arrangement of this type should be discussed, not merely "understood," and written instructions and contact information handed over. It is helpful, if possible, to seek a commitment from an alternate permanent caregiver. An owner should also consider making a bequest of money to the caregiver in her will to cover the expense of caring for the dog. Although the will can also describe how the money should be used, there is no automatic monitoring or enforcement mechanism.

Pet Sanctuary or Rescue Group

If you are unable to arrange for a caretaker, you may wish to explore the possibility of directing that your dog be placed in the care of a pet sanctuary or rescue group. A few sanctuaries

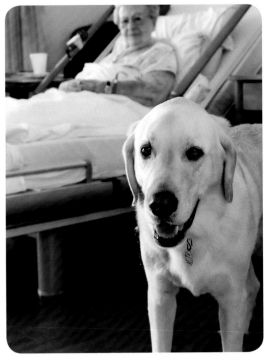

Ask someone you know to be a temporary caregiver to your dog in case of emergency.

and animal welfare groups maintain "retirement homes" where dogs can live out their lives, but most animal welfare organizations cannot promise long-term care for pets of deceased owners. It is important that you carefully investigate, visit, and choose the organization. You must negotiate the details of an agreement by fully discussing it with representatives of the group you choose. You can stipulate that the group try to find a good home for your dog and that it agree to care for the dog throughout his life if no satisfactory home is found.

In return, the organization will ask that a cash bequest be included in your will to cover the cost of caring for your dog, and the requested amount may be quite large.

It is mandatory that you talk with the group and not simply name a shelter or organization to receive your dog. Although devoted to the well-being of companion animals, shelters, sanctuaries, and similar organizations do not have the space or the funds to care for your dog indefinitely.

Pet Trust

A pet trust is a fairly new legal development that allows an owner to provide for a dog's care in her will. Because it is not legally possible to leave money directly to a pet, a trust is established to receive the money intended for the pet's care. This device is in use in 37 states and the District of Columbia.

Should you decide to use this option, work with a lawyer to establish a trust in your will. This involves selecting as a trustee an individual or a financial institution to receive and hold the funds that you have decided to leave for the care of your dog. The trustee will disburse funds to a caregiver whom you have chosen to take care of your dog. The trustee is charged with monitoring the dog's care according to instructions that you have outlined in the trust document.

There are many questions to be answered in establishing a pet trust. Who can be a good caretaker for your dog? Is she willing and able to do this? Should you name an alternate caretaker? How much money should be placed in the trust? What care instructions should you leave? What type of decisions do you want the caregiver to make about veterinary care should the dog become seriously ill? Do you want your pet to be buried or cremated? If there is money left over after your pet passes away, who should be the beneficiary of this sum?

It is important to consult an attorney about establishing the trust. Animal welfare groups can provide information and guidance about pet care trusts and similar arrangements.

Euthanasia of a Surviving Pet

If your dog is extremely old or in extremely bad health, it may be appropriate to direct that he be humanely put to rest if he survives you or if you are not able to care for him. It is not appropriate or fair, however, to direct that a healthy dog be euthanized in these circumstances, and many veterinarians are unwilling to do so. Instead, for your own peace of mind, make every effort to provide for your dog's care if he should outlive you.

RESOURCES MADE EASY

Books About Pet Loss

- Association for Pet Loss and Bereavement, www.aplb.org (contains bibliography about pet loss and bereavement)
- Brown, Robin Jean. *How to Roar: Pet Loss Grief Recovery*. Napa, CA: Lulu Press, 2005.
- Carmack, Betty J. *Grieving the Death of a Pet*. Grove City, OH: Augsburg Fortress Publishers, 2003.
- Kowalski, Gary. *Good-bye Friend: Healing Wisdom for Anyone Who Has Ever Lost a Pet*. Novato, CA: New World Publishing, 2006.
- Sife, Wallace. *The Loss of a Pet*. New York, New York: Howell Book House, 2005.

Euthanasia Guidance

- American Veterinary Medical Association (AVMA): www.avma.org
- Association for Pet Loss and Bereavement: www.aplb@aplb.org; 718-382-0690

Pet Cemeteries and Cremations

- Delta Society: www.deltasociety.org; 425-679-5502
- International Association of Pet Cemeteries (IAOPC): www.iaopc.com; 518-594-3000

Pet Hospice Care

- American Animal Hospital Association (AAHA): www.healthypet.com
- Nikki Hospice Foundation for Pets: www.pethospice.org

Pet Loss Support Hotlines

- American Society for the Prevention of Cruelty to Animals (ASPCA): 800-946-4646 pin#140-7211
- Animal Medical Center, NY: 212-838-8100
- Chicago Veterinary Medical Association: 630-603-3994
- Colorado State University College of Veterinary Medicine: 303- 221-4535
- CONTACT of NJ: 856-234-4688
- Cornell University Veterinary Students: 607-253-3932
- IAMS Pet Loss Support Center and Hotline: 888-332-7738
- Iowa State University College of Veterinary Medicine: 888-478-7574
- Michigan State University College of Veterinary Medicine: 517-432-2696
- Ohio State University: 614-292-1823
- Pet Grief Support Service of AZ: 602-995-5885
- Tufts University College of Veterinary Medicine: 508-839-7966

- University of California-Davis School of Veterinary Medicine: 916-752-4200
- University of Florida Veterinary Students: 352-392-4700 ex. 4080
- University of Illinois Veterinary Teaching Hospital: 877-394-2273
- University of Minnesota College of Veterinary Medicine: 612-624-4747
- University of Pennsylvania School of Veterinary Medicine: 215-898-4529
- Virginia-Maryland Regional College of Veterinary Medicine: 540-231-8038
- Washington State University College of Veterinary Medicine: 509-335-1297

Pet Urns, Memorials
- Angel Ashes: www.angelashes.com
- Close to our Hearts: www.closetoourheartspet memorialboxes.com
- Everlife Memorials: www.everlifememorials.com
- Paws 2 Heaven: www.paws2heaven.com
- T&S Pet Memorials: www.tspetmemorials.com

Providing for a Surviving Pet
- American Animal Hospital Association (AAHA): www.healthypet.com

- Humane Society of the United States (HSUS): www.hsus.org/petsinwills; 202-452-1100

Support Groups and Professional Counselors Directory
- Delta Society: www.deltasociety.com; 425-679-5502

Index 265

PHOTO CREDITS

Cover, title page: Lobke Peers (Shutterstock)

Mary Jane Checchi: 5, 32
Isabelle Francais: 55, 57, 60, 63, 65, 74, 83, 85, 86, 154, 161, 162, 166, 187
ryasick photography (Shutterstock): "Money Saving Tip" icon
Illustration on page 130: Angela Stanford
Jean Fogle, 136, 142, 229, 230

Shutterstock:
jean schweitzer, 4; Feverpitch, 6; Suhendri Utet, 7; Shutterstock, 8, 27, 35 (bottom left), 45 (bottom right); Hannamariah, 9; ZM Photography, 10; absolute, 12; zemfira, 14; Ivonne Wierink, 17; Frances L Fruit, 19; Russ Beinder, 21; Glenda M. Powers, 23; marikond, 24; Erik Lam, 29, 36 (top left), 39 (bottom), 41, 61, 188; Natalia V Guseva, 30; Anyka, 34 (left); Eric Isselee, 34 (right), 36 (bottom right), 39 (top), 44 (bottom left), 45 (bottom left, top right), 67, 105, 109, 153, 169, 174, 178, 195, 200, 261; Phil Dale, 35 (top left); Elliot Westacott, 35 (bottom right); Annette Shaff, 36 (top right); Andraz Cerar, 37; Chin Kit Sen, 40; vnlit, 42; Lerche&Johnson, 43; Mushakesa, 44 (top right); Utekhina Anna, 47, 53; einstein, 48; Ken Hurst, 51, 234; Justin Black, 68; Tammy McAllister, 70; Leah-Anne Thompson, 72; Maxim Urievich Lysenko, 75; Joy Brown, 77 (top); HTuller, 77 (bottom); Marcy J. Levinson, 78; Alexey Stiopp, 79; Tootles, 80; iNNOCENt, 81; Steve Lovegrove, 84; Elliot Westacott, 87; Judy Ben Joud, 88; Scott Bolster, 89; Matt Antonino, 90; John S. Sfondilias, 92; Philip Lange, 94; Ivonne Wierink, 97, 116, 192, 201, 210, 212, 224; Pierdelune, 99; Vinicius Tupinamba, 101; Glenda M. Powers, 102; AVAVA, 104, Erwin Wodika, 106; Justin Paget, 108; Joy Brown, 111; Chin Kit Sen, 113; Vikki, 114; Sarah Salmela, 115; Somer McCain, 118; Jean Frooms, 122; Willee Cole, 124; Losevsky Pavel, 133, 145; Peter Betts, 135; marilyn barbone, 141; Lobke Peers, 146; Kerioak-Christine Nichols, 147; illusionstudio, 148; Multiart, 150; kudraska-a, 156, 157; Sarah Salmela, 158; Alice Mary Herden Vision-Vault LLC, 164; iofoto, 59, 170, 223; Justin Paget, 173; Waldemar Dabrowski, 177; Michael Pettigrew, 180; Alex Valent, 182; afarland, 184; Sergey Laverntev, 185, Bonita R. Cheshier, 190; David Lade, 196; arena-creative, 198; jivan child, 203; Michael Zysman, 206; Tatjana Brila, 208 (top); Cameron Cross, 214; GW Images, 215; Peter Baxter, 216; steamroller_blues, 219; Anne Kitzman, 221; Eric Cote, 231; Karla Caspari, 236; dundanim, 238; Smart-foto, 239; aceshot1, 241; Natalya Lakhtakia, 243; Richard Thornton, 246; Pieter, 247; Galina Barskaya, 248; Alexy Stiop, 250; federico stevanin, 257; Dennis Sabo, 259

DEDICATION

TO CHARLOTTE

ACKNOWLEDGEMENTS

Special thanks to Abby Saffold, Ellen Linck and Karen Gilbert—always patient, upbeat and encouraging—and to my favorite veterinarian, Kathleen Dougherty. Also thanks to: Scotlund Haisley, former Executive Director of the Washington Animal Rescue League; Lisa LaFontaine, President and CEO, Washington Humane Society; Katherine Burton; Margaret Collins; Angela Maldonado; Hal and Lynne McCombs; Carrie Smith; Jeff Van Grack; Jane West; all my friends, canine and human, on the "dog path" in Westmoreland Hills who share their stories with me; and to the many dogs, trainers, and veterinarians I have learned from over the years. My heartfelt gratitude to the generous people who rescue, foster, care for, work and sacrifice to save dogs from neglect and abuse. Because of them many marvelous dogs have been saved, and I have been privileged to adopt a few of those special dogs.

I have been so very fortunate to work with agent Kate Epstein and editor Heather Russell-Revesz.

John Vincent, you lift my spirits and "Big John"—you make it all possible.

ABOUT THE AUTHOR

Mary Jane Checchi is the author of *Are You the Pet For Me? Choosing the Right Pet For Your Family*, and a member of the "50+ club." Her pet articles have appeared in *Dog and Kennel*, *PetLife*, *Big Apple Parent*, *Georgia Family*, and petcity.com. She has owned and trained dogs all her life, has assisted with animal rescue groups, and as a member of PAL (People Animals Love) she visits Washington area nursing homes, hospitals, and other facilities with her Collie. Mary Jane resides in Bethesda, Maryland, with her husband and dogs. Her website is www.checchibooks.com.

NATURAL with added VITAMINS
Nutri Dent ®
MD
Promotes Optimal Dental Health!

Dogs L♥ve'em! ™

AVAILABLE IN MULTIPLE SIZES AND FLAVORS.

Nylabone ®

Trusted For Over 40 Years

MADE IN THE USA

Our Mission with Nutri Dent® is to promote optimal dental health for dogs through a trusted, natural, delicious chew that provides effective cleaning action...GUARANTEED to make your dog go wild with anticipation and happiness!!!

Nylabone Products • P.O. Box 427, Neptune, NJ 07754-0427 • 1-800-631-2188 • Fax: 732-988-5466
www.nylabone.com • info@nylabone.com • For more information contact your sales representative or contact us at sales@tfh.com   TS446